hc

THE TAMING OF THE
DRAGON

EDWARD I & THE CONQUEST OF WALES

WAYNE BARTLETT

SUTTON PUBLISHING

First published in the United Kingdom in 2003 by
Sutton Publishing Limited · Phoenix Mill
Thrupp · Stroud · Gloucestershire · GL5 2BU

British Library Cataloguing in Publication Data
A catalogue record for this book is available from the British Library.

ISBN 0-7509-3217-1

Typeset in 10/12 pt Baskerville.
Typesetting and origination by
Sutton Publishing Limited.
Printed and bound in England by
J.H. Haynes & Co. Ltd, Sparkford.

Contents

*To the special
people in
my life*

Welsh Pronunciation

The double consonant 'dd' is pronounced as 'th', but 'th' and 'd' are pronounced as in English; 'f' is always pronounced 'v', while 'ff' is the soft 'f', and the sounds of 'y' and 'u' (the short 'oo' form) are interchanged except in the final or single syllable where 'y' often reverts to its short 'ee' sound. A circumflex accent lengthens the vowel, as in tŷ ('tee') – a house.

The Welsh 'ch' is a guttural 'c' as in 'loch' and not as in 'chair', 'rh' is a soft guttural 'r', for which there is no English equivalent; thus we find in the name Rhys Fychan that the 'y' in Rhys is pronounced 'ee' but in the first syllable of Fychan is 'oo' as in 'book': *ghrees voohan*. Stress normally falls on the penultimate syllable.

The Welsh 'w' is pronounced 'oo', as in 'who', hence 'fawr' (big) is pronounced 'va-oor'; while the famous 'll' of Llywelyn is hardly capable of rendering in print but is something like a softly aspirated 'hl', tossed off with a flick of the tongue.

Examples: Machynlleth, pron. Ma-hun-hleth. Llanybydder, pronounced Hlan-u-buther (*Llan* meaning a religious parish).

There are no dipthongs in Welsh, each vowel is pronounced separately: hence, 'ai' is pronounced 'ah-ih', 'ei' as 'eh-ih', 'au' as 'ah-ee', etc, although in common speech the separate sounds are elided. Welsh soft, nasal and aspirate mutations are notoriously difficult, generally following feminine forms, vowel endings or prepositions; the reader may spot them in place names in which, for instance, an initial 'm' (as in Magor) has mutated to 'f', or the 'b' in Bangor has become a 'm'.

1. The major territorial divisions of Wales in the medieval period.

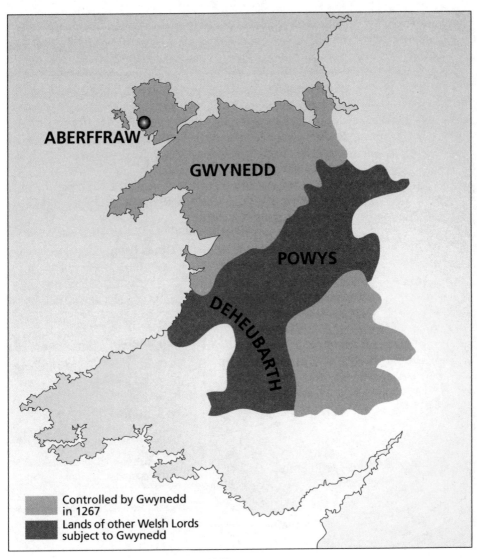

ABERFFRAW

GWYNEDD

POWYS

DEHEUBARTH

Controlled by Gwynedd
in 1267

Lands of other Welsh Lords
subject to Gwynedd

2. Gwynedd and other Welsh territories in 1267.

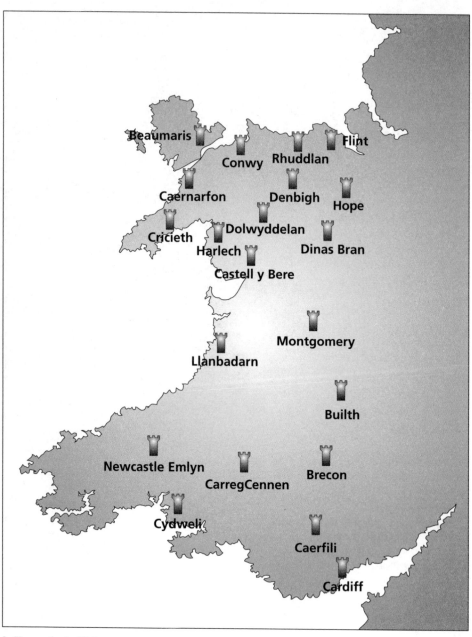

3. *Key castles in Wales.*

Introduction

In my youth, I spent many holidays in Wales, where I first became interested in medieval history. As an impressionable adolescent, it was impossible to visit the castles that remained from that time, still in some cases substantially intact, without my imagination working overtime, creating vivid pictures of great battles and sieges from times long past. I knew nothing of the history behind these massive bastions but that mattered little; what I did not know, my mind created. There was marvellous raw material to inspire such musings: majestic Caernarfon, staring imperiously out over the Menai Strait, and compact Conwy – even to someone who knew little about its architecture it was still obviously a marvellous example of the castle-builder's craft. Of them all, a castle less kindly treated by the passage of time inspired me the most. Carreg Cennen, poised precariously on its wild limestone eyrie, was to me the ultimate castle, remote, powerful, and far removed from those signs of modern 'civilisation' that can so easily obliterate the sense of the past that emanates from out-of-the-way places steeped in history.

But despite the impression they made as gigantic examples of military architecture, the stones of these castles were mute about their history. They could be explored with the aid of guidebooks that outlined the events that caused them to be built. But the collective knowledge these afforded did not give me an adequate understanding of the wars waged in Wales by King Edward I of England and how these conflicts encouraged him to grasp the north of Wales in a granite fist. Nor did my school education help. History lessons invariably concentrated on more modern events. The conquest of Wales, as far as I remember, was never alluded to, not once. It was as if Wales had always been connected by an unbreakable umbilical cord with its larger English neighbour.

Only when I reached adulthood did I begin to read more widely on the subject, and several things became clear. One of the most important was that the culture of Wales was very different from that of England, the one no less worthy of respect than the other. Wales had a history of its own, which deserved to be better understood by anyone who wished to appreciate the place of Britain in the world. I also learned that history cannot be neatly packaged. Origins and endpoints must be established for historical topics but they need to be chosen with care. Events do not happen in isolation, and without understanding the causative factors that shape events history can make little sense.

This is particularly true of the Edwardian conquest of Wales. To the uninitiated, one of the greatest surprises involved in studying these events is that much of thirteenth-century Wales was already occupied by English barons. Indeed, large tracts of the country had been occupied by English Marcher lords for over two centuries by the time Edward I invaded. Edward only completed a process that had been in train for some time. Then there are the Welsh themselves to consider. Llywelyn ap Gruffudd, the great hero of Welsh resistance, could not claim the full support even of those Welshmen whose lands were free from the control of English lords. When he died, accusations of treachery on the part of his own countrymen accompanied him to his grave. Among the armies of his enemies were as many Welshmen as Englishmen, and sometimes more. Simplistic accounts of this history that present it as a war between two races are therefore clearly wide of the mark.

The story of Edward I's conquest of Wales is full of drama, intrigue and passion. But the records that describe it are often less than helpful. The chroniclers are brief on detail and contradictory, though their shortcomings are compensated for by other sources of evidence about the period. The most obvious are the great castles of Wales themselves; yet the stones too can mislead, as by the middle of the fourteenth century many of them had already fallen into disrepair. But there are other sources, less dramatic perhaps but equally important to the historian. Contemporary administrative documents outline in great detail such matters as the cost of the war, the composition of the armies and where they were at a given time. English records of the time present an entirely English perspective, but nevertheless provide a goldmine of information for historians.

It was mined magnificently at the beginning of the twentieth century by a teacher, J.E. Morris.[1] It is a seminal point in the study of the conflict, a Rubicon crossed, following which no analysis of the events that took place would ever be the same again. A century later the conclusions of Morris still stand worthy of respect. His achievement was all the greater as this was the only book he ever wrote. It is a masterpiece of research, meticulously investigated and carefully crafted. Even now, it is the first reference point for anyone who wishes to understand the wars.

Such a testimonial may appear to question the need for another book on the subject. In my own defence, I would suggest that, while many of Morris's conclusions remain as valid as ever, with the passage of time, unsurprisingly, further information about the conflicts has been uncovered. Numerous academic articles during the twentieth century have examined different aspects of the war. Journals such as the *Welsh History Review* have brought new areas of research within the reach of an extended readership. Developments in the study of military, social and political history have made Wales in the thirteenth century look a very different place than it did to earlier historians. There have been new biographies, including two monumental works on the two major protagonists in the struggle.[2] The cumulative effect of this is to make a new analysis of the Welsh wars valuable, not to nullify the sterling work undertaken by Morris, but to bring it up to date with an accessible overview.

The Welsh wars were not merely a trial of wills between two strong-minded individuals, nor were they wars of great battles. There are many characters in the cast. The major engagements that took place were on a much smaller scale than the decisive battles of the Middle Ages, Crécy, Poitiers and Agincourt. The resources of the Welsh princes were restricted and the Welsh used guerrilla warfare instead. The English raised some very large armies but, in keeping with the character of warfare at the time, rarely kept them in the field for very long. Ultimately, economic factors were to play their part: protracted warfare was proportionately as expensive then as it is now. A great logistician, Edward used his advantages far better than previous English kings had and he deserves credit for it. This is not to say he had no faults. He had many, and they will be examined to the full. But they should not diminish his achievement in conquering Wales and bringing it into his kingdom, something no English monarch had previously achieved in anything other than name.

Neither should the achievements of the Welsh be underestimated. They fought gallantly and hard, and some at least refused to surrender their independence even when their cause was lost. A number paid the ultimate price for their resistance. But they had missed their moment. It is tempting, if futile, to speculate on what might have happened if the events of the late 1270s had occurred thirty years later. It is unlikely, given the disparity in available resources and geographical proximity, that the Welsh would ever have fought and won their own Bannockburn, but one can never be sure. If the vapid Edward II, rather than his more warlike father, had been the opponent of Llywelyn ap Gruffudd the course of British history might perhaps have been very different.

One other point needs to be explained before considering these great events in more detail. Several chapters begin with quotations from Gerald of Wales; as the more informed reader will know, Gerald stopped writing half a century before the events described. I make no apology for this apparent anachronism, however. Gerald's view was not so very different from that of his near-contemporaries who followed on closely behind him. He knew his country – for Wales was his home – and its people better than most, and he wrote in a style that no one else of that era could emulate. It is fitting that we should take into account the views of a man who could see strengths and weaknesses in both Welsh and Englishmen, for there were many examples of such qualities evident on either side.

The Welsh wars were crucial in the evolution of Britain. They brought Wales once and for all into a union, albeit often difficult, with England. They marked the end of an independent Celtic state in the west of Britain. For a time, the culture of Wales itself was under threat. Some would argue that it still is. The efforts of those in Wales in modern times who seek to ensure that the Welsh language not only survives, but thrives, speak eloquently of a culture that is determined to assert its individuality. The course of British history might have been much altered if the wars fought between the English armies led by Edward I and the Welsh led by Llywelyn ap Gruffudd had not evolved in the way that they did. Whether this would have been for better or worse is for others to debate. But there is no doubt that without the joining together of England and Wales events in subsequent centuries could well have been very different.

CHAPTER ONE

The Land of the Dragon

*The English are striving for power, the Welsh for freedom; the English
are fighting for material gain, the Welsh to avoid a disaster; the English soldiers
are hired mercenaries, the Welsh are defending their homeland.*[1]

The maxim of Gerald of Wales is still a familiar refrain heard in various
forms by English 'settlers' arriving in Wales today; a reminder to them
that, while they may have won a war seven centuries ago, the battle still
rages on the moral high ground. However, the conquest of Wales in the
late thirteenth century was not a single, dramatic event, the brutal,
unannounced steamrollering of one small, self-governing nation by a
larger, greedier neighbour; rather, it was the inevitable outcome of a long
series of 'policing' actions to contain bitter internecine quarrels, border
disputes and land grabs and raiding on both sides of Offa's Dyke, set
against the growing confidence and centralism of the English monarchy,
which coincided in turn with the gradual collapse of existing power
structures and the old social systems in Wales.

Arguably, the conquest of Wales, if 'absorption' is too politically
charged a word, happened over two centuries, not just the few years of
Edward I's invasions between 1277 and 1283, and was as much economic
and social as military. The English 'victory' was the culmination of a
series of campaigns, occasionally major, more often small-scale, that
overcame sporadic Welsh resistance and resulted in the creation of an
enlarged and acquisitive English dominion. But it would not be accurate
to represent Wales as a unified nation during this time; unity was hardly
universal, even England was obliged to recognise the quasi-autonomous
status of the Marcher lords, and Welsh nationalism was more the end-
product than the cause of the process. Welsh-born men fought on both
sides in the Welsh wars and later played their own, heroic part in the
growth of British empire, wealth and global power. Edward's triumph
cannot be fully understood, therefore, without putting it in the context
of the events that preceded it, and of changing Welsh social structure and
tradition over this period. The character of the king himself must also
bear some examination.

Exactly where to start an analysis of the chain of events that led up to the final subjugation of Wales is of course an arbitrary decision but it would be true to say that 1066, that pivotal date in English history known to every schoolchild, was in its own way equally decisive for Wales. When Harold Godwinsson, a well-known adversary of the Welsh after his decisive campaigns in the country in 1063, fell under the combined assaults of Norman archers and well-armed cavalry at Hastings, he left not only England open to the Norman invaders but also, in the longer term, Wales. For Duke William of Normandy, the triumphant commander on the day, had brought over to England with him men of determination, vigour and courage who were now deserving of reward; and, most pertinently of all, who possessed an unquenchable desire for land and conquest. It was these Norman lords who exposed frailties in the fabric of Wales that the English would fully exploit.

It was a while, however, before William could be completely confident of his position in England, the primary focus of his campaign. He could not afford to embroil himself in Welsh affairs while his main target was still unsecured. So the Welsh lived out their lives, at least for a short time, largely unaffected by events across the Wye. Their distinctive society, with its links to an earlier Romano-Celtic tradition, and a distinctive form of Christianity, went about its business as it had done before 1066. The respite, however, was to be brief.

Largely owing to its remoteness, Welsh society at this time was quite unlike that of most of the rest of feudal northern Europe. It was, first and foremost, a hierarchical society with rigid demarcations – one where men were, above all, conscious of their status. According to Welsh law, even the value of a dog would be assessed differentially, according to the status of its owner.[2] Status was conferred not by wealth or possessions but by right of birth, passing down through the generations from one dynasty to the next. Although wealth and status of course often went together, the relationship was not an inviolable one. Because a man was relatively wealthy it did not mean that he had an elevated status, and because he was poor it did not mean that he had none. The crucial factor was ancestry – bloodline.

These social distinctions showed themselves particularly in the law. The Welsh legal system had developed a sophisticated value structure whereby, instead of the crude 'eye for an eye' mentality of Norman law, monetary compensation on a predetermined scale for a range of offences was the norm. The level of compensation depended on the status of the person offended against. Similarly, if a man made an oath, its reliability was deemed to rest on his status. With this went another concept, that of honour. Honour was everything; an offence against an individual was not only one which potentially occasioned actual bodily harm or loss of wealth but, most importantly of all, impugned his honour, which could only be restored by adequate public recompense for the harm done to it. Although there would be great changes to Welsh society during the medieval period, the concept of honour was one factor that was to remain a more or less constant factor through the centuries.

Of all the distinctions of status that Welsh society made, perhaps the most common at the start of this period was between those who were free and those who were unfree. It was similar to an Athenian model of society where men who were fortunate enough to be born freemen considered themselves superior to their unfree counterparts; *superiores viri* ('superior men') as that great chronicler of the Welsh, Gerald of Wales, described them. But there was in this an irony. The freemen of society considered themselves superior even as the structure upon which they ultimately depended for their power was already crumbling. For the Welsh social system, enviable in many ways as it was, possessed one Achilles heel that was inevitably to undermine the collective strength of the people and that was land, and the way it passed from one generation to the next.

The concept of partibility was enshrined at the heart of Welsh law. It meant that land was passed on equally to all of the owner's surviving sons rather than, as in the Norman system of primogeniture, to one principal beneficiary. It is difficult to overstate the effect of this process, which implied a continual subdivision of estates into ever-smaller parcels, to be jealously coveted and quarrelled over. In one example, the estate of Iorwerth ap Cadwgan, who lived in the early 1200s, was, by 1313, divided between twenty-seven of his descendants.[3] Such an approach might seem equitable, particularly if one happened to be a younger son who would at least gain some benefit from the arrangement (rather than having to go into the Church or do knightly service), but it led to a progressive weakening of Welsh society, just when the feudal power of England was in the ascendant. As we shall see, the frustrated ambitions of younger brothers who felt they deserved better were to play more than an incidental role in the final conquest of Wales.

Welsh society was also characterised by a complex web of loyalties. The distinctions alluded to between free and unfree men did not remain static during the medieval period and, by the fourteenth century, these had become increasingly irrelevant as the lot of the unfree changed markedly. But as these distinctions became ever more artificial, others took their place. One level of loyalty was that to family. Ancestry played an important part in defining a man's position in society. As a race, the Welsh gloried in their prestigious ancestors, calling on ancient traditions and mythical writings to demonstrate their origins in much more glorious times. They traced their bloodlines back to classical roots: to Brutus, who fled from Troy and founded a new kingdom in Britain.[4] They yearned for the days when Britons would rule in the land once more and restore the heritage lost to the Anglo-Saxon and, more recently, Norman adventurers. In later centuries, the Arthurian tradition frequently placed the seat of Romano-British resistance to Saxon incursions in the fastness of the Cambrian hills.[5]

There was another, more fundamental, level on which Welsh social structures were built, and on which native Welsh society still functions to some extent today. Extended family units had come into being, typically defined as encompassing those males who shared a great-grandfather in common. Combined with the importance of status, and central to the protection of honour, this naturally led to people taking a keen interest in their own ancestry, and that of their neighbours. Family links lived on in the lengthy genealogies which the bards, perpetuators of Welsh oral tradition, recited in their poetry. Ancestry was also confirmed and celebrated in something as apparently mundane as a surname: a man with the name of Llywelyn ap Hywel Fychan ap Hywel ab Einion Sais, for example, clearly demonstrated his antecedents, foreign though they were![6]

Kinship ties were important, particularly in the context of the shared responsibilities that they entailed; but, while it gave apparent strength and unity to the clan, the principle of kinship ultimately threatened its autonomy, offering a useful bargaining chip to any neighbouring warlord demanding loyalty, and able to exploit the fact that a kinsman was obliged to offer himself as a guarantor of the good behaviour of other, potentially troublesome members of his extended family.

Over time, inevitably, there was less willingness to accept the burdens of kinship. Instead, men became conscious of their place in the wider community, and local loyalty began to supplant that of kinship. Men might still glory in their pedigree but they gradually became aware of an extended unit, the community in which they lived, and responsibility towards neighbours increased in significance. By the twelfth century, the local community, the vill (in Welsh, *tref*) was establishing itself as a critical layer in the complex web of loyalties. By this time, clearly designated geographical boundaries were being defined, eventually becoming administrative areas within which taxes might be raised or justice administered. The vill would also make itself responsible for maintaining its pastures and meadows and regulating the rights of the community to access these. The collective responsibility of the vill expressed itself most clearly in the law and its enforcement. Judgement often took the form of arbitration at a local level, an attempt to find a compromise solution to problems, that would manage to preserve a degree of harmony and concord within the community. So engrained was the process that Edward I, who otherwise launched a series of radical amendments to the Welsh legal system, allowed it to be retained in disputes concerning land.

Within this already multidimensional construct of loyalties, another strand can be identified, one which crucially was to take on much greater importance in the twelfth and thirteenth centuries; that of formalised lordship. Lordship came in several forms. As more and more of Wales came within the orbit of the English crown, so did the king of England become increasingly a source of law: a feature which is particularly marked just before, during and immediately after Edward I's wars against the Welsh. But the situation was further complicated because, at the same time, Welsh lords attempted to increase their own power. Llywelyn ap Gruffudd is an excellent example of this trend but there were many others, of whom Llywelyn ap Iorwerth and the Lord Rhys of Deheubarth are two of the more famous. These great princes of Wales attempted to formalise their power over those who lived in their lands, in the process irritating and sometimes alienating those on the receiving end of their actions. The result was a period of social upheaval in Wales, the structure of which altered much between 1066 and 1277. In the process, a great deal of friction was created, leading in turn to the formation of tensions that an opportunistic neighbour, as England undoubtedly was, could exploit to great effect.

All these divisions emphasise one point that is crucial to an understanding of medieval Wales. It was emphatically *not* a country; it was a region, or more accurately a collection of autonomous and shifting states, connected by language, customs and culture. Even when, during the thirteenth century in particular, one Welsh prince would assume prominence, other Welsh lords would still retain a large degree of independence. They might recognise him as their leader but it was a recognition that worked only within defined limits. Each of them would feel justified in developing his own local policy. This trend was supported by geography; for a relatively small land (only 8,000 square miles), Wales has a significant number of internal divisions created by mountains, bogs and river valleys. The end result was a loosely defined coalition epitomised by local flexibility and freedom of action and, as such, often lacking coordination and unity.

The economy of the country was historically shaped by its geography. It was a region of mountains and hills, forests and marshes, and this created its agricultural profile. The upland areas were unsuitable for arable farming and, as a result, pasturage was the predominant agricultural feature of Wales. There were sheep, though the quality of Welsh wool was not as a rule highly regarded until later in the medieval period. The major object of value was cattle. Where possible, rents were paid in cattle, gifts of cattle were held in high esteem, and tax records demonstrate the preponderance of sheep to cattle.[7] (There is even a link in the language, the word *da* meaning both 'good' in modern Welsh, and 'cattle' in old Welsh.) There was certainly to be a change in this situation, as sheep were to become much more important to the Welsh economy with the passing of time. English settlers and monks, especially the Cistercians, would drive this process forward in the first instance; but there was inevitably an assimilation of their ideas by the Welsh men and women living in close proximity to them.

Some arable farming did take place in the country. The geography of Wales, taken as a whole, might have militated against the growing of crops but there were a number of localised exceptions to this rule. Anglesey was the most famous, its fertile soils making it a critical area for supplying the rest of Wales, especially Gwynedd, with cereals. There were also a number of less significant areas that were able to supply their produce to smaller communities around Wales. Oats was much the most common crop, and this in itself is suggestive as it grows better than other crops in cold conditions and hilly terrain. However, barley, rye and wheat were also grown, along with peas and beans. During the two centuries following the Norman conquest of England, arable farming became far more important in Wales. Yet, even then, soldiers fighting in Simon de Montfort's army could protest at the lack of variety in the Welsh diet, complaining at the monotonous fare of meat, cheese, milk and butter – the principal output of an agricultural system that was still primarily focused on pasturage.

Although Wales was still essentially a rural country when Edward I subdued it, there were a number of important changes to its economy in the two centuries preceding the event. At the start of this period, Wales was a poor country with an underdeveloped economy. By the time of the English conquest it was, in relative terms, still poor – but much had changed. At the outset, in the eleventh century, its leaders basically formed a warrior aristocracy. However, fundamental changes were to take place as England evolved, and her colonists crossed the disintegrating frontiers to occupy land that had been conquered in former Welsh territory. The Wales that they found was, generally speaking, a non-monetary economy. Trade was conducted substantially through barter. There were few markets or fairs, and no towns of substance.

In 1066, there was no settlement in the country that might remotely be thought of as urban. Once more, intruders from over the border changed all that. As the Normans began to probe into Wales and conquer and settle territory there, they brought with them their castle-building skills. In these they had at the time no equal. They were capable of throwing up an earth motte topped by a wooden tower and surrounded by a palisaded bailey in incredibly short order. Many of these castles were eventually replaced by more permanent stone structures. Around them, settlements were established to supply their material needs. A number of these became, in relative terms at least, sizeable towns; and, within half a century of the arrival of English settlers in Wales, towns like Cardiff, Cydweli, Pembroke, Striguil (Chepstow) and Rhuddlan were well established. But it was not only in 'English' sectors of Wales that towns of a sort could be seen evolving. Llanfaes in Anglesey saw 30 ships a year arriving before the Edwardian conquest – a relatively small number, perhaps, but indicative of some external trading activity. Coastal settlements also developed at places like Bangor and Caernarfon. These were small, admittedly, but they were the precursors of much larger communities in the future.

But, to come full circle, the one commodity that was more vital than any other was land. Wales is a country where rugged (rather than high) mountains are generously spread, from Snowdonia in the north, via the Cambrian Hills to the Brecon Beacons in the south, from the Preseli Hills in the west to the Berwyn Mountains in the east. The spread of these mountains and hills made communication difficult; their configuration led to settlements being widely and inconveniently dispersed. There were also coastal marshlands, punctuated by a number of river valleys probing far into the hinterland, again interfering with communication and complicating settlement patterns. Cultivable land was therefore a precious resource: even the law recognised its unique importance with a specific injunction that 'chattels are perishable and land is eternal . . . Therefore land is neither to be given nor exchanged for chattels'.[8]

The pressures on land were exacerbated by several factors: the concept of partibility, already discussed, was the first of these, breaking the territory down into smaller and potentially less viable units. But the period was also one of population expansion, part native and in part fed by the influx of settlers, who began to Anglicise areas like Pembrokeshire to a very marked extent, long before the reign of Edward I. Increasingly, the people of Wales became marginalised, forced to cultivate land that was previously waste, making what was already a harsh life even more difficult. Such pressures help to place the wars of Edward I in some kind of context as the logical conclusion of tensions that had been building up for some time.

Within Wales, then, the region was divided into a number of smaller kingdoms. Three in particular were prominent in the medieval period, namely Gwynedd, Powys and Deheubarth. Competition between them (particularly the first two) was intense. By the time that Edward I had launched his first assault on Wales in 1277, certain positions had been reached. Mountainous Gwynedd was the last great bastion of the independent Welsh princes, the one remaining kingdom that refused to be assimilated, albeit that her princes were nominally vassals of the English crown. However, Powys had to all intents and purposes passed over into the English camp, subservient to the kings of England. After a glorious flowering in the late twelfth century, Deheubarth had found it impossible to maintain its position: it had divided internally and, with the breakdown of unified Welsh power, hungry English lords had nibbled away at its boundaries.

To describe the frontiers of these kingdoms is a thankless task: they changed frequently and an accurate delineation is therefore impossible. However, in general terms the kingdom of Gwynedd was based on Snowdonia and Anglesey. It was subdivided geographically into Llŷn, the promontory in the north-west of Wales on which Cricieth stands, Arfon, Eifonydd, Arllechwedd and Ardudwy. The territories of the Perfeddwlad – 'The Middle Country' – to the east of the Conwy were increasingly disputed with the English and formed the point of greatest friction with them, the friction being greater because this was the spot where Gwynedd, the strongest Welsh kingdom during the years before Wales was finally subdued by the English, abutted on to the lands of ambitious lords and kings who wished to take the region as their own. This was in many ways unavoidable: there were strong historic and regional ties between the Perfeddwlad and the remainder of Gwynedd and it was not unusual to have landowners holding property in both areas. Gwynedd had increased its strength relative to the rest of Wales during the twelfth century (with the exception of Deheubarth towards the latter years of that time) but its final flowering occurred during the thirteenth, when, under two outstanding princes named Llywelyn, Wales moved away from being a number of independent principalities to something approaching one, chief of which was Gwynedd.

Powys was formed of the lands of central Wales that bordered England. Again, there were territorial sub-divisions within its borders, reflecting older historical roots; areas like Ceri, Mailienydd, Gwytheyrion, Arwystli. Politically, Powys split in the late twelfth century. The northern part of the region, land in the valley of the Dee, passed to a lord named Madog in 1191, and that part of Powys subsequently became known as Powys Fadog. The remainder passed to a lord named Gwenwynwyn ab Owain Cyfeiliog, and was subsequently known as Powys Gwenwynwyn. Powys Gwenwynwyn later became a pivotal player in Anglo-Welsh relationships but the division reduced the status of Powys below that of Gwynedd and Deheubarth.[9]

Politically, Powys now found itself in an almost impossible position, squeezed between an irresistible force and an immovable object. The irresistible force came from the east and south where the Marcher lords of central Wales, especially the Mortimers, pushed forward into Welsh territory at every opportunity. The immovable object was Gwynedd, and Powys found itself in mortal danger, trapped between these two. Hemmed in on both sides, Powys Gwenwynwyn particularly was faced with two unpalatable options. The first was to disappear, subsumed within an expanded Marcher lordship, or Gwynedd, or probably both. The second was to survive with her powers much reduced, subservient either to England or Gwynedd. Judging rightly that future power lay there, Powys aligned herself with England, especially under the lordship of Gwenwynwyn (died 1216) and his long-lived son, Gruffudd ap Gwenwynwyn (died 1286). Inevitably, this brought Powys into conflict with Gwynedd, a defining characteristic of internal Welsh politics in the thirteenth century.

Deheubarth lay in the south-west of Wales. Within its boundaries much of what had been Dyfed, at one time a powerful force in the region, was subsumed, although English incursions here from soon after the Norman Conquest were to have a dramatic effect. Ceredigion, adjacent to what is now Cardigan Bay, was another part of Deheubarth, along with the regions of Cantref Mawr and Cantref Bychan. Deheubarth was to achieve much in the late twelfth century under the leadership of the Lord Rhys but on his death declined markedly. It suffered greatly from the persistent advances of ambitious English settlers, a process that resulted in an inexorable shrinkage in area, culminating in the thirteenth century. By the time that Edward I led his armies into Wales the power of Deheubarth was effectively spent, though within its borders there were still enough men of courage and resourcefulness to pose problems for any would-be invader.

These three kingdoms were prominent in the unsuccessful attempt to resist the English advance, with Powys Gwenwynwyn opting to support the English cause rather than resist. They by no means controlled the whole of Wales though. Other areas of the country, with equally proud traditions and heritage, disappeared beneath the advancing tide unleashed when William I crossed over from Normandy and took England. Gwent was one of the first to go, followed by Morgannwg. Brycheiniog, the region around Brecon, long remained a place of disputed ownership. Yet crucial though English control of such areas was, its completeness should not be overemphasised. There was no neat absorption of, for instance, Gwent into a Marcher lordship. Although large portions of such regions might become Marcher territory, some areas – especially in heavily wooded and hilly terrain – might remain in Welsh hands until very late on in our period. So, for example, might Llywelyn ap Gruffudd make a bid for the lordship of Gwent just a few years before the Edwardian conquest.

* * *

Having looked briefly at the nature of Wales, it is time to turn to the evolution of Anglo-Welsh relations. Resistance to Duke William, soon to be King William I, in England was patchy. The Norman war machine crushed resistance across the southern parts of the country with ruthless efficiency. Everywhere, their motte and bailey castles mushroomed. William had brought over a large army with him from Normandy. Inevitably, in the aftermath of the Conquest he was faced with a considerable debt to pay to many of his warlords. Their major interest was in land, and large parcels of English territory were divided up among them. But the land available in England was more limited than their lust for material gain. New opportunities therefore had to be found for them.

Generally speaking, the north of England proved initially more resistant to the Normans than the south. The result was that expansionist Norman pressure was pushed westwards. Wales seemed to offer them excellent prospects. The land was not united, a collection of autonomous territories with little cohesiveness between them. There was no overarching ruler in Wales, but rather a number of small princelings who acted independently. William was not overly concerned if there was resistance from the Welsh, which was inevitable given their penchant for war and their proud heritage. His lords fought for themselves primarily rather than for him and while they were occupied fighting the Welsh they could not cause problems in England. He therefore gave them licence to advance into Wales and help themselves to as much territory as the force of their arms could conquer.

There were other advantages accruing to William from this course of action. The Welsh were a potential threat, not to the wellbeing of his kingdom as a whole, but certainly to peaceful governance in various parts of it. They had a long history of cross-border raiding. The existence of a strong baronial presence in these potentially volatile frontier lands would act as a buffer against these raids. For this reason also, it made good sense for William to encourage his barons to develop fiefdoms on the Welsh borders – provided only that they did not become too strong and aggressive as a result. Thus, the Marcher lords were let loose on the Welsh.

There were a number of initial successes for the Norman adventurers who quickly tried their luck in Wales. Frontier castles were built, lowering aggressively westwards towards the heartland. Some of them would play a part in Welsh affairs for centuries to come. Greatest of them all in those early years was the castle built at Striguil, better known as Chepstow, by William Fitz Osbern. He constructed the first castle at Striguil within a few years of Hastings (he was to die in 1071). Its purpose was clear enough, being described in modern times as 'not so much defensive as to provide a secure base for future advances'.[10] It was an important site, evidenced by the fact that the castle was built of stone at a time when most were constructed of timber. This particular fortress was clearly here to stay.

Despite the attractions of this expansionist policy, it was not without its risks for William. His barons had an independent streak, and royal control was irksome to them. There were soon rumblings of discontent from the Marches leading to open rebellion. William put this down and took the opportunity to involve himself more in Marcher affairs, perhaps already regretting the free rein he had given the Marcher barons, as those who had installed themselves in the frontier lands between England and Wales, the Marches, were known. For some time thereafter, the Conqueror took a much more proactive role in south Wales. Only one Welsh lord effectively stood against him, Rhys ap Tudor, the ruler of Deheubarth, in the south-west of the country. Even he however was eventually forced to yield. In 1081, the Conqueror processed across south Wales to the city of St David's, at the extreme western tip of Wales. At the time, it can have seemed little less than a triumphant progress across the country.

The situation further north was also characterised by dynamism and activity. Roger of Montgomery built a castle at Shrewsbury and from here advanced into central Wales. Another was constructed soon afterwards, named Montgomery after his ancestral homelands in France. The north of Wales was threatened from Chester, where Hugh d'Avranches assumed prominence, surrounded by several lieutenants who had come over from Normandy with him. His principal supporter, his cousin, who became known as Robert of Rhuddlan, was the archetypal Norman adventurer: reckless, headstrong, acquisitive, thirsty for battle. A small borough was established at Rhuddlan by him, an early sign of the introduction of towns into Wales as an instrument of consolidation. According to Domesday Book, by 1086 there were eighteen burgesses within the borough, and the town had its own church and mint.

Once the Conqueror died in 1087 the control that he had begun to exercise over his lords, primarily in the south of Wales, loosened markedly. His successor, William Rufus, was happy enough to let his lords act with more or less complete independence in the south. The barons there grew more difficult to control as a result. However, this situation changed greatly with the accession to the throne of Henry I in 1100. He was a stern man, conscious of his rights, in many ways of the same stamp as Edward I. There was soon to be confrontation when Roger of Montgomery died, to be replaced by his son, Robert of Belleme. Henry's accession was not uncontested; Duke Robert of Normandy had also launched a bid for power. He was supported by Robert of Belleme but was ultimately overwhelmed by the king. Robert of Belleme was sent to Normandy in exile, and with him went his brother, Arnulf of Pembroke. Coinciding as it did with the death of the earl of Chester, who was succeeded by a minor, all of a sudden the north and central Welsh Marches were left largely leaderless. The situation did not last long. Seizing his opportunity, Henry quickly moved into the vacuum that had resulted and appointed his own officials to oversee the territory. This benefited him and his kingdom in the short term but in the long term did not help the Anglo-Normans and their position. It meant that the forces directly opposing the Welsh of Gwynedd were reduced in strength and vitality, allowing the princes of Gwynedd to recover.

The removal of Arnulf from Pembrokeshire also left a vacuum. His lands were divided up among several Norman lords; for the time being at least there would be no predominant Norman baron in the area. Instead, Henry encouraged a number of Flemish emigrants to settle there, and south-west Wales became and remains today one of the most Anglicised parts of the country. Gradually, Norman incursions in the south intensified. The region, especially the coastal plain, was more open to invasion than the lands to the north. In addition, a relatively open seaboard allowed the Normans to use their ships to assist the advances made. Large tracts of the south came under Norman rule, although where the land lay on the fringe of wilder hills at the head of the various river valleys, that domination was never absolute nor necessarily permanent. The castle of Cydweli, for example, changed hands with some regularity. But inevitably some lords – such as the Clare family – became more prominent than others.

The death of Henry I gave Wales some respite, largely because of the instability of England in the years after his death. England was about to find itself embroiled in civil war, presenting the Welsh with an opportunity to recover some of the ground that they had lost. After

Henry's death in 1135, the Welsh launched a number of raids, in the course of which several prominent Norman lords were killed. Henry's successor, Stephen, initially responded energetically – but subsequent raids launched from Gwynedd met with more Welsh success. From Gwynedd, the Welsh raiders pushed down into Ceredigion, much of which had passed into the Norman sphere of influence. They also entered into alliances with men from the south of Wales. It was for the Normans a dangerous situation. A disunited Wales – in truth, more often than not the norm – made relatively easy pickings for Anglo-Norman adventurers. But a determined alliance between the leaders of various Welsh territories on the other hand was a portent of real difficulties. So it proved. An Anglo-Norman force set out from Pembroke to intercept a Welsh raid and was crushed in the subsequent battle, giving the Welsh an opportunity of which they were quick to take advantage.

The position of the Welsh improved still further as England slid inexorably towards civil war while Stephen struggled to control his barons. The king found himself in opposition to Matilda, daughter of Henry I, who coveted England for herself. A number of her supporters came from the Welsh Marches. As her allies there found themselves dragged into the war in England, their attention was diverted, leaving them dangerously exposed to Welsh raids. The Welsh seized the opportunity, capturing a number of important Marcher towns including Oswestry. It was an unwelcome change of fortune for the invaders, who for so long had achieved a steady stream of success. However, when the civil war ended and England found herself with a new monarch, Henry II, their attention returned once more to Wales. Henry was a ruler who shared a number of Edward I's characteristics: tough, strong and possessed of that infamous Plantagenet temper – the 'black bile' as it was sometimes known. He launched a full-scale attack on Wales at the head of a large force, which appeared to spell disaster for the Welsh. But when disaster did finally threaten, it was not the Welsh who were to find themselves in the gravest peril.

Henry advanced into Wales in 1157, the third year of his reign. His plan of action was not without its merits. An English fleet sailed offshore, helping to keep the army supplied. Perhaps the advantages that he appeared to enjoy lulled Henry into a false sense of security. He set off into the thickly wooded area south of Hawarden, leaving much of his army behind. In so doing, he made two fundamental mistakes. A good commander never divides his force without an excellent reason for doing so. And, in unfamiliar territory, to set off without first of all deploying a strong screen of scouts is the height of folly. Henry was quickly to find out the seriousness of his miscalculations. One minute he was enjoying what seemed like an unhindered progress through north Wales, the next he was fighting for his life. The Welsh, experts at guerrilla warfare in a landscape that they knew intimately, launched a ferocious ambush on his depleted force. Henry barely escaped with his life. When he subsequently launched a raid on Anglesey, recognising its importance as a source of supply for Gwynedd, that too met with little success.

Despite these successes for the Welsh, the superior resources available to the English told in the end and Owain, prince of Gwynedd, was finally forced to sue for peace on unfavourable terms. The allegiance he swore to Henry though was little more than a charade. Only a few years later, Gwynedd was in revolt once more. Henry, a man who did not take kindly to being crossed, resolved to solve his Welsh problem once and for all. Rather than risk open battle, Owain retreated into the impenetrable mountains, daring Henry to come and find him there. Henry played right into his hands. Instead of advancing along the coast, he opted instead to attempt to cross the featureless Berwyn Mountains. In the process, he came up against the greatest ally of the Welsh – the climate. In medieval times, Wales was renowned for its inhospitable weather. It showed itself at its worst now. The mists came down, making the landscape more featureless than ever. The already-inadequate tracks turned into quagmires in the rain and became impassable. In such conditions, the large size of Henry's army became a handicap. Supplies ran out and Henry was left with only one option – an ignominious retreat back to England. It was a chastened, humbled and angry king who returned across the border. In an act of gratuitous spite, he blinded several of the hostages he had previously taken in an attempt to secure the good behaviour of the Welsh.

The English made more progress further south, however. Here, the Marcher lords grew stronger. On occasion they suffered reverses, such as when the Welsh attacked Llandovery in 1162. But these Welsh successes were localised and often carried out with little support from the Welsh in the north. Eventually, the Welsh in the south reached an accommodation with England. The Lord Rhys, prince of Deheubarth, assumed a prominence that no Welsh lord in the south had attained for many years. Realising however that his prospects of military success against the English were limited, he instead offered homage to Henry. In return, Henry was prepared to give him considerable autonomy. It was a relationship that worked surprisingly well. Rhys would be a loyal supporter of the English crown and he was, in return, largely left to his own devices. He in fact set a precedent; subsequent Welsh lords in

Deheubarth would look back on his time as a golden age and try, without success, to emulate his achievements.

* * *

Henry now decided to send a major expedition to Ireland, led by the earl of Pembroke, Richard 'Strongbow'. There were not only English troops in this army; there were also a good number of Welshmen, happy to join at the prospect of plunder. Welsh troops had fought with the English before, for example in the civil wars during the reign of King Stephen, and the involvement of Welsh troops is in itself suggestive. Politically, it showed that many Welshmen were pragmatists and by no means universally wedded to the cause of an independent Wales. Many indeed would fight alongside the English in the armies of Edward I at a later stage.

Following the death of Henry II, Wales was about to enter a new age, an era when her princes would assume a prominence that had been lost to them for several centuries. There were two outstanding princes who were to be the leaders of Gwynedd during the thirteenth century. The first of them was Llywelyn ap Iorwerth, the second Llywelyn ap Gruffudd. The first Llywelyn was an ambitious man, as evidenced by the fact that he married an illegitimate daughter of King John of England, Joan. This did not stop John of England advancing his interests in Wales and, for a time, it seemed as if the vassaldom of Wales was about to be complete. John marched deep into the country. He was, despite the generally bad press he has received from historians, an efficient organiser and his success presaged the greatest possible danger for Llywelyn. But, for the Welsh, the darkest hour was to be the one immediately before the dawn. An amazing renaissance was about to be launched.

The high-water mark of John's advances was to be reached in 1212. By this time, much of Wales appeared to be under his control. Soon after, instability in England once more took his attention elsewhere. John's English problems offered the Welsh the prospect of a recovery. That these hopes were not altogether in vain was largely because, although much of the south of the country, particularly in the coastal belt, was by now in the hands of Marcher lords, the principality of Gwynedd was still an intact, if dangerously threatened, entity.

It was in this environment that Llywelyn ap Iorwerth, a heroic figure in Welsh history, came to the fore. He was of course helped by events in England, and he was even more fortunate when John died in 1216 and was replaced by Henry III, who was a mere child at the time. Even allowing for these conditions, Llywelyn's success was remarkable. Just three years after being at his lowest ebb, in 1215 he took Shrewsbury. He then broadened the scope of his operations, sending aid to rebellious Welshmen in the south of the country. A number of towns, including Swansea, fell to them. In 1216, he fell on Powys, the prince of which was a supporter of the English. When there was a dispute over the government of Deheubarth, Llywelyn offered himself as a mediator. Whether by force of arms or diplomacy, Llywelyn was quick to seize every chance that came his way. But he was not foolishly ambitious and made no equivocation in offering homage to Henry III while at the same time increasing his autonomy. It was a fine balance to strike but Llywelyn managed it superbly well.

Llywelyn did not manage to retain all of his gains permanently. The dynasty of William Marshal, earl of Pembroke, one of the greatest of all the medieval baronial dynasties of England, fought back against Llywelyn and recovered some of the lands that they had lost. As Henry III grew into a man, he too was not slow to profit from a number of the opportunities that came his way. He captured Montgomery from Llywelyn and then launched further campaigns in 1228 and 1231. Although these achieved little military success, there were political gains, such as the receiving of homage from several Welsh princes. However, Llywelyn was far from finished. He launched a large raid of his own in 1231, conquering the fortresses of Brecon, Hay, Radnor and Montgomery. Cydweli and Neath were also sacked. It was a powerful reminder to Henry that Llywelyn was far from a spent force.

Llywelyn was ambitious to confirm his supremacy over the other Welsh lords, and claimed for himself the title *princeps Aberffraw et dominus Snowdonia* (prince of Aberffraw and lord of Snowdon), the first part of the title emphasising his claim to prominence over other Welshmen. Although English kings might resist this claim, his fellow countrymen often acknowledged its accuracy. But like all men he was mortal, and the greatest danger to his achievements was that his successors would not be able to protect them.

It was a threat of which Llywelyn was all too well aware. He had two sons. Gruffudd, the eldest, was illegitimate, while Dafydd was born from his marriage with Joan. Traditionally, illegitimacy would prove no obstacle to Gruffudd succeeding him. But both the English crown and the Church were opposed to any such idea and, in theory, the man born in wedlock, Dafydd, would be a more acceptable choice to them. Llywelyn saw that this might have a powerful effect on the viability of Gwynedd and he therefore resolved to appoint Dafydd his sole heir. It looked superficially a simple enough proposition. The Papacy had no wish to see an illegitimate son inheriting and English law equally frowned on sons born out of wedlock. Further, Joan – the mother of Dafydd – was Henry of England's half-sister. But Henry saw in the situation an opportunity. A divided Gwynedd could only weaken the fabric of Wales and make it easier to achieve his ambitions of supremacy. He therefore tried to manipulate the situation to his advantage and prevaricated rather than agreeing to the proposal.

His initial response may not have appeared unhelpful. His government noted and accepted the arrangement in 1220, to be followed by official ratification from the Pope, Honorius III. In 1228, Henry accepted Dafydd's homage for the land that would be his when his father died. However, a decade later in 1238, Llywelyn invited the lords of Wales to pay homage to Dafydd in advance of his eventual succession. When he got word of this, Henry acted promptly and negatively. He advised Llywelyn that his actions were premature and the English would only agree to a watered-down version of the oath that Llywelyn wished to use. The inference was that Henry did not want the lords of Wales swearing homage to the prince of Gwynedd when he felt that by rights their homage should be given straight to him. The act of homage had profound importance. It was a sacred act of allegiance, a moral contract, binding in the eyes of God, and it tied a man to his liege lord in such a way that the arrangement was, except in very exceptional circumstances, unbreakable.

The dispute revolved around the position of the prince of Gwynedd in the hierarchy of Wales. For some time – at least since the days of Henry II – the king of England had been nominal overlord of all Welshmen. Llywelyn, as a result of his extended period of success, had effectively created a position for himself as *primus inter pares* in the country. In this role, he was accepted as a man who held a superior position over all the lords of Wales and who would, if he had his way, pay homage to the crown of England on behalf of them all. It would give him great power and influence in Wales, something that Henry III was acutely aware of and would go out of his way to counteract.

This difficult situation was exacerbated still further because Gruffudd, who had clearly lost out badly in this particular scenario, was a man of strong emotions and actions. He was hardly likely to accept the loss of his birthright to his younger brother with equanimity. Llywelyn tried to soften the blow by offering him various positions of responsibility but with limited success. He was given lands to govern in Meirionydd and Ardudwy but he was soon removed from them in a way that suggested that he was not the most efficient or honest of administrators. This happened in 1221, soon after Llywelyn's original declaration of his plans for the succession, and Gruffudd was then employed in a military capacity. All was not well though between Llywelyn and Gruffudd and by 1228 the latter was in custody. He would remain there for six years. His position was improved somewhat when he was given some lands of his own but it did not bode well for a smooth handover of power.

In 1240, Llywelyn died. Dafydd quickly sought out Henry III to swear allegiance to him and secure his position. He hoped that in return his accession in Gwynedd would be unchallenged. A formal agreement was signed to mark the occasion, with terms that were harsh for the Welsh. Dafydd revealed his political inexperience by signing it, for it tied Wales much more closely to England. The terms stated among other things that the Welsh lords should give homage direct to the English crown in future, a marked diminution in the status of the prince of Gwynedd. There were also problems from within Wales itself. The relationship between Gwynedd and Powys had been strained for some time. The lord of Powys, Gruffudd ap Gwenwynwyn, was involved in territorial disputes with Dafydd, which had their genesis in the time of Llywelyn. It was decided that a commission would be set up to arbitrate on this dispute. On the commission would be a number of English lords and a papal representative, as well as two prominent Welshmen, Ednyfed Fychan and Einion Fychan.

The greatest challenge however came from Dafydd's half-brother, Gruffudd. He was married to a persuasive and clever woman, Senena. She took her case to Henry III, arguing that Gruffudd had wrongfully been deprived of what should have been his. Shortly after succeeding to the Princedom of Gwynedd, Dafydd had captured Gruffudd and thrown him, and his son Owain, into Cricieth Castle. Senena protested at the injustice of it all. With an understanding that surely owed more than a little to a cynical exploitation of the situation, Henry showed much sympathy for her case and sought to divide the Welsh. Dafydd showed little sign of accepting this situation and in the summer of 1241 Henry marched into Wales at the head of an army to force him to moderate his stance by freeing Gruffudd and Owain, and to divide his lands with his half-brother.

*   *   *

Dafydd was a disappointment as a prince of Gwynedd. He was not without abilities, but he rarely showed them to their best effect. He had first of all been outmanoeuvred in the political game. He was now about to be outwitted in the military arena. There was one cardinal rule that any prince of Gwynedd had always lived by and that was to ensure that, in the last resort, a final defence could be maintained in the fastnesses of Snowdonia. However, in the war that followed Dafydd committed an unforgivable error and allowed himself to be cut off from this bastion of last resort. He was left with no option but to seek terms, which were harsh indeed. Dafydd was forced to hand Gruffudd and Owain over to Henry for safekeeping. Henry could use these men as invaluable pawns in the future. Worse was to follow. Llywelyn had recovered a great deal of land from England in the days of King John. Dafydd was now forced to hand much of this back, effectively taking the country back to the position in which it had been three decades previously. The homage of all Welshmen was to be given direct to the English crown in the future. It was a devastating blow. It has been argued that it was not a decisive one but it was certainly a situation from which Dafydd personally never recovered.[11]

Ostensibly, Gruffudd and Owain would remain with Henry until he had resolved how lands in Gwynedd would be allocated to them; in the event, there is no evidence that this subject was ever seriously considered by the king. All Henry wanted was to have the men in his power as a way of ensuring the good behaviour of Dafydd. If Dafydd behaved, he could hope that Gruffudd and Owain would be kept well out of harm's way and he would be left to his own devices. If however he did not act in a way that Henry felt was acceptable then the king would support their cause enthusiastically. So Gruffudd was taken to London to be kept behind the grim walls of the Tower for the foreseeable future. He had merely swapped a prison in his own country for one in a foreign land. Dafydd did his best to improve his position. He suggested to the Pope that Wales should become a papal fief, an innovative plan but one which did not come to fruition. He also adopted for himself a new title, prince of Wales. It was a proud boast but an empty one and merely served to aggravate Henry III still further. Dafydd's ambition and courage far exceeded his abilities.

Wales was now slipping inexorably down the slope that led to domination by England. The English crown appeared to be growing more powerful by the year, while the last stirrings of an independent spirit within Wales began to fade forever. There seemed little hope for the country, whose survival as an independent region appeared to be on the verge of extinction. But in the shadows a young, ambitious and very talented member of the ruling dynasty of Gwynedd was about to make his appearance. Llywelyn ap Gruffudd was the son of that Gruffudd who was now incarcerated in the Tower. He had not yet made much of an impression on Welsh affairs. But the second Llywelyn's moment for greatness had now, at last, arrived. Because Gruffudd had been deprived of his inheritance, so too ultimately had his sons. It was a thought that must have preyed frequently on the mind of an intelligent, ambitious young man like Llywelyn. But even as these events were being acted out, another player was entering the stage. In 1239, a child was born who, in manhood, would bring Wales irrevocably into the orbit of the English crown.

CHAPTER TWO

Edward the First

Valiant, prudent, wise and bold:
and adventurous and fortunate in all feats of war.[1]

When Prince Edward of England was born on 17 June 1239, there was a
great outpouring of joy among the population of the country. He would
ultimately be crowned King Edward I of England, though in fact this was
an inaccurate appellation explained by that strange quirk of English
history which insists on numbering English kings from the Norman
Conquest onwards. There had been several Saxon kings of England
named Edward and it was after one of them, the saintly Edward the
Confessor, that the young prince was named. Edward's father, the pious
but ineffectual Henry III, was deeply inspired by the example of the
Confessor and he would expend a great deal of money and effort on
rebuilding his abbey church at Westminster. It was his greatest legacy to
future generations, a magnificent, uplifting monument to a reign that
did little to merit it.

There are few records of the young prince's early years but those that
survive suggest that he enjoyed a fairly typical upbringing for the times.
He was farmed out early on, to be brought up away from the presence of
his father and mother. Details of his education are sketchy but as a grown
man he not only spoke French, the everyday language of the English
court at the time, but he could also converse in English and he had some
understanding of Latin. Outdoor pursuits would have taken up an
important part of his developmental years too; riding and hunting, as
well as falconry, a hobby that he would take very seriously indeed as a
grown man.

Of his youthful character, there are not many references on which to
construct a hypothesis but surviving sources paint a picture of a young
man that is not altogether flattering. One of the livelier chroniclers of
the day, Matthew Paris, describes how the young prince, then a strong-
willed teenager, was involved in a very unpleasant incident. A youth for
some reason or other caused Edward offence and, in response, the prince
ordered his entourage to cut off one of his ears and gouge out an eye. If

he acted like this when he was young, wondered Matthew, what would he be like when he was a man with real power in his hands?

Another contemporary writer described Edward as a leopard, a beast regarded by medieval commentators as an animal of contradictions, untrustworthy and duplicitous. Therefore he had the attributes of the lion, Leo, brave, proud and fierce. But alongside these characteristics he also bore the mark of the 'pard', a creature that could not be relied upon.[2] The analogy is not without supporting evidence. There is certainly plenty to suggest that he was a man of violent temper, capable of erupting at a moment's notice. Later on in life, one of his daughters – with whom he generally enjoyed a good relationship – did something to arouse his ire. In a fit of blind rage, he picked up her coronet and flung it on the fire. On the wedding day of another daughter, Margaret, a squire enraged the king, as he then was, causing him to lose his temper. In a violent attack, he beat the squire, doing him so much damage that he later felt obliged to pay the substantial sum of £13 6s 8d as compensation. He was clearly not a man to be crossed lightly.

That there was also a devious side to his character is readily apparent. During the civil wars in England between Henry III and his brother-in-law, Simon de Montfort, Edward led a force to relieve the garrison at Gloucester, which was under siege at the time. After breaking into the town, the position changed drastically when a party of rebels under the command of Earl Ferrers appeared. Realising that the forces arrayed against him were too strong for him to defeat, Edward sought a truce. This was successfully negotiated, whereupon Earl Ferrers went away. As soon as he had left, the prince threw a number of the citizens into prison and laid a heavy ransom on Gloucester; both actions were against the terms of the truce. From what we know of Edward, he would easily have justified this volte-face to himself by arguing that the truce had been forced out of him under duress, and that a prince was under no obligation to comply with terms wrung from him under such conditions. But acts such as this did nothing to enhance his reputation.

A full consideration of Edward's early life is out of place in a book examining specifically his campaigns in Wales but there are two events in particular that had a bearing on his later career. The first of them concerned the lands granted to him by his father when still a prince. It was customary at the time for a young prince to be given lands to govern from which he could both draw an income and also learn the art of government. When still a youth, Edward was to receive a number of lands from his father. There was no doubting which was his own particular favourite. The region of Gascony, in the south-west of France, was warm, fertile and rich. It is easy to understand why a young man could fall in love with such a place. This was the start of a life-long attachment as far as Edward was concerned; the land was a source of provisions and men that he would call upon frequently in the future, not least during his Welsh campaigns.

As far as Edward's Welsh involvement is concerned, the most relevant grant of land took place in 1254 when he was given large amounts of territory in Wales. Most of these belonged to the lordship of Chester and were found in the north-east of the country, in the region known as the 'Four Cantreds' or, to the Welsh, Perfeddwlad. There were, however, other lands in the south, such as the famous 'Three Castles' of Grosmont, Skenfrith and White near Abergavenny. The timing of the grants is significant; at about this time, Llywelyn ap Gruffudd was establishing himself as an emergent force in the country. His rising power in Wales coincided with a period of harsh rule under Edward. We should be careful before blaming the young English prince for this. He was after all still an inexperienced youth and it was his advisers who should take the majority of the blame. Indeed, to an extent the repressive regime that was in evidence when Edward was given these lands was very much a continuation of what had gone on before.[3] Neither was Edward quite as free to act unilaterally as might superficially appear to be the case. Henry III still played a prominent role in the conduct of Welsh affairs during these years and Edward himself appears only to have made a brief visit to Wales, in July 1256.

As for Chester, there was persistent grumbling from the Welsh in the north that the English were attempting to impose English modes of law on the territories that they held, and that they were trying to subsume them within the wider lordship of Chester – accusations that uncannily resemble those made against the English nearly thirty years later, when Anglo-Welsh relations reached a point of absolute crisis. The 'high-handedness and insensitivity' of English officials led to 'a mounting sense of outrage and resentment in Wales'.[4] In 1256, the Welsh population of those lands in the north-east of the country that were ruled by Edward decided they could take no more. In an attempt to prevent their assimilation into a way of life that they neither understood nor cared for, they launched a full-scale revolt against their English masters. They appealed to Llywelyn ap Gruffudd for support, and he came to their aid. It was the start of a decade-long period in which the star of both Wales itself and Llywelyn in particular was definitely in the ascendant.

Llywelyn achieved astounding results in the north of the country, where Edward appears to have had markedly inadequate resources at his disposal to resist the advances of the Welsh forces. His initial successes appear to have spurred Llywelyn on to more ambitious plans. Not restricting his campaign to the lands of the north, he also attacked Meirionydd and then moved on Builth. In the process, he attacked the lands of various Marcher lords such as Roger Mortimer in mid-Wales, and the earl of Gloucester. The sequence of events is absolutely striking. Repression by the English in lands that they ruled in Wales, particularly in the form of the imposition of English law and customs, fuelled resentment that, in its turn, manifested itself in a violent counter-reaction. Llywelyn, an opportunist of the first order (like Edward himself) availed himself of the chance to advance his position as a result, and in the process brought himself into conflict with some of the key Marcher lords. These events were, in these respects at least, a carbon copy of the later wars in Wales and the circumstances that led up to them.

It was apparent to Edward and his advisers at a very early stage that they lacked the wherewithal to reverse initial Welsh successes but appeals to Henry III for help fell on deaf ears. In a response that eloquently typified Henry's general ineptitude as a king, he grumbled that the situation was Edward's responsibility and that he should sort it out himself. It was an analysis that ignored certain key facts. The land might be Edward's but he needed adequate resources to govern it. He was a young, inexperienced man and he needed support if he was to learn to be an effective governor. Henry had anyway continued to play a dominant part in Welsh affairs when it suited him to do so. And, if the revolt were to proceed unchecked, then it would have repercussions outside the lands immediately ruled by Edward in the north of the country.

Henry deserves to be most criticised for failing to appreciate this last fact in particular. Because of his inactivity, things went from bad to worse for the English. The largest force that they had available was sent to the south, towards Llandovery. Edward was not personally involved in subsequent activities there, and leadership of the force was delegated to the earls of Gloucester and Hereford. Their campaign coincided with the Welsh winter, a wet, cold time of year that more than lived up to the reputation of Wales for inhospitable weather. The English trudged around in the mud aimlessly, and achieved virtually nothing in return for all their efforts.

Soon after, a decisive event took place which meant that Henry III's policy of sitting imperiously on the sidelines was no longer a tenable position. A Welsh noble in the south of the country, Rhys Fychan, asked for English help in restoring his influence in the region. It was a good opportunity for the English to take advantage of internal Welsh divisions and advance their own position as a result. A force was despatched under the command of Stephen Bauzan to assist Rhys. There was nothing wrong with this general strategy but at a crucial moment in the campaign Rhys changed sides. Bauzan's forces were led straight into a trap; when it was sprung, a heavy defeat was inflicted on them. The reverse forced Henry's hand: splendid isolation was no longer an option. On 1 August 1257, he summoned a force to meet him at Chester.

*   *   *

In the expedition that followed, Henry was to demonstrate his inadequacies as a military commander to the full. Nevertheless, for Edward the campaign was not without its uses. The young prince accompanied his father on the campaign – despite the assertion of Matthew Paris that he was at odds with Henry and wanted nothing to do with it – and in return received an invaluable lesson. Edward was about to find out exactly how not to conduct an expedition in Wales. It was an experience that he would never forget and, when he returned to Wales twenty years later, he was fastidious in avoiding a replication of the mistakes that dogged Henry's campaign in Wales.

The route that the English followed was a well-trodden one as far as would-be conquerors were concerned. The English would advance from Chester along the coast and threaten Gwynedd. To achieve success, however, the army would need to be maintained by a steady flow of supplies and this required that a sophisticated logistical operation be set up. It transpired that the challenges involved were far beyond the capabilities of Henry III to deal with. Supplies soon became a problem. The resilience of the Welsh, their ability to make the most of the terrain to employ their well-practised hit-and-run tactics, further strained the English. The advance began to slow and then stopped completely. It was soon followed by an undignified retreat, with the departing English, demoralised, tired and hungry, chased remorselessly by the exultant Welsh rebels.

These experiences were crucial in advancing Edward's military knowledge and giving him invaluable insights into the way that a successful war could be fought on Welsh territory. At the end of this somewhat chaotic expedition, there was one fact that was abundantly clear. The rising fortunes of Llywelyn ap Gruffudd, at this stage very much in the ascendancy in Wales, meant that for some time to come the balance of power between the English and the Welsh would be tipped towards the latter.

Edward was still learning both how to fight and how to rule his lands, but even at this early stage of his life certain personal characteristics were already becoming clear. Surviving accounts from the time suggest that Edward's lands were run in such a way that every effort was made to ensure that profit from them was maximised. Income from them was surprisingly high given the actual wealth of the lands involved. The implication is that Edward was a hard master, who put his own personal gain ahead of most other considerations. Accusations such as these were to be made against Edward in many of his lands throughout his life and their consistency suggest that he was indeed eager to profit from all his territories.

But of all the formative events in his early life, perhaps the most crucial were those of the late 1250s and early to mid-1260s, when England was to find itself in the grip of a violent and bloody civil war. This was the second great formative experience for Edward, with regard to future Welsh affairs. The catalyst for the conflict stretched back into the past, drawing on an ongoing struggle between monarchs and barons for power. Perhaps the most famous incident characterising these tensions was the civil war in England against King John, which culminated in the signing of Magna Carta in 1215, but it was by no means an isolated example of what happened during the period. Magna Carta was not entirely the defining event that a simplistic examination of history might suggest. The underlying problems that led to its signing were not irrevocably solved and were in fact to resurface again with dramatic results during the reign of Henry III.

The immediate reason for the crisis in Henry's reign was the ambitious Earl of Leicester, uncle to Edward through marriage to Henry III's sister, Eleanor. Simon de Montfort is one of the most striking baronial figures in English medieval history. Intensely ambitious, he brought relationships between the English monarch and his subjects to a very different level than they had ever been before. Simon was a man of contrasts, capable of inspiring great loyalty from his close allies but also of alienating men either through his excessive ambitions or his arrogance. A man who believed in getting his own way, he played a crucial role in Edward's life while the young man was still maturing. It is perhaps more than coincidence that we see something in Edward during later life of de Montfort's determination to get his own way.

It was a combination of circumstances that finally brought matters to a head, listed by one modern historian as including a hatred of Henry III's half-brothers, who played a prominent part in the government of the day; resentment at Henry's ill-founded attempts to involve himself in hopelessly over-complicated foreign adventures; dissatisfaction at the outcome of events in Wales, and widespread opposition to the way that local government was conducted in England.[5] A council in April 1258 was summoned to discuss the situation. Opposition to the rule of the king was so powerful that he was forced to agree to terms that both he and Edward, who was also present, found particularly humiliating. A committee of twenty-four men was to be created to begin discussions concerning the reform of the nation's affairs; twelve of them were to be chosen by the barons themselves. On 30 April, Henry III and Edward both swore to be bound by the terms that the committee would eventually decide on. Both men were proud of their position and status and the nature of the agreement must have meant that the opposition was indeed powerful and that the position of the monarchy was relatively weak. One can easily imagine the effect on Edward, an impressionable youth who would demonstrate repeatedly throughout his life that he was acutely aware of the importance of his position.

There would be other humiliating instances in the years ahead, which helped to emphasise the weakness of the crown. The collective impact of these imminent years of strife and anarchy was to give Edward a sense that the rights of the crown had been unnaturally interfered with. When he became king, he resolved, he would spend much of his reign attempting to restore what he perceived to be the excessively reduced powers of the monarchy. An understanding of this facet of his character is crucial to an appreciation of the events of his reign, especially with regard to his actions in Wales, where it is noticeable that one of the key factors leading to the first Welsh war in 1277 was the refusal of Llywelyn ap Gruffudd to pay homage to him as the new king of England, as the latter was bound to do.

It was during the years of greatest tension in England (1258–67) that relationships were forged, both positive and negative, crucial to the development of future Anglo-Welsh relations, and which led ultimately to the invasion of Wales in 1277 and its final conquest in 1282. In developing acquaintance with men who would later come to be among his key advisers during those years of warfare in Wales, Edward also encountered sometimes difficult relationships with some of the Marcher lords. Their ambivalence towards the centralising tendency of the English crown presented an opportunity that a strong Welsh prince, such as Llywelyn ap Gruffudd, could – if he played a wise political hand – exploit to his advantage. A strong and assertive English king could threaten the autonomy of the Marcher lords as much as he challenged the independence of Wales. Events were to take place during those years which would define the relationship between Edward and the de Montfort family, who would themselves be part of the catalyst leading to war with Wales. And all the time, Llywelyn ap Gruffudd would avail himself of the opportunities given by dissension in England to advance his own interests.[6]

Other events conspired to show Edward in a dangerously ambitious light. When Henry III travelled to France in 1259, Edward saw an opportunity to benefit from his absence. He attempted to do so, first of all, by advancing the interests of his own allies. One of them, Roger Clifford, was given custody of the 'Three Castles' in the Welsh March, which played such a strategically important role in the region. The name of Clifford should be noted – he will appear again in the crucial early days of the Welsh war of 1282. But this was just the beginning of Edward's ambitious plans. Rumours reached Henry in France that were, to say the least, alarming. The stories in circulation suggested that Edward was set on nothing less than the crown of England itself. Henry was concerned enough to arrange a prompt return home, in the meantime summoning a number of his magnates to meet him in London with their men-at-arms. Prominent among them was the earl of Gloucester, a Marcher baron with whose family Edward would often be at odds. As the earl descended on London, so too did Edward with a large number of armed men. For a time, confrontation seemed likely. But Edward, realising that the right time had not yet come, backed down and a peaceful resolution was negotiated.

What bearing do these events have on the later history of Wales? First, they show Edward as an ambitious individual, driven by thoughts of his own aggrandisement. He was still, after all, a young man, and it is hardly unusual for young men to be excessively ambitious. Edward was especially so. This sense of ambition does much to explain his later adventuring in Wales. The events of this traumatic period also show just how diametrically opposed the interests of Edward and some of his Marcher lords could be. Gloucester opposed Edward's ambitions so much that he was prepared to trade blows with him in order to protect his own position. This demonstrates how deep internal divisions in England and the Marches were, divisions that the Welsh might indeed take advantage of – at least in the short term.

Llywelyn was not slow to avail himself of the opportunities afforded to him. Late in 1262 he attacked the Marches, with some success. English feathers were ruffled. Edward was abroad at the time and hurried back to England. Frantic despatches had been received from Peter de Montfort, in charge at Abergavenny, to say that his position was precarious. Desperately, de Montfort told his superiors that 'if [the Welsh] are not stopped they will destroy all the lands of the king as far as the Severn and the Wye; they ask for nothing less than the whole of Gwent.'[7] It was clear that support for Llywelyn came not just from the north but from right across Wales. Worryingly for the English, other Marcher lords were decidedly reluctant to come to de Montfort's aid, a strong indication of where their loyalties lay. An expedition was summoned and put under the command of Edward in person. He was at Hereford by 3 April, for here a treaty was agreed with Dafydd, the brother of Llywelyn – a man who would be at different times both an ally and the bitter enemy of Edward. But, apart from this, little was achieved in the campaign. The Welsh adopted their traditional hit-and-run tactics, launching guerrilla assaults and then disappearing into the forests and mountains of their country so that the English forces could not work a decisive position for themselves. But this campaign must again have proved a useful learning experience for Edward.

* * *

The campaign in Wales presaged a massive deterioration in conditions in England itself. Since the agreement of the so-called Provisions of Oxford in 1258, the country had found itself under great stress but out-and-out civil war had so far been avoided. However, the momentum now enjoyed by the reform movement was very powerful. Simon de Montfort, building on deep-rooted tensions in the country, was determined that the programme of reform continued to push forward. On the other hand, Henry III, supported by Edward, was determined that the rights of the crown should not be further diminished. Indeed, he was set on reversing many of the changes that he had already been forced to acquiesce to.

De Montfort had spent some time abroad, leaving England in 1261. When he returned in 1263, he was set on advancing his cause still further. He sought alliances that would help him to achieve the desired results. There was one area in particular that proved to be a fertile source of support for him: there had been a change of the most profound importance in the Marches. Richard, earl of Gloucester, had died in 1262. Relations between the old earl and the crown had not always been easy. The late earl's son and successor would prove to be an even more difficult man to deal with.

Richard's successor as earl of Gloucester, Gilbert de Clare, was an ambitious and radical young man. Holder of a significant part of the Marches where Marcher lands bordered those of the Welsh in the south of the country, he was in a crucial position. His resources and influence were significant enough to play a vital role in the balance of power, both between the English and the Welsh and between the forces of reform and those of the crown. He had already shown his independent spirit when ordered by Henry III to take an oath of fealty to Edward. He had refused to do so, marking the start of a long and often difficult relationship with the young prince, which would continue to be troublesome when the latter became king. There was a great deal of support for the reformers from the Marches, which was decisive in worsening the position of the monarchy. An irresistible drive for change threatened to deluge the crown. London turned on the king in support of it and he was forced to take refuge in the Tower to protect himself.

Nevertheless, de Montfort was not quite able to create a position of irreversible advantage for himself. There are several reasons why this may have been so, most of them beyond the scope of this book. But there is one factor of especial relevance to an understanding of Anglo-Welsh relations at this time. The records show that, on 18 August 1263, a number of important men with interests in the Marches declared their support for Edward. One name in particular needs to be noted: John Giffard was not, at least at this time, a consistent supporter of Edward. He would however later become one of his most trusted confidants in Wales, as well as a significant beneficiary of Edward's largesse after his campaigns there. This declaration of support for Edward, and by definition the royalist cause, is an important development and there is one factor that perhaps explains it more than any other.

If de Montfort was to succeed in fulfilling his ambitions, he needed to take advantage of the disaffection of those who were naturally interested in discomfiting the crown. There was one man in particular who was keen to take advantage of such discomfiture. Independent-spirited, ambitious and opportunistic as he was, the weakening of the royalist position would open up all kinds of possibilities for Llywelyn ap Gruffudd. Therefore, it is perhaps not surprising that de Montfort began discussions with the Welsh prince with a view to winning his co-operation. But the effect of this was not altogether positive for de Montfort. By seeking the support of Llywelyn, de Montfort was weakening the support he received from the Marcher lords, to whom the Welsh prince was a bitter and dangerous rival. It was a policy that would come back to haunt de Montfort with personally catastrophic results.

England was sliding, out of control, towards the abyss of civil war. Law and order began to collapse. In the Marches, it fell apart completely. John Giffard launched a bitter attack on the lands of Roger Mortimer and his holdings in the mid-Welsh Marches. At his side were the sons of Simon de Montfort, another Simon and Henry (the elder Simon was at the time out of action due to a broken leg). There was another significant participant in the attack on the Mortimer lands – Llywelyn ap Gruffudd. Within months of agreeing to support Edward, Giffard had allied himself with both the reform movement and the Welsh. Although this tangled political web would mutate constantly, as those involved in it changed allegiances, the underlying trend was for supporters of the de Montfort cause to find themselves in alliance with those of Llywelyn, with the Marcher lords holding the crucial balance of power in the equation.

This alliance posed a great threat to royalist interests and Edward was quick to react to it. The prominent role that the young prince was taking in military affairs by this stage is notable (though he was accompanied on this expedition by Richard, Duke of Cornwall, himself a very prominent figure as the king's brother and a key player in politics both inside and outside England). His expedition met with some success, with the castle at Hay being seized and Brecon surrendering; these lands were handed over to Roger Mortimer, who would be a crucial supporter of the crown, both now and in the future. Soon after, the city of Gloucester was taken by the rebels (it was here that Edward demonstrated his flair for duplicitous trickery referred to above).[8]

An unstoppable momentum towards all-out war was now evident. Soon after these events took place, on 6 March 1264, Henry III summoned his feudal levies to meet him at Oxford. Ostensibly, the Welsh were the pretext; the army was assembled to constrain Llywelyn and his supporters. This was however merely a front for the real purpose of the summoning of the army, which was barely concealed within the text of the summons that 'those who are against us are not written to'.[9] The army was purportedly to be used in an attempt not only – and in fact not at all – to put down rebellion in Wales but rather to crush those who wished to bring it about in England. When the English king marched out with his army a month after the force assembled at Oxford, the banners of war at its head led them, not westwards to Wales, but north-east towards the army of the rebel barons at Northampton.

In the civil war that followed, initial baronial successes were to be outweighed by an ultimate royalist triumph. In between, the royalist cause was to see some very dark days indeed. At times, Edward's life itself was under threat, though the possibility of his enemies deliberately eliminating him should not be over-stressed as he was a very powerful bargaining chip. But the cumulative effect of his experiences must have been to harden an already stern character, and when the later inflexibility and harshness of Edward the king is witnessed, we should perhaps bear in mind the formative experiences endured by Edward the prince.

Edward was quick to advance on the Marches. He attacked Humphrey de Bohun, who had allied himself with the baronial rebels, and took Huntington and Hay, handing these and Brecon over to the safekeeping of Roger Mortimer. But the seminal battle at the outset of the war took place on 14 May 1264 at Lewes. It was the first major battle that Edward had been involved in (the skirmishing he had witnessed in Wales and elsewhere was a very different type of warfare) and it would be another painful lesson for him. Edward played a personally courageous and successful part in the battle but he was still on the losing side. The enemy captured both the king and Edward. The barons would only agree to harsh terms. Both King Henry and Edward were to be kept as virtual prisoners. It was a brutal humiliation for the prince. It would not be stretching a point too far to say that the impulsive youth had learned a lesson that would markedly affect his future attitudes towards war.

Warfare was about much more than glorious battles and impulsive sorties. It was ultimately about victory. Heroic defeat ran a very poor second to methodical, unglamorous success.

The triumph of Simon de Montfort, though seemingly overwhelming, was not yet completely decisive. In the aftermath of the battle, he released several of the Marcher lords such as Roger Mortimer and Roger Clifford. He perhaps reasoned that, with the king and his heir in custody, he did not need further sureties and would be better placed to win their favour by giving them their freedom. This turned out to be a miscalculation of epic proportions. Not only would the Marcher lords combine later to great effect to lead an irresistible fightback against de Montfort but it was a move that must have infuriated Llywelyn ap Gruffudd, who was, as we shall see, at odds with these barons and would have welcomed their extended removal from the political stage.[10] But it would be some time yet before this became clear. For now, it appeared that things could hardly get worse for the royalists. There were some areas that held out for the king and his son – Bristol for one was held by another future supporter of Edward in Wales, Robert Tibotot – but these were times of great danger for the prince. When, for example, the castle at Wallingford, where he was held, was attacked by supporters attempting to free him, the commander of the garrison threatened to fire him out of the castle in a catapult. It is little wonder that, as king, Edward I was so determined to assert his authority given the experiences of these desperate days.

Events were about to move decisively against Simon de Montfort and it was the Marcher lords who were to tip the scales in Edward's favour. Most prominent among those to change his allegiance was Gilbert de Clare, earl of Gloucester. He felt threatened by the alliance between de Montfort and Llywelyn ap Gruffudd, which implicitly challenged the large landholdings that were his in the Welsh Marches. There was not a defining moment when it could be said that de Montfort had lost the support of Gloucester, rather a gradual but definite deterioration in relations between the two. This was marked enough to require the cancellation of a tournament which both factions were due to attend in February 1264, as it was feared that open violence might break out.

That these fears were well-grounded is evidenced by events shortly afterwards. Gloucester openly broke with de Montfort and threw in his lot with other Marcher lords. At his side were several long-term supporters of the royalist cause such as William de Valence, as well as others who had also switched allegiances, like John Giffard, all names that would figure prominently in Edward's later campaigns in Wales. This shift in the balance of power was made decisive by a dramatic development following in the wake of these events.

Edward was still a prisoner, now kept at Hereford. Why he was detained in such a volatile area is something that few with the benefit of hindsight will understand but it was a serious error of judgement by Simon de Montfort. The prince, like many contemporary young men, was an avid horseman and he was allowed to go out riding in the countryside around his prison. One particular day, he was particularly selective about the horse that he chose. He tried several mounts before he chose one that he believed particularly served his immediate purpose. When he was out in the open country, he dug his spurs into his steed, which charged away from the body of guards accompanying him. Knowing that he had chosen a horse that was more than a match for any of those ridden by his guards, he disappeared enthusiastically into the distance, pausing only to shout back to his bewildered captors that he wished them well and asking them to give his regards to his father whom he would see again soon.

The escape was clearly a pre-arranged plot. Edward made his way straight to the castle of Roger Mortimer at Wigmore. His position had changed radically. Soon after, he joined up with the forces of Gloucester. Seeing that a wind of change was sweeping the country, large numbers flocked to his side, especially from the Marcher lands. The army that was subsequently formed moved first of all on the city of Gloucester, which was taken. Simon de Montfort in the meantime assembled a force of his own to meet the threat. He spent a good deal of time trying to recruit Welsh forces to his army but with only limited success. The Welsh did not wish to fight outside their own lands and perhaps Llywelyn ap Gruffudd had anyway perceived that a potentially decisive change in fortunes had taken place. De Montfort's efforts in Wales did him little good and he was eventually forced by events to return his attentions to England, his ambitious plans for recruitment in Wales largely unfulfilled.

His army eventually found itself opposite that of Edward and Gloucester at Evesham, where there was a crossing of the Severn. Battle was joined soon after. The brutality of the fighting demonstrates how deep emotions were running in England at the time. The battle was a bloody one, with no quarter given. De Montfort arrayed his men defensively in a circle but he was handicapped from the start as the Welsh troops that he had managed to recruit were overrun and quickly broke and fled, their hearts not in the battle. Inexorably, the troops of Edward and Gloucester pushed forward, bunching de Montfort's men closer and closer together. The tide began to flow decisively in favour of de Montfort's enemies. Eventually, de Montfort fell. With him died the hopes of his followers. The royalist army was decisively victorious.

Edward's ferocity towards the man who had become one of his bitterest enemies evidenced itself in the aftermath of the battle. As a gruesome relic of his triumph, de Montfort's testicles were cut off and sent to the wife of Roger Mortimer. When King Henry was subsequently released, he and his son began to confiscate the lands of the rebels. A mopping-up operation began, with all of de Montfort's residual support gradually evaporating. But although the royal triumph seemed total it was in fact not quite so. In 1267, Gloucester's allegiance changed again. Unhappy at the severity with which King Henry and Edward continued to punish the rebels (in terms of land confiscation rather than actual executions it should be noted) he formed an army and marched menacingly towards London. It was not an out-and-out revolt, rather a clear statement to the crown that it could not govern exclusively as it wished. Even though the war had been won, conditions had changed. There was no going back to the old ways. The king had to take due account of the interests of his leading barons.

These events play an important part in the story of the English conquest of Wales. Not only was there significant Welsh activity at the time (which will be considered in more detail below) but also there are a number of other highly relevant features. It had become clear that in any consideration of affairs between England and Wales there was a third force to consider, namely the Marcher barons. In many respects, they formed a semi-independent power bloc of their own. True, they owed allegiance to the English crown – but they often acted in their own best interests alone. Geographical remoteness and tradition both encouraged this trend towards autonomy. But this bloc was not a coherent entity. There were great tensions between the Marcher lords themselves, a natural enough phenomenon as, in many ways, they were direct rivals. Both Llywelyn and Edward were acutely aware of the enmity felt by some Marcher lords towards others. Their tactics towards them would however be different, reflecting differences in the status of each man, and the resources available to them.

Llywelyn, of course, attempted to take advantage of rivalries between the barons, and tried to seize land to expand his domain. However, in the process of picking off parcels of land as they appeared to be ripe for the taking, he was embarking down a dangerous road. This *ad hoc* opportunistic approach risked forcing the Marcher lords collectively into an alliance against him. A better approach would have been to play one off against the other.

For Edward, the situation was different. The civil war would not have been won without the aid of the Marcher lords, Gloucester's assistance in particular being crucial. Yet it would be expecting too much for Edward to be excessively grateful for this. It was a salutary reminder of just how reliant he was on the power of the barons. The events of these years appear to have affected him deeply. They set the tone for his kingship when he eventually acceded a few years later. His reign would be characterised by an unceasing effort to assert the rights of the crown. On many occasions he would attempt to further his own position at the expense of that of the barons. It rarely threatened all-out conflict (although at times matters did get too close for comfort) but there were many occasions when Edward sought to advance his interests in other ways. Among other things, this meant that Edward would be likely to react firmly to any sign of trouble in his kingdom. It also meant that he would enforce his rights when men refused to give him the honour that was due to him. It was a lesson that Llywelyn ap Gruffudd would have done well to heed.

During these years some important new relationships had been forged. The war ended with Roger Mortimer a particularly strong ally of King Henry and his son. Indeed, even when a number of Marcher lords had allied against the crown in the black days of 1263–5, he had remained loyal. This would be recognised shortly afterwards when Mortimer would assume a position of much importance in the government of the land. As well as those who had been consistent supporters of the crown, such as William de Valence, there was also John Giffard. Other relationships were formed with men perhaps less well known than Mortimer but still destined to play an important part in the future of Wales. One such was Robert Tibotot (or Tiptoft), found as a knight in the garrison at Bristol in 1264 and profiting greatly from the break-up of lands after the civil wars. He would later accompany Edward on crusade and become a trusted warrior in the Welsh wars, eventually being made justiciar of West Wales in 1280.[11] Hugh Turberville, too, had supported Edward even when the prince was in captivity. A Marcher lord, who in 1263 had been made constable of both Carmarthen and Cardigan castles, he would later fight in both Welsh wars and eventually become constable at Castell y Bere.[12]

But with Gloucester, the relationship was clearly strained. In the aftermath of the civil wars, Edward appears to have wanted heavy terms to be imposed on his defeated enemies. One such foe, Robert Ferrers, earl of Derby, was ordered to pay a fine of £50,000 if he wished to keep his lands, a quite preposterous sum that was far beyond his means. As a result, his lands were forfeit. Gloucester strongly opposed this harsh stance, and did his utmost to insist on a greater degree of moderation in the dealings of the crown. For a while in 1267, it appeared that Gloucester's men would come to blows with those of Edward, though confrontation was eventually avoided with some difficulty. The bond between Gloucester and the crown was far from an unbreakable one. Acrimony was never far away when the two men were in the vicinity of each other. At one stage, personal insults and rumours began to circulate, including one that Edward was altogether too friendly with Gloucester's wife. At any event, the strains between the two were great enough to cause one eminent historian to remark that 'Edward's policy in the Marches in the late 1260s was directed not so much against the Welsh as against Gilbert de Clare, earl of Gloucester'.[13] These factors collectively formed a significant part of the equation as far as Welsh affairs were concerned.

* * *

During the thirteenth century, thoughts in the Marches were to turn more towards governance and less towards conquest. It is ironic that this was at a time when a resurgent Gwynedd had pushed the Marcher borders back, leading to violent confrontations that were, relatively speaking, on a very large scale. The Marcher lords therefore were refused a chance to consolidate just at the moment when they wished to do so. For, as the twelfth century drew to a close, so too did the period of relatively easy English conquests in Wales. The lowland areas were by now largely conquered. These were the easiest to capture. The areas that remained free were wild, remote and hostile, and the Welsh who lived there were determined, brave and fierce. Their conquest would bring little economic gain to the English and subjugation of them, a desirable military objective certainly, difficult – given the talent of the Welsh living there to melt into the landscape rather than foolishly offer battle when conditions were unfavourable to them. Further conquests offered only diminishing returns to the Marcher lords.

The position of the Marcher lords was a paradoxical one. They had strong connections with both English and Welsh camps but ultimately acted independently of either. The nature of this unusual state of affairs is best evidenced by the fact that Roger Mortimer, staunchest supporter of the English crown, was married to Gwladus, sister of Gruffudd, and therefore was uncle by marriage to Llywelyn ap Gruffudd himself. There is documentary evidence that Mortimer supported Llywelyn in his attempts to establish himself in opposition to Dafydd, the price of which was an undertaking from Llywelyn that he would not attempt to take any lands in Gwethyrnion and Mailienydd which were claimed by Mortimer.[14] Their position meant that they had to engage in political and/or military dialogue with the Welsh; at the same time, their feudal ties meant that they had to maintain a relationship with the English crown, as evidenced by their involvement in the civil wars in England. Further, many were not exclusively Marcher lords, but also held lands in England, emphasising their relationship with the king (Roger Mortimer offers one of the few exceptions to the general rule: his lands were concentrated in the

March). To this extent at least the Marcher lords had an interest in the state of both the crown and of Wales.

But they also enjoyed a unique degree of autonomy within their Marcher lands. Even here, they owed allegiance to the crown but that homage was a lot more tenuous that it would have been in a lordship in England. They developed their own laws; not one code that could be described as 'Marcher law', but each territory having its own local variations, drawing on a variety of foundations, be it Welsh law, English common law or feudal custom and conventions. Thus was one Marcher lord, William de Braose, able to exclaim in 1199 that the royal writ did not apply to his Marcher lands and no royal judges held court there. Lawyers who worked in the interests of the king may have been far from content with this degree of independence but the rights of the Marcher lords, hard-won and now long-established, would only in the end be overturned after the passage of centuries.

The unique nature of the March, and the unrivalled freedom of its lords, may have been, as one commentator has said, 'an anachronism, a survival from an age of conquest',[15] but it was crucial in the context of Welsh affairs. It effectively divided Wales into two (three if one also considers the land owned directly by the English crown), known as *pura Wallia* (ruled by Welsh princes) and *marchia Wallie* (the March of Wales). Its relative independence should not however obscure the fact that royal power still affected its evolution. In the face of a resurgent Welsh counter-attack, royal support became crucial and the Marchers furthered their ambitions most when allied to the royal cause. Such periods of co-operation were only driven by mutual interest and were interspersed between times when the Marchers and the crown were at odds with each other – but they were still important to the success of large-scale military campaigns in Wales, as the wars of Edward I were to illustrate very well indeed.

* * *

With the civil war over, Edward turned to his mind to other things. He was especially keen to go on crusade before he became king and he turned his attentions to preparations for this. His wish was to be fulfilled, though the expedition would be far from the unqualified success that he desired. But much in him would change during his absence. When he left England he was a young prince whose character had been shaped by adversity, keen to earn glory and honour on his mission. When he returned, with that desire for glory largely unfulfilled, it would be as a fully-fledged king, acutely aware of his rights and prepared to enforce them with all the vigour that was necessary.

CHAPTER THREE

Llywelyn the Last

A man for Wales was bold, I name him, Manly Llywelyn,
best man of Welshmen.[1]

The respective positions of Edward, prince of England, and Llywelyn of Wales could not have been more different at birth. Edward was born to become the king of a powerful and relatively wealthy nation. His birthplace was the great Palace of Westminster, the apartments of which assumed an opulence that previous generations could not even imagine. Henry III was a lover of fine things and the thirteenth century was an era of great commercial expansion, which fuelled his love of luxury. The king had his own favourite colour scheme – green spangled with gold stars – which was employed liberally in his palaces. Westminster would soon be resplendent with the magnificent double towers of the king's great abbey. Adjacent to Westminster, the city of London drove forward energetically in the interests of commerce and profit as it grew rapidly. By the following century, London would have 35,000 inhabitants, dwarfing the next largest city – York – with 11,000. The scale, grandeur and wealth of all this was something that Wales could not hope to rival.

The contrast with the conditions into which Llywelyn ap Gruffudd was born could not be more marked. There is no clear record of when he was born. There has even been dispute over who his mother was, although Llywelyn's latest biographer asserts confidently that he was born of a legitimate relationship between Gruffudd ap Llywelyn and his wife, Senena.[2] He was the second of four brothers, all of whom would play a crucial role in his later life. The eldest, Owain, would enjoy a difficult relationship with him, as indeed would his two younger brothers, Dafydd and Rhodri.

It was not just with respect to its wealth that Wales differed from England. The political structure of the country was very different. As it was in reality a series of small principalities with a shared racial origin, rather than a united political structure, unifying Wales was a massive undertaking. This was the challenge that faced any man who would claim to be pre-eminent among the lords of Wales, and it is important to recognise from the outset that it would take a combination of favourable circumstances allied to outstanding personal qualities if any Welsh lord or prince wished to stake such a claim. In one of those accidents of timing that shape history, such a unique synthesis of factors was present in Wales in the middle part of the thirteenth century.

The lack of detail about Llywelyn's birth extends even to when it took place, although opinion tends towards a date somewhere in the early 1220s. But by the time that he was a young man it was clear that here was someone with strong ideas, striking character and exceptional abilities. He was also prepared to back up his words with decisive actions. When independent Wales found itself divided as a result of the civil wars that marred its political landscape in the opening years of the 1240s, Llywelyn – still only twenty or so – found himself in opposition to his uncle, Dafydd, holding territory in the 'Four Cantreds', the Perfeddwlad, against him.

Llywelyn's situation changed dramatically in 1244. His father, Gruffudd, was still a prisoner of the English, along with his elder brother, Owain. Life in the Tower sat uncomfortably with Gruffudd. Remote from his homeland, and powerless to intervene while Dafydd strengthened his position there, the long, frustrating hours of inactivity gnawed away at him until he could take it no more. He decided to attempt an audacious escape from his grim prison. The date he chose for this could not have been more appropriate, given his origins – St David's Day, 1244. He planned to climb out of the window and down an improvised rope made of bed-sheets. Accordingly, during the still hours of darkness, he lowered the sheets from the window of his prison room and began to climb gingerly towards the ground, far, far below. But the long days of imprisonment had told on him. The weight of his frame was too much for the sheets to support. They tore, and Gruffudd plunged to his death.

Henry III released Owain soon afterwards. There was great indignation in Wales at the news of Gruffudd's death, and tension rose irresistibly. The English king probably wished to use Owain as a means of causing internal division in Wales but, if this was his plan, the execution of it was fatally flawed. It would be many months before Owain actually returned to Wales and, by the time that he did, the position of his younger brother was far stronger than it might otherwise have been. Owain's absence from Wales at what transpired to be a crucial time gave Llywelyn invaluable breathing space. It was an opportunity that a man of Llywelyn's talents would not need a second invitation to take advantage of.

News of Gruffudd's death stoked up the flames of war in Wales once more. By 1245, Dafydd had taken up arms against England again. Much of Wales was with him. At Dafydd's side rode Llywelyn. The significance of this was profound. Dafydd had no heir and had agreed with Henry on a previous occasion that if he were to die childless then Gwynedd would pass to the English crown. By raising himself in the estimation of the lords and people of Gwynedd, Llywelyn was advancing his cause greatly as many there had no wish to see Gwynedd become just another possession of the English crown. The English king took up the challenge and planned to invade Gwynedd to enforce his rule over the rebellious Welsh.

Henry's plan of campaign was straightforward. It was similar to that adopted before on a number of occasions, and it also closely mirrored the tactics that would be used thirty years later by his son, the future King Edward I. His main army would advance along the north Welsh seaboard towards Deganwy, while, from the other direction, an army made up of troops shipped in from Ireland would lay waste to fertile Anglesey and deprive the Welsh of crucial food supplies. Henry's troops however ran out of supplies and were harassed by guerrilla raids. The English army therefore had little option but to negotiate a truce and withdraw. The performance of the Welsh, and Dafydd in particular, was creditable. It earned the respect of his people, one of whom, the poet Dafydd Brenfas, would write of him that 'he was a man who sprang, great joy of the people, from the true royal lineage of kings'.[3] After a traumatic, often difficult, reign Dafydd had carved for himself an honourable niche in the history of Gwynedd, though it would be virtually his last contribution to his people.

The English cause was assisted by the death of Dafydd on 25 February 1246. After his demise, Welsh unity began to disintegrate, a situation helped along no doubt by the eventual return of Owain soon afterwards. Owain, however, found that Llywelyn's position was now too strong within Gwynedd for him to be ignored in the future government of the region. It was therefore decided that Gwynedd would be divided between them. This did not of course make for firm government and the arrangement was fraught with difficulties from the outset. The situation would be made even worse by the attitude of Henry III.

In Henry's eyes, Gwynedd was his and the lords who ruled there did so only because he had given them title to do so. In many ways, it was just another barony for him to hand out as he saw fit. There were of course local differences, particularly with regard to the tradition and culture of Wales, which mean that this simplistic analysis overstates the case, but Henry at any event refused to recognise the arrangement. He argued that Dafydd held the land from him and therefore it was he who was the ultimate arbiter of how the succession should be settled. He claimed that Dafydd had indeed agreed to this arrangement before his death and that, in the absence of an heir, the territories that he held would pass to the English crown.

Owain and Llywelyn were not at the time in a strong enough position to resist Henry's forces, and they were therefore left with little option but to agree to peace on his terms. Given the stance that he had adopted by insisting that the lands they held were in his gift and that they had no automatic right to them, those terms were not altogether unreasonable. By the agreement sealed at Woodstock on 30 April 1247, he confirmed them in their position. There were, however, strings attached and these constrained the ambitions of the brothers significantly. They were to recognise Henry's claims to ultimate authority over them and the Perfeddwlad was to be handed over to him, markedly reducing the size of their territories. Further, the claims that they had made to Meirionydd were denied to them. They were limited in terms of territory to Gwynedd alone.

Henry was well satisfied with this arrangement. Gwynedd was divided in two, and he hoped for further opportunities in the future. When Dafydd and Rhodri came of age, they too would lay claim to land held by the brothers. The cohesiveness and unity of Gwynedd would be further weakened. If their claims were resisted then civil war would break out again, and the Welsh would soon be busy fighting each other. Other features of the settlement emphasised the subservice of Gwynedd to the English crown. The region was to provide feudal levies to the king when called upon to do so, another illustration of the way that Gwynedd, in Henry's eyes, had become just another part of England.

There were other signs elsewhere in Wales of attempts to 'anglicise' the country and bring its structures more into line with England's. These were especially noticeable in the land of Deheubarth, where there was much reorganisation of the region on English shire structure lines. These factors are extremely important as a part of the process by which Wales was subsumed into England. The subjugation of the Welsh princes and the reduction of their power, alongside the imposition – or perhaps, more accurately, confirmation – of feudal duties owed by the Welsh to England, provides irrefutable evidence that Edward I only built later on the policies already developed by his father.[4]

Owain and Llywelyn returned to Gwynedd. The Treaty of Woodstock was undoubtedly a serious blow and it was a truncated principality that Llywelyn and Owain governed now but it was at least something to build on. They were faced with some difficult choices about how they would rule. The two options were either to govern as co-rulers or to divide the land between them. The former would surely have been unworkable. Government by consensus between two ambitious men would have been very difficult. It was therefore agreed that Gwynedd would instead be divided between them and each would take a portion to govern in his own right. But the specifics of the division are interesting, as they bear witness to the powerful position that Llywelyn had managed to build for himself while Owain had been absent in England. It was Llywelyn who took Snowdonia, the place of last refuge, protected jointly by the castles of Dolwyddellan and Dolbadarn and those far more impenetrable walls of the Snowdon massif itself. He therefore governed the more secure area.

It was perhaps inevitable that this unsatisfactory arrangement would not last for very long. It is almost a surprise that it survived for six years. But then, in 1253, a crucial breach occurred that was to have immense results for the future of Gwynedd. And the catalyst of important changes for the first, but most decidedly not the last, time was Owain and Llywelyn's younger brother, Dafydd. Like Llywelyn, he was most definitely ambitious and he determined to stake his claim for a share of the land of Gwynedd. In order to further his aims, he presented himself to the English court. Soon afterwards directions were sent to the rulers of Gwynedd, directing that they should give to Dafydd what was his 'according to the custom of Wales', i.e. the system of partibility discussed in Chapter 1.[5] The injunction was followed by a directive to the English authorities in Chester to offer, within limits, support to Dafydd if he needed it. It set a dangerous precedent for Wales, and not just for Gwynedd alone. Similar instructions to share out land were sent to Gruffudd ap Madog, ruler of Powys Fadog, soon afterwards.

It comes as little surprise that Owain and Llywelyn were very reticent indeed to hand over any of their lands to their assertive sibling. Apart from anything else, the interference of the English had ominous implications for the future. There was more than a hint of irony in the situation, the humour of which would have been lost on the brothers. The Welsh jealously guarded their rights and customs, and would later go to war to protect them. In this instance, however, the instructions from England were not to comply with English law but rather to ensure that Welsh traditions were observed. Since the situation threatened a great deal of personal damage to the ambitions and status of Owain and Llywelyn, their prevarication is understandable.

A commission was set up to examine the claims of Dafydd. Its composition cannot have encouraged Llywelyn as it included Alan la Zusche, the unpopular English administrator at Chester, John Lestrange, a long-established Marcher lord, and Gruffudd ap Gwenwynwyn, whose support for the English crown and its policies was well known. It appeared that Llywelyn was the primary object of the commission's efforts, the implication being that Owain had already compromised whereas his brother had not.

Before the commission could deliver its conclusions, however, the situation was dramatically changed. Owain had already opted to give some land to Dafydd, but Llywelyn continued to resist. Dafydd therefore joined forces with Owain and marched on Llywelyn. Their two armies met at Bryn Derwin. Few details are known of the battle, which was probably fought in June 1255, though the poet recorded that Llywelyn fought like 'a lion in a host and fearsome in combat'.[6] Surviving accounts describe the engagement as being 'brief and decisive', suggesting that although the battle was not fought for long, it was violent while it lasted. The end result was clear enough though: both Owain and Dafydd were captured. For Dafydd, it was to be just one incident in an often turbulent relationship with his elder brother as, soon after, he was restored to his good graces. For Owain on the other hand the future was much bleaker. After his capture, it would be twenty-two long years before he tasted freedom again. It is important to note that some in Gwynedd thought that Llywelyn was unduly harsh in his treatment of his brother, who was the elder sibling and had, as far as can be ascertained, not been a bad ruler of his lands. It hints strongly at a ruthless streak in Llywelyn.

Just over a year after his triumph at Bryn Derwin, Llywelyn felt confident enough to push on to invade the Perfeddwlad. Of the 'Four Cantreds' of the region, which were now under English rule, conditions were especially problematic in three of them (Rhos, Rhufoniog and Dyffryn Clwyd) and were therefore conducive to the success of Llywelyn's incursions. Although the English had tried to establish a settlement at Deganwy, which they hoped would help to subdue the area, the venture had not been a great success, either strategically or administratively. The success of English rule here was not helped by the harshness of those appointed to govern the land. The administration of Alan la Zusche (appointed in 1251) was particularly stern and was to generate a groundswell of support for Llywelyn among the oppressed Welsh inhabitants of the region.

In 1254, the land had been handed over to Prince Edward as part of the territories awarded to him by his father in Wales. Alan la Zusche however stayed as the chief administrator of the region until 1255. The harshness of English rule proved more than the Welsh in the Perfeddwlad could bear, and they lobbied Llywelyn to help them. Encouraged by the absence of both Henry III and Prince Edward in Gascony, Llywelyn intervened. When he launched his raid into the region in 1256, he was assisted by a lord from the far south, Maredudd ap Rhys Gryg, who was to play an important part in Anglo-Welsh relationships in the future. Llywelyn needed no second invitation to enter into these lands. The Perfeddwlad (with the exception of Teigingl, which abutted the border with England) was almost an integral part of Gwynedd and the settlement of 1247 that removed it from the direct rule of the princes of Gwynedd was in many ways artificial. Its character, its people and its customs were Welsh and the imposition of a method of government that was alien would inevitably generate friction, the sparks from which were always likely to ignite a flame of rebellion at some time.

By December 1256, all of the Perfeddwlad, with the exception of Deganwy and Diserth, had fallen to Llywelyn. He then turned his attention to the land of Meirionydd, an area much coveted by the princes of Gwynedd. This too fell to Llywelyn, with the former Welsh lord in the area, Llywelyn ap Maredudd, fleeing to England. Llywelyn now turned his attentions far to the south, to the region of Deheubarth. Given his alliance with Maredudd ap Rhys Gryg, this was a not unsurprising development. Maredudd wished to restore the patrimony of his illustrious predecessor, Rhys Gryg, which had been controlled from the fortress of Dinefwr, now in the hands of Rhys Fychan, the bitter rival of Maredudd and a major stumbling block in the way of the achievement of his ambitions.

The very success of Llywelyn was about to threaten his plans. Rhys Fychan had turned to England for help.[7] It was this request that encouraged Stephen Bauzan to lead his forces to Rhys's aid. Even as he did so, Ceredigion rose in support of Llywelyn. In the meantime, Maredudd had been able to reclaim a large part of what he perceived to be the lost inheritance of Rhys Gryg. Bauzan left his base at Carmarthen on 31 May 1257 and soon after reached Llandeilo Fawr, where he set up camp. During the night, the forces of his Welsh opponents encircled his position, waiting impatiently to launch a dawn attack on his unsuspecting men. The attack was pushed home with ferocity, and the English only managed to survive with difficulty. By the dawn of the next day, Bauzan was on his own, Rhys Fychan having decided to throw in his lot with his fellow Welshmen. The English found themselves under attack once more. Dinefwr, their original objective, was no longer a viable target for them and they instead took to the higher ground and tried to make their way to Cardigan. Here they were attacked once more, at Cymerau, this time with disastrous results. First of all, most of their supplies were lost. Worse was to follow, as in the battle itself they suffered heavy casualties, with some chroniclers asserting that 3,000 men were slain.

Ironically, Rhys's change of allegiance was to pose Llywelyn great problems. Thus far, the prince had achieved amazing results. He had attacked the lands of Gruffudd ap Gwenwynwyn in the mid-Welsh Marches and, although Gruffudd managed to retain his castle at Welshpool, many other lands were taken. In the process, Llywelyn found himself at odds with the Marcher lords, particularly Roger Mortimer –

but also in the south around Cydweli and Gower, where the castle at Swansea was burned down. However, now that Rhys was loyal to him, it meant that some of the lands previously given to Maredudd ap Rhys Gryg in return for his support were handed back. This alienated Maredudd and made him a tempting target as an ally for the English in the future. He was infuriated at Llywelyn's decision to deprive him of the lands that he had so long desired, and indicated that he could be tempted to desert him in the future. It was an advantage that the English were quick to press home.

The desultory campaign that Henry III subsequently waged in Wales did more harm than good to the English cause. After dallying at Chester for some three weeks before entering Wales, when it eventually set off the army quickly ground to a halt. Seeing that little positive result was likely to accrue from these half-hearted attempts, a number of prominent Welsh barons threw in their lot with Llywelyn. When Henry retreated, after the ships that were to join him and assist in the attack on Anglesey had failed to appear, he had achieved virtually nothing for his unenthusiastic efforts. There was however one ray of hope for the English cause to arise as a result of this lacklustre expedition. It came from Deheubarth, where an offer had been made to Maredudd ap Rhys Gryg that, in return for his support, the lands he had desired for so long and which, for a tantalising second, he had actually held before they had been returned to Rhys Fychan, would be his once more.

In October 1257, Maredudd journeyed to London where he paid homage to Henry in the presence of some of the key Marcher lords, such as the earl of Gloucester and Patrick de Chaworth of Cydweli. In the following year, some form of accommodation was reached between Llywelyn and Maredudd but, clearly founded on mutual mistrust as it was, it was at best a transitory arrangement. Under the terms of the deal, Maredudd would provide hostages for his good behaviour – hardly a positive sign. The inauspicious beginnings to this reshaped relationship were an entirely appropriate portent of things to come. Before long, Llywelyn had invaded Maredudd's lands and chased him all the way to Cydweli. Soon after, a counter-attack was launched by Maredudd in the company of Dafydd, Llywelyn's brother, who had thus far continued to support the English since he had deserted Llywelyn's cause, and also Patrick de Chaworth. It was a sizeable force but it was bested by the Welsh in battle and forced to abandon its attempts to recover Maredudd's lost lands for the time being.

Llywelyn could not fight this war forever. He did not have the riches to wage a constant war of attrition against the English. Sooner or later, he would need to employ other skills to further his ambitions. It was time to consolidate his position in Wales, and he could only achieve this by reaching an agreement with Henry III that ratified his status in the country. The extent of his ambitions needs to be noted from the start. Never was full independence a viable option. Instead, Llywelyn strove for a situation where he was recognised by all men, especially the king of England, as the most prominent man in Wales. In the feudal structure that he sought to build, all other lords in Wales would do homage to him for their lands, and he in turn would do homage to the king of England. To the achievement of this objective he would devote his efforts, his resources and his skills for the next decade. He was prepared to pay heavily in return for recognition of his position. If he were to achieve his desires and obtain formal ratification of his situation to the extent that he desired, he would have achieved something far greater than even Llywelyn ap Iorwerth, 'The Great', had achieved.

* * *

The long road to recognition began in 1258. Llywelyn first sought to formalise his position by encouraging the Welsh lords to swear allegiance to him. Given his striking results so far, many were moved to do so. But this was in many ways the easy part. Far harder would be the process of achieving appropriate recognition from the king of England. Nevertheless, he wrote to Henry in that same year, in terms that showed well enough what he sought. He used a term that had been used previously only by Dafydd ap Llywelyn when he was at odds with Henry. In his approaches, Llywelyn entitled himself *princeps Wallie* – Prince of Wales.

This was not the only significant change to the political landscape in 1258. Nobles from Scotland visited Wales, and an agreement was signed signifying mutual support between the two lands. It was an ambitious policy in its own right but almost as interesting as the alliance itself were the signatories to it. Top of the list on the Welsh side was of course Llywelyn himself. Next however was a name of great significance – Dafydd, his brother. Judging that the wind had changed direction significantly, Dafydd had changed tack and decided to support Llywelyn.

The deterioration in the English situation that led to the civil war as recounted earlier in Chapter 2 proved something of a double-edged sword for Llywelyn. The breakdown of royal power in the country did mean that Llywelyn could make a number of short-term gains while the Marcher lords were distracted by events in England and the king was powerless to intervene. But the situation also posed him problems. After the great advances he had made in the past two years, he needed recognition to build on the material gains he had made. The distractions of Henry III in England and his relative weakness meant that a decisive solution could not be agreed.

The negative connotations of the internal situation in England showed themselves very clearly in the negotiations undertaken at Oxford in 1258. Llywelyn was invited to send representatives to the council as one of the major items on the agenda was the Welsh situation. It was planned that the council should consider the renewal of active hostilities in Wales so that Llywelyn could be brought to book for his temerity in recent times. In the event, the course of the conversations was very different. The Marcher lords present there, the most prominent of whom were Gloucester and Roger Mortimer, argued that the time was not right for war as the issue of English reform needed imminent resolution.

But this was not the good news that it seemed for Llywelyn, because instead those present began a lengthy period of procrastination, which would deny him the opportunity that he so much desired to negotiate some kind of recognition of his enhanced status and power. As Marcher lords, whose own selfish interests were greatly affected by the power of Llywelyn, they would not countenance any agreement that might threaten their own position. Instead, they refused to enter into any serious discussions about the Welsh situation. In the event, a truce was agreed at Oxford but this was not what Llywelyn wanted. He wanted peace on something like his terms, and a temporary cessation of hostilities was far from this outcome. He was prepared to pay a good price for what he really wanted. As an unmarried man, he could use his own personal status as part of any proposed deal, and one of his suggestions was that he should marry a niece of Henry III. He was also willing to pay a good deal of money in return for recognition, though an offer to pay £200 annually for the next eighty years offered little short-term attraction to the king. But all these plans came to nought, and Llywelyn could only look on in frustration as England began to trundle towards the abyss of civil war.[8]

He was instead left to turn his attentions back to Wales, and in the absence of any positive advancement of his position in England, once more resorted to the battlefield. There was an outbreak of fighting in Dyfed, where Llywelyn was forced to intervene against the recalcitrant Maredudd ap Rhys Gryg. But by the end of 1258, Maredudd was in Llywelyn's custody, where he would remain for three years, and one more obstacle to Llywelyn's recognition as the pre-eminent lord of Wales was removed. By the end of 1259, Llywelyn – who had still seen no movement in England as far as his position was concerned – decided that it was time to force the issue. Prince Edward was now involved (albeit temporarily) in England as a supporter of the reform movement, which was at that time composed partly of a number of Marcher lords who would brook no agreement with Llywelyn that threatened their own status and position.

Llywelyn therefore launched an assault on Builth, one of Roger Mortimer's possessions. Although it did not fall at the first attempt and a truce was brokered, this was only a temporary resolution to the problem. The attack was renewed in 1260, and on 17 July the castle fell to Llywelyn, possibly because of treachery. Rather than attempt to hold the castle, Llywelyn instead burned it to the ground and denied its use to the English. This significant triumph for the Welsh happened at a time when Llywelyn's representatives were in London discussing improved relations with the crown, and the English king must have been extremely angry at what he would have regarded as duplicity on the part of the Welsh. It was nevertheless arranged that negotiators would be sent to the ford of Rhyd Chwima, close by Montgomery, to discuss a renewal of the truce. The ford, a border crossing-point between England and Wales, was frequently used for such meetings and had an important symbolic status as far as Anglo-Welsh relations were concerned.

It looked for a time as if matters would still come to a head in 1260. Henry summoned his lords to bring their levies with them to Chester on 8 September of that year. Then, just a week before this date, a truce was patched up once more. There was though a subtle distinction within the terms of this agreement that was quite important. The truce was to last for two years and both Henry and Llywelyn were to retain possession of the lands that they currently held. Llywelyn was therefore allowed to keep the areas he had conquered in the past few years, albeit that the long-term future of these territories was not yet clear. In the process, Henry also recognised Llywelyn as the legitimate voice of the Welsh people. The agreement was duly sealed, the leading authorities signing up to the arrangement being Henry III and Prince Edward on the one hand and Llywelyn and Dafydd on the other.

This truce by no means secured even short-term stability on the frontiers of England and Wales. There were frequent tensions and a number of subsequent meetings at Rhyd Chwima, where attempts were regularly made to repair the damage caused by the friction. It was still after all a period of truce, of abstention from armed conflict, rather than a period of peace, which is a different thing altogether. The tensions that regularly rose to the surface suggested turbulent undercurrents that would sooner or later lead to far greater problems, and so it proved. In 1262, the truce broke down altogether. A number of Marcher lords were unhappy at Llywelyn's increased strength and resolved that they would not accept his much-improved position. Prominent among them were

Hamo Lestrange (particularly active around Chester and Montgomery) and Roger Mortimer.

At this crucial moment, strange rumours began to spread that Llywelyn had contracted a serious illness and subsequently died. In the event, stories of his demise were decidedly premature but they were believed in some very high places. Henry III certainly credited the news and sent out instructions to his advisers about how the Welsh situation should be handled. On no account was Dafydd to be recognised as Llywelyn's successor. He was not the first-born of Llywelyn and there was an elder brother still alive, although he was living in captivity. In addition, Wales was not an independent territory but held by the English crown, and it was therefore for the king to decide how it should be dealt with. The lords of Wales owed homage to Henry, and it now seemed an opportune time to reassert his authority.[9] The stories were untrue and there is no certainty that Henry's instructions ever became anything more than a private communication between him and his officials. However, events soon afterwards were to demonstrate that Llywelyn was very much alive. There was to be a distinct hardening in Llywelyn's attitude soon afterwards, and it is tempting to speculate, although with no conclusive evidence, that Llywelyn had become aware of Henry's instructions issued soon after the unfounded rumours of his death. But it is equally likely that after years of protracted and ultimately futile discussions, Llywelyn's patience had finally run out.

The castle of Cefnllys was a particular bone of contention between Mortimer and Llywelyn. Llywelyn claimed that the terms of the recent truce prohibited castle building in the Marches but that Mortimer had ignored these to advance into Welsh territory and provocatively begin construction of a castle here. While construction was still in progress, on 29 November 1262 the Welsh attacked the men building it. This move was a success and Llywelyn soon after took land close to the castle at Wigmore, the ultimate seat of Mortimer's power and on the borders of England itself.

Llywelyn's hardening attitude is evidenced by other aspects of his relationship with the English at this time. Although Llywelyn had called himself 'Prince of Wales' in 1258, he had thereafter assiduously avoided formally using the title, the adoption of which Henry III might have considered provocative. But in 1262, Llywelyn renewed his use of it, writing to Henry and using the title 'Prince of Wales and Lord of Snowdon'. His caution put to one side, Llywelyn would continue to use this title for the rest of his days. It was an intimation that attempts for a peaceful resolution of the Welsh situation had failed and that all-out conflict was now likely. For his part, Henry was angry at the renewed conflict in Wales, which came at a time when the situation in England itself was still volatile. He would have been even more perturbed had he realised how much support Llywelyn enjoyed from among the Welsh living under Marcher rule, for example in the country around Abergavenny and in many of Mortimer's territories. The situation was compounded still further by the reticence of those not directly affected, such as Humphrey de Bohun, earl of Hereford, to involve themselves in sorting the problem out.

In 1263, Llywelyn gathered together a large force, said by some chroniclers to consist of 180 horse and 10,000 footsoldiers, and moved on Gwent. His assault met with a determined counter-attack from Peter de Montfort in which the Welsh were forced back. King Henry now decided to have no more to do with the conduct of the campaign and passed over control of all matters to Edward. It was a defining moment because Edward and Mortimer were subsequently to establish the understanding that would have such important results for Anglo-Welsh affairs in the future. Another crucial development was one more change of allegiance on the part of Dafydd. Why he should desert Llywelyn at precisely the moment his powers appeared to be in the ascendancy is difficult to understand but, at any event, on 3 April 1263 he formally entered into a compact with Edward.

Llywelyn also turned his attention to the mid-Welsh Marches. He attacked the crucial border garrison at Montgomery and then beyond towards Clun. He suffered a check to his ambitions here but the wider context was to change dramatically soon afterwards with moves towards open civil war in England. Llywelyn's improved position was evidenced by support for his cause coming from an altogether unlikely direction. Gruffudd ap Gwenwynwyn was a long-term ally of England and had indeed been brought up there. He was traditionally at odds with Llywelyn but a combination of factors meant that he deemed a change in tack to be in his best interests. He had been in dispute with a Marcher landowner, Thomas Corbet, over disputed territory adjacent to Powys Gwenwynwyn, Gorddwr. He was also territorially ambitious and he was acutely aware of the precariousness of his position given the change in the political environment within Wales. It was a difficult choice for him to make but he reckoned that it was a dangerous and potentially untenable position for him to be in if he continued to sit in the opposite camp to Llywelyn when the latter was clearly in the ascendancy.

The terms of the agreement that was made between Llywelyn and Gruffydd give an insight into the nature of such undertakings at the time. It was noted that 'the lord Gruffudd, of his own free will, did homage for himself and his heirs and, placing his hand on holy objects, swore fealty to the lord Llywelyn and his heirs'.[10] In return for his fealty, all the lands taken from Gruffudd a few years previously by Llywelyn were returned to him. Llywelyn also undertook that, if in the future Gruffudd's castle at Welshpool should be lost – by no means a remote possibility, given its forward position – then he would provide a suitable castle for him in its place. In the meantime, conquests made in Powys would be shared between them. ·

Gruffudd's support for Llywelyn, and his proximity to Marcher territory, boded ill for the English lords who held land in the close vicinity. There was one in particular who had reason to be apprehensive about this state of affairs and it was indeed not long before Roger Mortimer found his lands under attack from the combined forces of Llywelyn and Gruffudd as they came together, according to one contemporary, 'with a great army to destroy the Marchers, and especially Roger Mortimer'.

All this happened as the civil war in England was about to erupt with its full fury. Even so, Llywelyn did not commit himself irrevocably to the de Montfort cause. Simon de Montfort was very keen to secure the support of Llywelyn and the resources that he might bring to the war and an understanding of sorts was reached between the two, but Llywelyn showed restraint in his commitment to him. On occasion, there was active co-operation between the two, such as the joint attack on Radnor (the date of this is unclear but was probably early in 1264), but support was by no means always aggressive or unquestioning. However, Llywelyn was still far from inactive. The involvement of the Marcher lords in the great events in England inevitably distracted them from the situation in Wales. While their guard was down, Llywelyn took steps to benefit from their distraction. In July of 1263, he moved through Hereford and Hay en route to Montgomery, threatening Mortimer's lands further in the process. These actions were not planned to further de Montfort's cause. They were rather actions that would primarily benefit Llywelyn.

It is tempting to see the civil war as a moment of supreme opportunity for Llywelyn, but it is important to keep its effects in proportion. He had already experienced a good deal of success before the outbreak of hostilities in England, and it would undervalue his achievements if this were not duly noted. And, as the civil war approached its denouement in 1265, it appears that Llywelyn may well have seen that de Montfort's moment had passed, and that he ought to maintain a degree of detachment. By this time indeed matters had reached a somewhat bizarre state. Henry III was in captivity and a number of pronouncements were made in his name, which clearly bore the stamp of Simon de Montfort. Many men believed that, were Henry in a position to act freely, many of de Montfort's decisions would be overturned.

It is in this context that the so-called Treaty of Pipton should be seen. Negotiations took place between Llywelyn and Simon de Montfort on Henry's behalf in June 1265. These discussions took place by correspondence and the two men did not meet as they evolved. Instead, they were conducted through representatives. Under the terms of the agreement made at Pipton, Llywelyn would pay the princely sum of £20,000 in return for lordship over all the other lords of Wales. In contrast to attempts sometimes made in the past to limit agreements with Welsh princes to their own lifetime, Henry agreed that these rights would pass to Llywelyn's heirs. All previous agreements, including the Treaty of Woodstock in 1247, were annulled. In return, Llywelyn recognised that the English king was his overlord and that he owed feudal service to him. Witnessing his seal were some of the greatest men of Wales, including Gruffudd ap Gwenwynwyn, Gruffudd ap Madog and Rhys Fychan.

Llywelyn also promised to provide military aid against the Marcher lords. This last requirement was the most pressing current need of Simon de Montfort. Simon progressed through Welsh lands in an attempt to drum up recruits for what he must have seen as a decisive battle but the results were poor. This suggests several things: that the Welsh were reluctant to leave their own lands to fight at this stage; that they were not decisively committed to the cause of baronial reform in what was after all to many of them another country; and, perhaps, that they saw that de Montfort was in a perilous position. So uncertain was de Montfort's position, indeed, that he provided hostages to Llywelyn as surety for the agreement.

So de Montfort went to meet his appointment with destiny at Evesham with few Welshmen at his side, other than the men of Humphrey de Bohun. Even they were only there because they had been called upon to attend by their lord. A number of them died at his side as he, in a brave final gesture, fought on foot with them so that he could share their fate. Humphrey was among the many men fighting alongside de Montfort killed in the battle.

In the aftermath of Evesham, the lordship of Chester, which had been taken by de Montfort, was returned to Edward. Llywelyn perhaps saw the threat that was likely to arise from the determined English prince, as he moved on the castle of Hawarden, which was taken and destroyed. He then retreated to Ewloe, the forward base of his defensive line. A truce was arranged soon afterwards, which was to last until 1267, the year that marked the zenith of Llywelyn's power.

Events had so far conspired against any permanent resolution of the Welsh situation. The chaos in England had militated against meaningful negotiations with Llywelyn. The country was divided and an agreement, such as the one confirmed at Pipton in 1265, meant little if it could be shown that the king had agreed to the conditions attached to it when he was under duress. A further complicating factor was the presence of so many prominent Marcher lords among the ranks of the party opposing Llywelyn. Of the three great Marcher lords (Gloucester, Mortimer and Humphrey de Bohun, earl of Hereford) two were opposed to de Montfort. They had very good reason to dispute any agreement that would strengthen Llywelyn's position. With their lands in close proximity to those of Llywelyn, they would be especially resistant to the agreement of 1265. Once the king was released, they too could be expected to argue against ratification of the terms.

Potentially, the defeat of de Montfort's cause at Evesham and the release of Henry III changed everything. The support of the Marcher lords had been crucial and their council would play an important part in the formulation of Henry's future strategy with regard to Wales. So too would the inclinations of Prince Edward, a man already noted for defending his rights and one who could be expected to resist any attempt to confirm Llywelyn in possession of the lands that he already held, especially of those he had taken in the 'Four Cantreds'. It was a complex situation and it required the talents of a skilled and respected negotiator if there was to be a resolution of the situation that was acceptable to both England and Wales. Fortunately, there was just such a man present in the country at the time.

Pope Clement IV, a Frenchman and himself a former papal legate to England, was keen that peace should be restored. Clement therefore despatched his legate, Ottobuono, in 1265 to do what he could to achieve this. When he left for England, de Montfort was still a force in the land and Ottobuono came armed with instructions that Llywelyn was to abandon any understanding with de Montfort on pain of excommunication. This stance became redundant with the death and defeat of de Montfort, and a change of direction was required from the legate.

Peace between England and Wales was not immediately possible, for several reasons. Peace in the latter was not achievable until peace in the former was secure; the two were inextricably linked. There were deep wounds left by the civil wars; trouble continued, even after de Montfort was dead and gone. Then there was also the nature of the agreement already made between Henry III and Llywelyn to be considered. Llywelyn was happy with the agreement more or less as it stood and would be unlikely to agree to any noticeable diminution of the powers vested in him by it, even though the king was under pressure to abandon it. It looked as if some tough negotiations were ahead.

The situation was further confused by ongoing tensions between Marcher lords, especially between Gilbert Clare, earl of Gloucester, and Roger Mortimer. Mortimer did particularly well in the aftermath of the civil wars, being granted significant tracts of land in England. Clare on the other hand benefited much less from the cessation of hostilities. Tensions between Mortimer and Gloucester, bitter rivals in the March, grew alarmingly and an attack by the former on Brecon in May 1266 was probably aimed at Gloucester, who had been awarded the town after the death of Humphrey de Bohun at Evesham. Llywelyn agreed a truce with Gloucester in the build-up to the latter's advance on London in 1267 but, again, an absence of war did not mean peace. Llywelyn was slow to take advantage of Gloucester's dissatisfaction, possibly because Llywelyn had been involved in conflict in Glamorgan, the hub of Gloucester's Marcher lands, shortly before.

The resolution of the difficulties between Gloucester and Prince Edward, which had for a time threatened imminent hostilities, was to have a significant impact on Anglo-Welsh relations. It has already been noted that peace in Wales was not possible until the situation in England had been resolved. The patching up of strained relationships in London left the way open for a settlement in Wales. Gloucester finally expressed his satisfaction with affairs on 18 June 1267. Less than a week later, Henry III wrote to Llywelyn in apologetic terms for not responding more positively to the initiatives made by Ottobuono for a peaceful settlement thus far. Now that Gloucester's concerns had been addressed, he expressed his willingness to meet Llywelyn at Montgomery on 2 August.

Negotiations did go ahead, though not as quickly as originally planned. They started on 28 August, at Shrewsbury rather than Montgomery. But it was quickly apparent that this time there was a genuine willingness to come to terms. The long years of tension and, latterly, open conflict in England had taken their toll and there was now a real desire for peace, which meant that both parties were prepared to compromise. On 21 September, Henry instructed Ottobuono to negotiate whatever terms he saw fit, with an undertaking that he would subsequently ratify them. By the 25th, representatives of both Llywelyn and the English crown had sworn that they were ready to abide by the terms of the treaty. The way was clear for one final, dramatic moment in which the treaty would be sealed. The major parties were about to meet in person.

On 29 September, Llywelyn presented himself to Henry III. The meeting took place at Montgomery. Although there is no certain knowledge of whether the assignation was at the castle or at the ford nearby, it seems probable that it was the latter. The ford of Rhyd Chwima was a time-honoured boundary between the two nations and it was a frequent occurrence at the time for meetings of this kind to take place at locations of such profound symbolic significance as a 'crossing-over' place. Llywelyn swore solemnly on the Holy Scriptures that he would abide by the terms of the treaty. He would give his fealty to the crown of England, accepting that he held his lands at the gift of the King of England. The lords with him, men such as his steward, Goronwy ab Ednyfed, added their own oaths. The treaty was formally sealed by King Henry and his son and heir, Edward.

Llywelyn gained much in return. Henry signalled that he was prepared to grant the principality of Wales to Llywelyn and his heirs. All other Welsh lords were to do homage to Llywelyn, with one notable exception. Maredudd ap Rhys Gryg, who had come to blows with Llywelyn a few years previously, was alone among the Welsh lords to pay homage directly to the English crown. All previous treaties and agreements that were at odds with the terms were to be annulled. There was only one important caveat: Dafydd was to be provided for under the terms of the arrangement, and various procedures were set up to settle this issue in the event of disagreement. The king sought a quick resolution of this particular problem, and it was laid down that the situation regarding Dafydd must be resolved by Christmas.

Llywelyn was to pay a heavy monetary price for his success. He had to hand over the sum of 25,000 marks to the king, with 1,000 marks due immediately and 4,000 by Christmas. Thereafter, payments were to be made at a rate of 3,000 marks per annum (about £2,000). This represented a huge burden for Llywelyn. It has been estimated, using what have admittedly been described as 'precarious calculations', that Llywelyn's income from his heartland of Gwynedd was perhaps £3,000–£3,500 per annum. From this must presumably be deducted some monies which would have gone to Dafydd after he was granted land in the region (maybe more than £1,000 per annum). Llywelyn would have had other income and such sums would put him among the wealthier magnates in the land. Estimates by contrast suggest that Gloucester had income of £4,500–£5,000 per annum from his lands and, at a later date the Earl of Lincoln, Henry de Lacy, £6,000. Other Marcher lords such as the earl of Hereford had income of only about £2,000 per annum from their lands.

Set against his likely revenues, then, the drain of £2,000 per annum was substantial. Llywelyn would of course have had other costs to bear. The sparse evidence that survives suggests that he did not live lavishly or extravagantly but he would have had dependants and servants to provide for, and his 'army'. In addition, although he could not afford to be a great castle builder, some money would have gone on constructing and maintaining fortifications such as Dolforwyn and Ewloe that he had ordered to be built. All in all, the suggestion appears to be that Llywelyn was perhaps overambitious in signing up to a treaty that bled his treasury at an alarming rate. It was understandable that he should do so in the light of the great personal rewards that he anticipated in return; but when, a few years later, he stopped making the payments because of what he claimed to be breaches of the terms, it is difficult to avoid the conclusion that he was anyway encouraged to do so by an affordability problem.[11]

The treaty defined exactly what territory would be regarded as being in Llywelyn's principality. Llywelyn was in a dual position, as the title he used of 'Lord of Snowdon and Prince of Wales' suggests. As Lord of Snowdon, his territory was fairly well defined – with one vital exception: 'Snowdon' applied not only to the mountains that lay at the heart of north Wales but also to the wider area of Gwynedd. Llywelyn ap Iorwerth had defined Gwynedd as consisting of not only the land to the west of the River Conwy, Gwynedd Uwch Conwy, but also the Perfeddwlad to the east of it, Gwynedd Is Conwy. The position of the Perfeddwlad was clarified under the terms of the Treaty of Montgomery; it would pass to Llywelyn. In the wider territorial sense, the designation 'Prince of Wales' was harder to define. Did the title mean 'Prince of the Welsh'? If it did, then the situation was far from clear because many of the Welsh lived in Marcher territories where his writ did not run. In the event, most of Deheubarth and Powys was considered as being part of the principality of Wales under the terms of the treaty, the lands of Maredudd ap Rhys Gryg excepted. Areas recently won by Llywelyn elsewhere were to be returned to the king, with the exception of a few towns, including Builth and Brecon.

But the position regarding other lands was less clear, and therein lay a source of potential friction in the future. Mailienydd, a crucial area abutting Mortimer lands, appears to have been one bone of contention. The section of the treaty dealing with this was ambiguous and suggests the formulation of a poorly defined compromise that was never likely to work. Mortimer wished to build a castle there, as he claimed the land for himself. Under the terms agreed, he would be allowed to do so, at Cefnllys. But Llywelyn could still claim to be lord of Mailienydd if he could prove that it was his by legal action. In other words, the issue of ownership was left unresolved by the agreement, a situation that hinted at future difficulties. Glamorgan also was not covered by the arrangement. It was an area that Llywelyn coveted, something that would bring him into potential conflict with the current Marcher lord, Gilbert de Clare, earl of Gloucester. When England and Wales veered towards conflict again a few years later, Glamorgan would be the catalyst. In this case, the silence of the treaty on the region was decidedly unhelpful.

The terms of the treaty must have pushed Llywelyn close to the brink of financial exhaustion. In 1283, when Llywelyn had lost his power and, indeed, his life, a review of his period of rule was instigated. Admittedly, it was not altogether objective, as the hand of Bishop Anian of St Asaph's, with whom Llywelyn enjoyed an uncertain relationship, can be detected behind it. But allowing for its possible bias, it is still suggestive. It describes Llywelyn as a harsh ruler, who introduced innovative ways of collecting taxation to Gwynedd that ignored age-old conventions. The number of officers employed to recover tax monies due had doubled. He also assiduously took advantage of all the monies from fines and other legal methods of recovering money that were available to him, such as the right of claiming wrecks on the shore (something that was on occasion to cause great difficulties with England). His people acknowledged that he could be generous on occasion but generally considered his rule hard. If all this were true, and it cannot be dismissed out of hand, then it is hardly surprising, considering the heavy responsibility placed on Llywelyn by the terms of the treaty.

But any misgivings that might have been lurking beneath the surface at the time would not have detracted from the sense of elation felt by Llywelyn after the Treaty of Montgomery was agreed. For nearly a decade, he had planned for such an event, for the moment when the King of England invested him as Prince over the Welsh. It gave him legitimacy, status and power, all the things that Llywelyn, an ambitious man, desired. At times in the past it may have seemed very doubtful whether such success was possible. The internal situation in England had for so long militated against any such recognition from Henry III. But now the time had truly come. Undoubtedly, Llywelyn must have had concerns about how he was going to pay for the privilege of the recognition that he had achieved, and just how willing the Marchers – not to mention Prince Edward – would be to make it work. But one emotion above all others would have been his companion as he rode back into the country that was now recognised as his, albeit as tenant-in-chief for the English king. As he travelled homeward, perhaps he recited to himself again and again with self-satisfaction, the contents of the treaty, especially that portion which explicitly stated that the English crown wished to 'honour the person of Llywelyn': recognition indeed. He was as the contemporary Welsh poet Dafydd Benfras proudly exulted, the 'royal son of Gruffudd, royal redeemer of his patrimony, the restorer of his lands'.

It was perhaps as well that Llywelyn as he rode with his entourage through the Brecon Beacons could not see into the future because, with great irony, the climax of his achievements would bring him little lasting joy. The effort of paying for the privileges granted him under the terms of the Treaty of Montgomery would stretch his country to the limit, and probably beyond it. And he would soon find that he would have to fight to protect those privileges, straining his finite resources even more. Perhaps the most successful of all medieval Welsh leaders, first among princes, Llywelyn ap Gruffudd was destined to be known to posterity as 'Llywelyn ein Llyw Olaf' – 'Llywelyn the Last'.

CHAPTER FOUR

Preparations for War

*Once [the Welsh] show signs of rebellion, no mercy should be shown
to them and they must be punished immediately.*[1]

Henry III died on 6 October 1272. Prince Edward, his heir, was far
away from England, having made his way on crusade to the east. The
venture had been abortive from the outset. The leader of the crusade,
King Louis IX of France, had died when it was barely underway.
Edward was late in joining the expedition and, when he caught up with
it outside Tunis, it was already on the verge of returning to Europe.
Accompanied only by his small English contingent, he pushed on to
the Holy Land. Once there, his tiny army achieved little, though the
ten-year truce that he negotiated with the Egyptian sultan, Baibars,
bought the now dying crusader kingdom in the east a little time. Apart
from that, the major event of note during the crusade was an attempt
on Edward's life. The prince was stabbed and for a time his life was in
danger but, being a young man with great physical strength, he
survived.[2]

He was already on his way home and had reached Sicily when he
received news of his father's death. It affected him greatly. Charles of
Anjou, his host and a fellow crusader, remarked on his great grief, which
contrasted markedly with the emotions shown when Edward received
news of the death of his son John. Edward replied that 'the loss of sons is
easy to bear, since more of them can be produced any day, but there is no
remedy for the death of parents, who are irreplaceable'. Such an attitude
might be understandable from a man who would sire fourteen children
with his first wife, Eleanor of Castile, only six of whom would reach their
teens, but it hinted at a harsh temperament.

The new king was in no rush to return to his homeland. Rather than
hurry back for his coronation, it would be well over a year before he
would land in England to take up his crown. His presence was needed in
Gascony where there was much unrest, but there were several other
events on his homeward journey that would have specific repercussions
for Edward and Welsh affairs in the future.

On his way back to England, the king stayed for a while in Savoy, from where his mother's family had originally come. The Savoyards continued to play an important part in English affairs; several of them, notably Otto de Grandson, a nobleman whose family hailed from the shores of Lake Neuchatel, would remain lifelong confidants of Edward. One of the places that Edward stopped at was the castle of St Georges d'Esperanche, which was not by this stage completed. While there, he probably met the architect of this impressive new fortification, one Master James of St George. The two men would renew the acquaintance spectacularly later on in their lives.

Edward also spent some time with the Pope, Gregory X, a man who had been elected pontiff while on crusade with Edward. It was of course a very sensible move politically for a new monarch to visit the Pope and secure good relations with him. But Edward's reasons for visiting Gregory were in part to seek retribution for the murder of his long-time friend, Henry of Almain. The two men had grown up in each other's company. Before sailing for the Holy Land early in 1271, Edward had received a message that his father was ill. Rather than return to England in person, he had sent Henry of Almain in his place to look after his interests. Henry's journey had taken him through lands in which lived Simon and Guy de Montfort, sons of that Simon killed by Edward's army at Evesham. In revenge for their father's death, they had in their turn struck down Henry of Almain. Edward now looked for retribution. He got it after a fashion, when the Pope excommunicated the murderers. No further action followed, however, and Edward marked the injury done him by the de Montforts personally. Anyone connected to the family could expect little mercy from him.

England was rapturous when Edward eventually arrived at Dover on 2 August 1274. He journeyed on to London where lavish preparations had been made for his coronation. He entered his capital in triumph on 18 August. The day after, he was crowned in the abbey at Westminster. It was a splendid occasion. Wine flowed from fountains for the people of the city to drink their new king's health. England looked forward confidently to a new beginning. It was a year of fresh hope, when even nature seemed to recognise that something unusual was happening: 'on the vigil of Saint Nicholas, there were earthquakes, thunder and lightning, the fiery dragon and a comet'.[3] The fiery dragon was an especially appropriate portent.

The coronation ceremony itself was a typically majestic occasion, but there were a few things of note that the more discerning observers would have marked. There was some debate about who should take what part in the ceremony. The archbishop of York was at odds with the archbishop of

Canterbury, Robert of Kilwardby, over the carrying of his cross and did not attend as a result. Edward also made an amendment to the traditional oath sworn at coronation ceremonies. He introduced a new vow that not only would he protect his people, he would also protect the rights of the crown. It was a clear signal that the new king had a well-developed sense of the supremacy of the crown and his own paramount position. It was an apt defining moment for the reign that was to follow.

There was one other matter of great significance. It was expected that the king's leading subjects would be present to give their homage to him. Not only were the leading magnates of the realm there, the King of Scotland was also in attendance. It was a tremendous occasion, as a contemporary chronicler makes clear:

> The king took up his crown and shone in glory before the peers of the realm. Also present, besides the citizens of London and of other towns and cities from all parts of the kingdom – who had vied with one another in bedecking themselves in a variety of rich clothes – was a large throng of earls, barons and knights, similarly decked out.[4]

But amid this gathering of the great and the good, there was one notable absentee. Llywelyn ap Gruffudd, Prince of Wales, was not in London nor was he anywhere near it. His non-attendance was notable. Attempts had already been made to persuade him to declare his allegiance to Edward, as under the terms of the Treaty of Montgomery he was bound to do. It was important to establish as soon as possible in the new reign that the king's lords publicly demonstrated their allegiance to the incoming king. Within two months of Henry's death, Llywelyn had been summoned to Montgomery to do homage to Edward, although the new king would not of course be present in person as he was then still far away from England.[5] But when the abbots of Dore and Haughmond turned up at the ford there to receive Llywelyn's homage, they wasted their time, for he did not come.

This was merely the first in a series of summonses that were sent to Llywelyn and ignored. He was invited to the coronation, as Llywelyn himself acknowledged when he wrote to his 'particular friend, Reginald de Grey', with rare irony given the damage that the latter would do to his country a few years later. But although he sent a gift of venison with the letter, he did not go to the coronation.[6] Injunctions to Llywelyn to attend on Edward followed with regularity. Soon after Edward's coronation it was noted that 'the king has not forgotten that he enjoined the messengers sent by the said Llywelyn to have a colloquy with the king at

Martinmas . . . in order that the prince might come to the king there and do his homage and other things according to the form of the said peace without further delay'.[7]

It was next arranged that Llywelyn and Edward would meet at Shrewsbury on 25 November. Three days before they were due to meet, Edward called the meeting off as he was suffering from an abscess. In the following year, another entry in the records noted the sending of a 'mandate to Llywelyn, son of Griffith, prince of Wales, whom the king has several times commanded to be at Chester to do his homage and fealty, to be before the king at Westminster three weeks after Michaelmas next to do so'.[8] But Llywelyn replied that he would not come, 'saying he remembered the death of his father Griffith, who fell from the Tower of London and broke his neck and died'.[9] Further summonses were despatched to Llywelyn in 1276 with equally unsatisfactory results. It became obvious that the Prince of Wales had no intention of giving his fealty to the new king.

This was not the only sign of Llywelyn's disenchantment with affairs. The terms of the Treaty of Montgomery, although in many ways quite satisfactory to Llywelyn, were expensive for him. Yet for a time, the annual payment was made in full. There were occasional problems and the payments were delayed from 1270 onwards. It has however reasonably been argued that this was because of Llywelyn's financial difficulties.[10] Certainly this time was a difficult one for the country as a whole. There were serious problems with the harvest in both 1270 and 1271. Even in 1273, Llywelyn insisted that, although he was experiencing problems, he had imposed a special tax and would continue to make the payments that were due. The records note the safe receipt of the sums due as late as 1274, with an entry in the Patent Rolls giving 'acquittance to Llywelyn, son of Griffith, Prince of Wales, for the receipt by the hands of the abbot of Chester of 3,000 marks for Christmas term'.[11] But the payments dried up thereafter, giving yet more substance to the impression that Llywelyn was spoiling for a fight.

There were a number of reasons for his intransigence. Not least of them was the difficulties that he had been experiencing with some of the English Marcher lords whose lands bordered on his. These had manifested themselves particularly in his relations with Gilbert Clare, earl of Gloucester. Gilbert had a patchy history. In 1264, he had fought alongside Simon de Montfort but in the following year he had been Edward's right-hand man in the defeat of de Montfort at Evesham. Then, in 1267, Gloucester had again changed tack, marching on London in an attempt to force Edward to be more conciliatory in his treatment of the rebels. In the process, he allied himself with Llywelyn.

In 1270, Gloucester, the holder of substantial lands in the south of Wales, started work on a new castle at Caerphilly. He had taken the lands from a Welsh lord, Gruffudd ap Rhys, in 1266. In the aftermath of the demise of Simon de Montfort, King Henry III had given Gloucester carte blanche to retain whatever land of Simon's or of his supporters that he could conquer in Wales.[12] It is not entirely clear how aggressively Gloucester took advantage of this concession but Llywelyn perceived the building of what was clearly going to be a substantial castle as a threat.

Gloucester had been present at Kenilworth Castle when it was besieged by the victorious royalist armies after the Battle of Evesham in 1266. Surrounded by water, the castle resisted for months before finally capitulating at the end of the year. A young, ambitious man such as Gloucester, still learning the skills required to succeed in medieval warfare, cannot have failed to have been impressed by the construction of the castle. It is surely no coincidence that, in part at least, the castle at Caerphilly (Caerfili) employed a similar design, though with many modifications, which show that the earl of Gloucester (or, at least, his architect) was a man with an enquiring and adaptive mind, capable of fusing together a number of different concepts and making his own mark through the castle he was now building.[13] The result was a fortress on a massive scale (the largest in Wales in fact) that even a king would be proud of.

Even before work began on Gloucester's massive new fortress there had been signs of tension. Llywelyn led his men into Glamorgan, part of Gloucester's territory, and by 1267 he was arguing that, as Gruffudd ap Rhys was a Welsh baron, he owed allegiance in the first instance to Llywelyn and that his lands therefore were part of the prince's territories. The situation may even have pre-dated 1266 and it is quite possible, though speculative, that Llywelyn had advanced into the region as early as 1265 when the civil wars in England gave him a window of opportunity. The truce of 1267 between the two men was nothing more than recognition that both needed a breathing space, especially Gloucester, who was then planning his move on London. At any rate, it was clear that both men had ambitions in Glamorgan and that any cessation of the dispute was not likely to be permanent. There were even hints that the negotiations around the Treaty of Montgomery were marked by behind the scenes wrangling on the future of Glamorgan, which was not satisfactorily resolved at the time. Such uncertainties would certainly help to explain the ambiguities in the treaty, the ramifications of which were already becoming apparent. There were a number of Welshmen in Glamorgan, especially in the uplands there, and their loyalty might well be suspect with a strong leader such as Llywelyn in the ascendancy.

When Henry III was presented with the cases of Llywelyn and Gloucester he recommended that the men should find an amicable, negotiated settlement to the dispute and suggested to Llywelyn that, if he wished, an action against Gloucester might be undertaken in the English courts. Whether or not this proved acceptable to Llywelyn we do not know, but it is most unlikely that Gloucester would have been satisfied to go along with what he would have seen as an unwarranted intrusion into Marcher affairs by an English court, as his rights would, in his eyes, have been seriously compromised as a result.

In 1268, Gloucester and Llywelyn tried to resolve their differences without the intervention of the king, something that neither man probably wanted. However, they could not do so. Henry therefore arranged for a consideration of their disputes to be held at the ford of Montgomery. The king instructed his son, Prince Edward, to examine the merits of the case. And so, at the ford of Rhyd Chwima, the very spot at which the Treaty of Montgomery was signed, Edward and Llywelyn met. It was in retrospect a defining moment. The two men were both at a crossroads. Llywelyn, by now a very experienced leader, whose status had both been secured and constrained by the Treaty of Montgomery, a powerful and proven warrior and a politically astute prince, had to see for himself what the treaty would mean for him in practice. If it were to mean anything the ambitions of Marcher barons such as Gloucester had to be kept in check.

Edward was on the other hand a rising power, a man who was on the brink of great things. Physically prepossessing, young, strong, ambitious, with his silvery-blond hair and his great height (hence his nickname of 'Longshanks'), he radiated vigour and energy. He was even then contemplating preparations for his departure on crusade, a glorious adventure. He was also on the verge of kingship, although of course he could not know when his father would die. When the two men were to meet again a decade later the situation would be very different, and many things would have changed. For now, the two men apparently got on well. Edward seemed to be sympathetic towards Llywelyn, partly perhaps because Gloucester was no friend of his.

There was one important issue on which Edward agreed with Llywelyn. Both Llywelyn and Gloucester had been arguing that Maredudd ap Gruffudd owed allegiance to them. Edward now decided in favour of Llywelyn. It was a decision that must have infuriated Gloucester, and he worked consistently to have it reversed from then on, though his fury did nothing to change Edward's mind. There were a whole range of other issues where no final agreement was reached, though Edward and Llywelyn left each other on good terms. Llywelyn sent a letter to King

Henry, saying how pleased he had been with the way that the meeting had gone, and the king replied that his son had also been delighted at the respectful way in which Llywelyn had treated with him. But Edward soon became preoccupied with his plans for the crusade and the foundations of good faith laid down by their meeting were not built upon.

When Llywelyn subsequently wrote to Henry seeking a decisive resolution of the dispute yet again the king said that he could not respond. It was his son's responsibility to adjudicate on the matter and he was now out of the country, having left in 1270. Edward would remain abroad for several years and his lengthy absence gave Henry an excuse to prevaricate. Llywelyn was faced with one of two options, neither of them palatable. He could back down and give up his claims to Glamorgan. These were anyway weak, and the scope of the Treaty of Montgomery generally suggested that the lands involved belonged to Gloucester. Or, he could launch an all-out attack on Gloucester.

In 1270, Gloucester was summoned to parliament to present his case. While in London, he took the opportunity to lobby support for a reversal of Edward's decision concerning the allegiance of Maredudd ap Gruffudd. It became clear that there was a good deal of support for Gloucester's claims in England. The time for a peaceful settlement had in any case passed. On 13 October 1270, Llywelyn's patience finally ran out. He marched his army to Caerphilly and caused serious damage to the castle that Gloucester was constructing there. The building of Caerphilly is a tangible demonstration of the tensions that were developing between Llywelyn and Gloucester. But the damage that Llywelyn caused in 1270 merely hardened Gloucester's resolve. He began work again early in 1271. The castle he now planned would be surrounded by lakes, the completed structure forming a vast amalgamation of land and water defences that would be immensely strong.

Gloucester had called Llywelyn's bluff by recommencing work. Now he was committed to war, the Prince of Wales had little option but to attack it once more. He declared angrily that, however strong the castle Gloucester was building might be, he would knock it down in three days. The castle was soon under siege from his men. Henry III was seriously perturbed and sent two of his bishops to intervene. They begged Llywelyn to refrain from his attacks and seek a peaceful solution. He was most reluctant to do so but he was eventually persuaded. It was agreed that the two men's representatives would meet at the ford of Montgomery in another attempt to resolve their differences. In the meantime, the bishops – as supposedly neutral parties – would hold the castle until its future was resolved.[14]

Soon after, Caerphilly was back in Gloucester's hands, retaken by subterfuge. It had been handed over to the safekeeping of the Bishops of Coventry, Lichfield and Worcester while its future was decided. Llywelyn had agreed to the arrangement provided that no 'walls, ditches or garniture [should be added] nor should any walls be raised, crenellated or changed'. Negotiations were arranged to take place in July 1272. But in February of that year, the constable of Cardiff Castle arrived at Caerphilly, requesting permission to check the stores held within the castle. Once inside, they left the castle gates open. Forty men-at-arms arrived soon after, turning the bishops' men out and taking over the castle. A letter from Henry III to Llywelyn soon afterwards apologising for this act could not alter the fact that Caerphilly was once more in Gloucester's hands. This time, it would stay firmly within his grasp.

* * *

Llywelyn's decision to involve himself in Glamorgan was perhaps one of his more serious mistakes. His claims there were weak, and would inevitably bring him into conflict with the earl of Gloucester, a powerful Marcher lord, who could prove a most difficult enemy to deal with. And, leaving aside the legality or otherwise of his claim to the lands involved and their lords, there were also pragmatic considerations to bear in mind. Glamorgan was far away from Gwynedd and his involvement there would stretch Llywelyn's resources seriously. It was a heavy gamble on his part, and he gained nothing for his efforts in the long run.

Problems were also evident in Llywelyn's relationships with Roger Mortimer. Mortimer had been building castles around his territories to an extent that was, in Llywelyn's eyes, contrary to the provisions of the Treaty of Montgomery. Llywelyn wrote to Edward asking him to stop the work, without success.[15] At about the same time he issued an overt challenge to Mortimer. He began to build a new castle of his own at Dolforwyn, near Newtown.

A message was sent from England telling Llywelyn to desist from his plans for Dolforwyn. Llywelyn well knew that Mortimer's hand was behind the command. He kept the messenger, the prior of Wenlock, waiting for several days before seeing him. He finally responded that he would do as he wished with his own lands; Edward was not then in the country and clearly, in his view, would not have issued any such order if he had been. He therefore carried on with construction work regardless. He shortly afterwards sent another message, complaining that Mortimer, who had been repairing the nearby castle of Cefnllys, was doing so in a way that was beyond the scope of the Treaty of Montgomery.

Llywelyn was also at odds with Humphrey de Bohun, who would become earl of Hereford in 1275 (the two men had come to blows over lands around Brecon). De Bohun submitted his claims to arbitration in England but he failed in his attempt to win wholesale support. De Bohun did however find a patron in the shape of Gloucester. The earl encouraged him to carve out a lordship for himself around Brecon, no doubt reckoning that this would distract Llywelyn from Glamorgan. De Bohun was encouraged by other local lords, who calculated that it would be very useful for them to have a buffer zone between their lands and those of Llywelyn. De Bohun's cause must have been assisted by the fact that Llywelyn did not have total unanimity of support from the Welshmen in the Brecon area. He was forced at one stage to take hostages to ensure the good behaviour of certain Welsh lords in the area, and it is noticeable that in Edward I's campaigns of 1277 these men were quick to lend their assistance to the English.

The aggressive nature of the Prince of Wales was sufficient to convert the waverers among the Marcher lords 'from being anti-loyalist to anti-Welsh.'[16] Later, Llywelyn would invade parts of Shropshire, depriving Peter Corbet, a Marcher lord there, of a sizeable part of his lands. So great were the losses sustained by Corbet that he was unable to meet his feudal obligations to the crown.[17] The March was soon virtually universally united against Llywelyn.

Llywelyn's problems with Roger Mortimer were especially dangerous. When Edward left for his crusade, Mortimer played a prominent role as one of Henry III's councillors. When Henry died, he was one of the new king's regents until his return to England. He was at the apex of politics in England and his enmity was a problem that Llywelyn could well do without. Gloucester too was very powerful, especially in the south, and de Bohun, although as yet in the earlier stages of his career, would also eventually rise to great heights. There was potentially great rivalry between these Marcher lords. However, by a combination of circumstances, mutual self-interest and greed and Llywelyn's poor handling of the situation, these three men in particular had been cajoled into forming a triumvirate which posed the Prince of Wales a threat of deadly proportions.

In 1274, steps were taken to set up arbitration to settle the disputes. The conciliation was to take place at the ford of Montgomery where the claims of Llywelyn would be examined by the earl of Warwick, Roger Clifford, William Bagot and Odo de Hodenet. Shortly after, it was recorded that the conciliation would take place within a month of Easter, and its primary aim would be to negotiate a truce between Llywelyn and Humphrey de Bohun. But such attempts led to few concrete conclusions and generally did nothing to lead to peace being restored.[18]

Llywelyn was not only at odds with the English. Some of his greatest difficulties revolved around his relationships with other Welshmen, not least his own flesh and blood. His brother, Dafydd, was increasingly frustrated at seeing power concentrated in the hands of Llywelyn. He was a fickle character, who had turned on his brother before. Dafydd clearly felt that he had not received his fair share of recognition in Wales and was ambitious for far greater power and influence. He found a willing ally in the shape of Gruffudd ap Gwenwynwyn of Powys who had been a frequent opponent of Llywelyn over many years. Matters came to a head in 1274. The construction of Llywelyn's castle and borough at Dolforwyn threatened Gruffudd's main base at Welshpool, and Gruffudd reacted aggressively to the threat it posed.

Together, Gruffudd and Dafydd devised an extreme plan. They resolved that they would kill Llywelyn. A date was set for the assassination – 2 February 1274. Until this time, Dafydd was to stay with Llywelyn's entourage, so that he could step into the vacuum created by his death. Dafydd's daughter was to marry Gruffudd's son and the regions of Ceri and Cedewain in Powys were to be granted to Gruffudd. But the weather intervened. A snowstorm on the night that the murder was to take place prevented the party that was to kill Llywelyn from fulfilling its mission. Soon after, news of the plot broke.

Gruffudd's son, Owain, was seriously implicated as the leader of the would-be assassins. He was taken hostage by Llywelyn. Gruffudd was also called to account by the prince. He was forced to renew his allegiance to Llywelyn and some of his lands were taken from him, among them the region of Arwystli. Gruffudd was warned that he would forfeit all his lands if he repeated his crime. But he was fortunate; his punishment could have been far worse. So too was Dafydd, who seemed to escape scot-free. Llywelyn's leniency is baffling and can only be explained convincingly if it is accepted that he did not yet know the full details of the plot against him.

Llywelyn still thought that the breach with the men who had plotted against him could be healed. They were very powerful influences in Wales and he would still by choice have preferred to have their assistance. He sent a delegation to Gruffudd's castle at Welshpool with a view to resolving the differences. Gruffudd received them amicably enough. However, when their guard was lowered the men were seized and taken prisoner. Gruffudd had passed the point of no return. Shortly afterwards, he fled over the border to England with Dafydd. Gruffudd was welcomed and allowed to settle at Shrewsbury, dangerously close to the Welsh border. From here, in the next year, 1275, he launched a series of raids on Llywelyn's territory. He flaunted the gains that he made from these, selling the plunder he had seized freely at Montgomery and Shrewsbury. He even took one of Llywelyn's men prisoner and brought him back with him, soon afterwards having him publicly decapitated.

Llywelyn reacted forcefully to the situation. In the words of the Brut y Tywysogion he 'overran all the territory of Gruffudd without opposition and set his own officers over it all'. He was understandably both angry and concerned that his potential killers had found shelter in England. He looked around for support. He did have one particularly useful ally, although he was far away in Rome. Pope Gregory X attempted to act impartially in his interventions in the disputes between England and Wales. However, although he could not be too fulsome in his support for Llywelyn, as this would have put him in a difficult political position, he appears to have had some sympathy with his predicament. Soon after these events in Wales, Llywelyn wrote to Gregory to explain his position. However, an unfortunate period of instability within the papacy caused Llywelyn problems. Gregory died in January 1276. His replacement, Innocent V, did not last the year, neither did Innocent's successor, Hadrian V. The next Pope, John XXI, did marginally better, lasting into 1277 but just at the time that matters in Wales were building to a fatal climax, the papacy was unusually weak.

The events of 1274 occurred just when Llywelyn was experiencing other problems which suggest that his grip on his territories was not as firm as he would wish. He fell out seriously with Anian, Bishop of St Asaph's. Anian wished to protect the position of the church in Wales. However, he came into conflict with Llywelyn, who was supported by the Cistercian order. The Cistercians indeed did rather well in Wales at the time. They took over a number of churches in Anian's bishopric. The bishop was not best pleased. Gregory X had set up a committee to investigate the disputes led by the abbot of the Premonstratensian foundation at Talley. The abbot sided with the Cistercians in the dispute. When Anian contested his findings, the abbot promptly excommunicated him. Matters were eventually resolved after a fashion but these events in themselves give evidence of instability in the country. Llywelyn was frequently at odds with Anian and such internal divisions hardly strengthened Llywelyn's position.

Soon afterwards there was another serious development that was guaranteed to inflame Edward I. Llywelyn had sided with Simon de Montfort during his wars against the crown. There were rumours current that Llywelyn was even now in discussion with the Montfortians. For the best part of a decade, discussions had taken place concerning a proposal for Llywelyn to marry Simon's daughter, Eleanor. Llywelyn now resurrected the idea. Edward was enraged by the plan. He told his advisers that the match would 'scatter the seeds which had grown from the malice which her father had sown'.

A marriage by proxy was celebrated in 1275 in France. Soon afterwards, Eleanor set out to take her place beside her new husband. Her crossing of the English Channel was a dangerous enterprise given the fact that Edward opposed the marriage. Her party made their way so far in safety but their luck finally ran out in the Western Approaches. Here, an English ship, probably under the command of Thomas Larchdeacon, a Cornish knight, lay in wait. The trap was sprung and the ship seized. Eleanor, along with her brother Amaury, were taken to England to enjoy the dubious hospitality of Edward, the avowed enemy of their family. Edward later attributed the seizure to divine providence but stories of such a fortuitous coincidence should be treated with a substantial degree of scepticism.

Edward was not slow to take advantage of the situation. A parliament was held at Westminster in 1276 to discuss those who were 'formerly disturbers of the kingdom'. There was one man, however, who was very much still a 'disturber of the kingdom'. Despite repeated demands, Llywelyn 'refused to appear in person. Nevertheless, he sent ambassadors to treat for peace, and offered no small money as ransom for the daughter of the earl of Leicester, whom he wished to take for his wife. But the king refused to consent to the marriage, and would not take the money that was offered to him, unless Llywelyn would restore all the territories which he had invaded, each to its lawful master, and repair the castles of England which he had destroyed.'[19]

Edward proceeded to ensure that he took maximum advantage of this opportunity. Amaury was incarcerated safely in close confinement behind the grim stone walls of Corfe Castle. Despite pressure from the papacy (Amaury was a cleric), he stayed there until 1278. It was not until 1282, seven years after his capture, that he was completely free.[20] He was released finally on condition that he left England and never returned. Eleanor was also kept in Windsor Castle, though as a gentlewoman and a cousin of the king the conditions of her confinement would have been much less arduous.

These factors collectively augured a dangerous future. Llywelyn's refusal to present himself to Edward was ill-judged in the light of Edward's view of kingship. Llywelyn had persistently refused to pay the homage due to him. Edward, with his passionate views concerning the rights of his crown, was unlikely to take such a blatant rejection of his authority with equanimity. Neither was he likely to look kindly upon

Llywelyn's friendly relations with the de Montforts. Llywelyn's proposed match with Eleanor appeared to Edward to be prompted by political motives and it was unthinkable that he would agree to it.

There has been a good deal of speculation as to why Llywelyn was so intransigent towards Edward. His attitude can only have arisen from overconfidence concerning the outcome of any war with the English. However, there are several factors which together might explain why Llywelyn misjudged the situation so greatly. It is important to remember that Llywelyn was a successful commander who had already tasted success against the English. Further, the Marcher lords by no means worked in unison. Rivalry among them was common, and their loyalty to the crown was by no means assured, as witnessed by the previous support of the Montfortian cause by some of them. Llywelyn may have hoped that he could take advantage of their disunity by a renewed attack on Marcher territories. However, if this was his analysis of the situation it was sadly awry; support for Edward was virtually unanimous in the campaign that was to follow. Llywelyn's inability to reach a long-term accommodation with any of the major Marcher lords was a failing that was to cost him dear.

Llywelyn would also have known of previous English campaigns against Wales, which had often ended in stalemate or worse for the invaders. Less than half a century had passed since Llywelyn the Great, his grandfather, had effectively ruled a virtually united Wales and had opposed the English crown with a good deal of self-assurance. Throughout most of the thirteenth century the Welsh had at most times held their own, and sometimes better. With a new, unproven king on the throne of England, Llywelyn may have reckoned that bold tactics could meet with success.

There was also the character of Edward as king to consider. He has accurately been described as 'a king unusually prickly about his regality: Llywelyn was just the first of many who was to discover that truth'.[21] And in that brief analysis perhaps lies the explanation of Llywelyn's actions. Edward was a new, unproven, untested king. But if Llywelyn indeed believed he could ignore the importance of protocol to a man such as Edward he was surely a poor judge of character. Here was a king who would insist on full recognition of his royal rights, as Llywelyn would find out to bitter effect.

*   *   *

As time passed, it became increasingly apparent that Llywelyn had no intention of presenting himself to Edward to offer the king his homage. He even wrote to the Pope explaining the reasons for his refusal to present himself, and asked the pontiff for his support in protesting against the capture of Eleanor de Montfort, a request that the Pope was sympathetic to. Edward finally lost patience and decided that he had no option but to bring Llywelyn to book by means of force. His mind was made up partly because, throughout 1276, the situation in the Marches deteriorated. Llywelyn continued to protest about the aggression of Roger Mortimer and Humphrey de Bohun, as well as Dafydd and Gruffudd ap Gwenwynwyn. Pain de Chaworth, a staunch ally of Edward and a fellow crusader, also attacked Welsh lands. At the same time, Llywelyn launched attacks of his own in the Marcher territories around Oswestry and Montgomery.

War had probably been inevitable since Dafydd and Gruffudd ap Gwenwynwyn had fled to England for protection. Given the character of Llywelyn and Edward, and their views of their relative status in their respective societies, the two were on a collision course from this point on. Edward wished to have the best of both worlds, to have a subservient Llywelyn in Gwynedd while at the same time retaining the friendship of Gruffudd, a long-time ally of England. Llywelyn on the other hand found it impossible to contemplate obeisance to Edward while his court harboured his would-be assassins. Llywelyn's advisers told him that he should not go to England and offer his homage until the situation with his errant brother and the recalcitrant Gruffudd had been resolved. Neither did the ongoing insensitivity of England help. The maintenance of Gruffudd at Shrewsbury, from where he raided into Wales, can hardly have endeared Edward to Llywelyn. And, when Llywelyn was asked to go to London, it is not unreasonable to assume that the fate of his father, kept as an English pawn until his failed attempt to escape, weighed heavily with him. Welsh hwyl, or brio, was almost certainly tempered with, if not fear, then (with good reason) caution for his own self-preservation in Llywelyn's persistent refusal to treat with the king.

Both Edward and Llywelyn were therefore at fault in the events that led up to the war. It has been suggested that the critical event was Edward's summons to Llywelyn to meet him at Chester in August 1275.[22] Both men were geographically very close to each other at the time, as Llywelyn had journeyed to the very borders of Wales but would not cross them; he did not feel that he could risk travelling to Chester, although he was at this moment at the extreme eastern edge of his principality. The king and the prince were little more than ten miles apart. But Edward could not bring himself to compromise. In his eyes, the short journey to meet Llywelyn could not be made without showing weakness. He had summoned Llywelyn to Chester, and to Chester the prince must come. As a result, perhaps the best and final chance for peace was lost.

Reckoning that war was now inevitable, Edward decided to muster his army at Worcester on 1 July 1277. Aware that he needed to maintain an aggressive defence of his borders with the Welsh until he was ready to go on the offensive, and also hoping to give himself a strong springboard for a full-blown invasion of Llywelyn's heartland in Gwynedd, Edward delegated special powers to some of his trusted lieutenants in Wales in November 1276. A writ of aid was issued to 'Roger Mortu Mori [Mortimer], appointed captain in these parts, against Llywelyn, son of Griffith and his accomplices'. This writ was to cover the territories of Shropshire, Stafford and Herefordshire. Similar writs were issued to William Beauchamp, earl of Warwick, who was to be Edward's captain for Cheshire and Lancashire and to Pain de Chaworth in West Wales.[23]

He also despatched a force of men from his own household to support these captains; their journey can be traced from records that show them receiving pay at London, Windsor and Cirencester. The existence of these household resources was vital, as it gave the king a ready source of warriors who could be put into the field at short notice. Included in the household forces were men with family names that would become very familiar in Anglo-Welsh affairs, like Knoville and Lestrange. Their tasks were varied, as they not only played a part in the fighting in the preliminary stages of the war, they also helped in the recruitment of troops. Some forty knights and seventy troopers from the household were sent quickly to Wales, arriving finally at either Oswestry on the borders or Carmarthen. In the meantime, John Beauchamp was appointed to the command of the castles at Carmarthen and Cardigan, and he soon had 100 cavalry to support him. It gave Edward the opportunity to keep Llywelyn in check while a full-scale invasion force could be assembled.

Such action was necessary because it would require a space of some months before any invasion force could be suitably prepared for an advance into the remote territory of north Wales, the most likely target for an invasion. The source of Llywelyn's power was to be found in Gwynedd and it was always probable that Edward would strike straight for the heart of Llywelyn's territories. In so doing, he would be both true to his character, which dictated that he look for a decisive result, while at the same time following the precedent of previous campaigns against the Welsh and the tactical lessons he had learned from his father's failures. There was much to be done before Edward was ready for such an assault. There was a shortage of horses and Edward was forced to send to France to replenish his stocks; the records note that on 12 December 1276 the port of Wissant was allowed to permit the transportation of seventy-five horses to England. This involved a significant outlay of funds. A horse might be expected to cost an amount that was equivalent to an entire year's revenue from a knight's lands.[24] Finding suitable numbers of horses was often a problem for the medieval commander. It has been estimated that a knight might need a minimum of five horses for a campaign, and there was the additional problem of looking after them during an expedition, with their daily requirement of four gallons of water – though, given contemporary English views of the climate in Wales, which have hardly changed to this day, the latter need was perhaps not expected to pose a problem.[25]

There were also manpower considerations to take into account. Since the days of King John, and the signing of Magna Carta, the English had been especially cynical about the use of mercenaries. However, this did not prevent Edward from sending to Gascony for thirty crossbowmen, the crossbow being a weapon much valued by Edward.[26] Gascony was a highly prized part of Edward's continental territories and he presumably reckoned either that such men did not count as 'foreign' mercenaries or, more likely, was not unduly concerned at the effect that their employment would have on public opinion in England; such considerations were secondary to the objective of a decisive victory in Wales.

Last but not least, Edward sent out summonses to his lords, requiring them to submit themselves with their feudal levies at Worcester on 1 July in the following year, 1277. Three separate sets of writs were despatched, the first of them sent to the great lords of the kingdom, the second group to churchmen and ladies and the third to local sheriffs, who would be responsible for collecting the remainder of the feudal levy. During the succeeding months, a great deal of frantic activity took place in all these areas and others, involving the accumulation of provisions to keep the army supplied when it did eventually move on Gwynedd. Previous English expeditions to Wales had failed largely because the organisation accompanying them had been amateurish; Edward was to demonstrate conclusively when the time came that he had learned the lessons of past campaigns well.

At this stage, Edward was already thinking about the future government of Wales. On 26 December 1276, at Cirencester, homage was received from 'Llywelyn, son of Griffin de Brumfeud' with the provision that, even if the rebellion were to end in the near future, future homage from him would be direct to Edward himself rather than via Llywelyn, prince of Wales.[27] This is an unambiguous sign that Edward already intended to change the nature of the government of Wales, however the rebellion ended. It was a major departure from the current situation whereby the homage of virtually all the Welsh lords was given to Llywelyn himself, who then in his turn swore homage on their collective behalf to Edward. The changed situation that Edward envisaged cannot have failed to reduce the status and influence of Llywelyn, while giving the English crown greater power. It was an approach that fitted well with Edward's attempts to enhance the rights of the crown at every opportunity.

Edward perhaps hoped that the Marcher lords and his household troops would keep the Welsh in check until he was ready to advance with his main force but in the event they did much more than this. The launching point of the main attack into Wales was to be the city of Chester. There is very little mention of aggressive activity in the records on the part of the English in this region of all those bordering Wales. However, the shortage of direct references in the records appears to be slightly misleading. A reference in the Patent Rolls of 24 January 1277 refers to fighting in the area south of Denbigh. It seems that there was some advance into north Wales at a fairly early stage, with the result that when Edward appeared with his main force later that year he was able to advance as far as Flint without fear of a Welsh attack.

There was one particularly significant member of the force at Chester, Dafydd, Llywelyn's brother. Dafydd was promised a great reward in return for his co-operation against Llywelyn. At what stage he was informally offered this is unclear. It was formally recorded in August 1277, when it was noted that a grant was made 'to David, son of Griffith, that in the event of the king conquering Llywelyn, son of Griffith, his brother, the King will restore to David and Owen his brother a moiety of the whole of Snowdon, and the Leyn, and a moiety of Anglesey and Pentlin; or if the king take the whole of Anglesey, the whole of Snowdon and Pentlin'.[28] In other words, Edward was publicly promising that Llywelyn's lands would be divided up between the English crown and Llywelyn's brothers, Dafydd and Owain. There was, in the small print of the agreement, something of a sinister undertone. Was the statement that Dafydd and Owain and their descendants were to 'come to our parliaments in England, as other earls and barons',[29] further evidence that Edward thought of Wales as no different than any other part of England? The precise details were, it is true, capable of variation and it is interesting to note that Edward had already clearly identified the strategic importance of Anglesey and very sensibly gave himself the opportunity of retaining control over the island. But it is clear that Dafydd was led to believe that he could expect to receive substantial recompense for his support of Edward.

Intense fighting appears to have taken place further south in the Marches of mid-Wales in advance of the main English campaign. Llywelyn himself was involved in the fighting, reflecting perhaps part of a sustained campaign to strengthen his position there (recent incursions into the territories of Peter Corbet have already been mentioned). The

Sheriff of Shropshire, Bogo de Knoville, whom Edward would use as an administrator in his Welsh campaigns on several occasions, was responsible for raising men and supplies to support the English forces in the area. His base was at Oswestry, where by December he had been joined by some of Edward's household troops.

The major English base in the area, though, was at Montgomery; among others, the dispossessed Peter Corbet was here. The Sheriff of Herefordshire also came to Montgomery to support the force. Work was put in hand to strengthen the defences of the castle, but the English by now had a sizeable force in the town and this appeared to Roger Mortimer, Edward's captain in the region, to offer the opportunity of an early counter-attack against Llywelyn. Accordingly, one was launched soon afterwards.

The fruits of Llywelyn's ambitions regarding the domination of the Marches in the region now came to fruition. His actions had merely served to unite his opponents against him. The first successes of Mortimer's troops included the recovery of Peter Corbet's lost lands in Shropshire. Then lands were recovered in Powys, the territory where Llywelyn's old Welsh adversary, Gruffudd ap Gwenwynwyn, had ruled; although these would, for the time being, remain in English hands, the support of Gruffudd for the English crown would not be forgotten and he would ultimately be well rewarded for his help. The Welsh were forced to burn down the castle of Dinas Bran rather than let it fall into English hands.

It has been noted that the forces here were unpaid by the crown.[30] This is a point of some significance. Many of the more prominent knights of the realm preferred to operate in this way, even though Edward would make much use of knights on his payroll during his campaigns. There were several reasons for this. It avoided the knight in question being subservient to the crown; he could therefore act on his own initiative and his obligation was limited. In theory, he could not be required to serve for more than forty days under the terms of the feudal levy, a situation that some of Edward's leading knights could take advantage of, as would be demonstrated during the later years of Edward's reign. By threatening to withdraw their troops at strategically critical times during campaigns, they could effectively attempt to manipulate the king's reliance on them to their advantage. A number of the leading barons therefore protected their privileges by adhering strictly to what was required of them under feudal law. This also meant that, should they conquer lands using forces paid for by themselves, they would be entitled to retain them by right of conquest. But if the forces conquering those lands were in the king's pay then the crown would be justified in retaining possession of the territories involved, even if they had previously been held under the direct control of a Marcher lord. This might explain why some of the Marcher barons involved were keen for early successes before Edward himself had arrived.

Their achievements were a tremendous start to the campaigns in the mid-Welsh Marches. The initial victories of the Marchers, later assisted by household troops, has led one commentator to claim that all that was left to Edward I when he appeared at Chester in July 1277 was 'to deliver the coup de grace'.[31] The position of the English in the Marches was further strengthened, in January 1277, by the arrival of a strong, paid force under the command of Henry de Lacy, earl of Lincoln, who would be one of Edward's most trusted leaders as well as a major beneficiary from the Welsh wars. It consisted of 100 cavalry in addition to the earl himself. There were seven bannerets with the force, including Otto de Grandson. These men, who were contracted for a period of 120 days (contracts of service were still normally based on the standard 40-day period required for unpaid feudal service or multiples thereof) gave a powerful boost to Mortimer's force, which was now over 150 strong in terms of its cavalry contingent.

There then followed a further advance by the English forces. A siege was laid to Dolforwyn Castle, the newly constructed fortress which had been such a source of angst both to the English and to Gruffudd ap Gwenwynwyn. In accordance with the custom of the time, it was agreed that if the garrison were not relieved by 8 April 1277, then the castle would be surrendered to the English. No relieving force appeared. Llywelyn could ill-afford to spare any troops, even if he had them, given the fact that the main English invasion had not yet even begun. Dolforwyn was accordingly handed over to Roger Mortimer. Mortimer in turn passed it into the hands of Gruffudd ap Gwenwynwyn for safekeeping.

Soon after, Builth – a strategically important frontier town around which wars between the Marcher lords and the Welsh frequently raged – was taken by the English. The advances of Llywelyn's Welshmen had first been checked and then reversed completely. In the mid-Welsh Marches at least the prince of Wales was firmly in retreat. So complete was the change in fortunes that Bogo de Knoville was able to hand over Oswestry to Roger Lestrange and join Edward for the main invasion. By May 1277, the paid force under the earl of Lincoln was effectively surplus to requirements and it was accordingly disbanded.

Slightly further south, the earl of Hereford, Humphrey de Bohun, took advantage of the collapse of the Welsh in the mid-Marches to assert his claims to the area around Brecon by force of arms. His claim was a tenuous one, but the outbreak of hostilities was a heaven-sent opportunity to further his cause while the Welsh were too distracted elsewhere to fight back. There was initially a good deal of hard fighting in Brecon. However, the superior resources of the English were eventually decisive, although Humphrey de Bohun required strong reinforcement to win through. After making the most of his opportunity there, he was free to report to Edward to fulfil his feudal obligations.

The southern coastal band of Wales had been in the English sphere of influence for some time, and Welsh resistance there was, in the absence of Llywelyn, futile. Pain de Chaworth led a force that included 75 paid cavalry. There were also 48 horsemen from Edward's household there, which probably gave a total, with the cavalry of the Marcher lords themselves included, of 160 horses. This gave Pain a very solid base on which to construct his offensive, and he duly probed along the Towy in January 1277. Although there are few details surviving of the campaign, it was clearly a successful one for the English. By June 1277, Carreg Cennen and Llandovery had been captured. Much of the area around Carmarthen and Cardigan passed to the crown, markedly increasing its stakeholding in the south. It was an important development, as much of the territory of what was formerly Deheubarth, traditionally a stronghold of powerful Welsh princes, passed to Edward.

There was one point of particular note for the future in Pain's campaign. One of the Welsh lords who submitted in the south was Rhys ap Maredudd. He was allowed to retain his castle at Dryslwyn and was required to assist the English army if called upon to do so, and to do homage to Edward for his lands later. Rhys submitted to those terms, apparently gladly, and he would for some time be a close ally of the English. However, the absence of greater rewards – the nearby castle at Dinefwr (Llandeilo) would have been a welcome addition to his lands – clearly rankled with him because he would, long after Llywelyn was dead and the cause of an independent Wales essentially lost, rebel against the English crown with personally catastrophic results.

The immediate fate of the castle at Dinefwr would have encouraged Rhys's ambitions. It was in the possession of Rhys Wyndod, who had originally sided with Llywelyn but deserted his cause and surrendered to Edward. He was allowed to keep most of his lands but not Dinefwr, which was retained by the king and handed over to Bogo de Knoville, his justiciar in the south, as a royal base. Edward's actions in this instance alienated both Rhys ap Maredudd and Rhys Wyndod, albeit in a different timeframe. Rhys Wyndod was later to face claims against him from John Giffard, who would become lord of Llandovery, and this would persuade him to side with Llywelyn in his later rebellion against Edward in 1282. It would end with his capture and imprisonment until his death.

On the other hand, Rhys ap Maredudd – who must have hoped to gain control of the castle when Edward took it for the crown – would never gain Dinefwr and, his ambitions frustrated, he would later launch a revolt of his own in 1287. His feelings typified the complicated local politics of Wales at the time. Twenty years earlier, Rhys ap Maredudd's father, Maredudd ap Rhys Gryg, had supported Llywelyn in a campaign against Rhys Wyndod's father, Rhys Fychan.[32] Maredudd later turned on Llywelyn but was captured and brought to book and spent three years in captivity. Relations between Rhys ap Maredudd and Rhys Wyndod were still strained as a result. Against the backdrop of feuds such as this, the prospects for Welsh unity were not encouraging.

While all this military activity was taking place, Edward was taking advantage of the time that it bought for him by ensuring that his preparations were as methodical as possible. The decisive element in the reverses suffered by the English in the past had almost invariably been the lack of logistical forethought by the invaders. Whether or not Edward was a military strategist of the highest order has been the subject of some debate. He was not essentially an innovator in a strategic or tactical sense but he was, if nothing else, a planner and organiser of rare ability. It is easy to argue that Edward should have won any war against the Welsh, given the mismatch of resources between the two armies involved. However, previous English armies of invasion had enjoyed similar superiority but had usually achieved little of permanent effect as a result of their efforts. It needed someone with outstanding organisational ability to maximise the advantages inherently enjoyed by the English. Edward was such a man.

Edward's preparations were extremely thorough. As well as continuing to send to France for more horses for his cavalry, he also called on abbeys in his realm to provide him with carts to transport his tents to the war. He ensured that his army would be amply stocked with both food supplies and military provisions. Large volumes of wheat and oats were ordered from Ireland, to be delivered to the invasion force's main base at Chester. He was a strong advocate of the crossbow, a fact that is amply illustrated by the fact that he ordered 200,000 crossbow bolts to be manufactured at St Briavel's in Gloucestershire.

There followed a period of hectic activity while England readied itself for war. Those required to provide feudal levies went about their duties conscientiously, for the early evidence from Edward's reign thus far was that he would view the actions of any of his subjects who shirked their responsibilities in a very dim light indeed. Many of the troops were infantry, the majority equipped as archers, though some were armed with lances. Generally speaking, the locality from which they came was responsible for the provision of weapons as well as men, although the crown did provide crossbows. Infantry was typically divided into sections of 20 men, each led by a vintenar, though in the Second Welsh war in 1282 section sizes increased to 100. Five 20-man sections were combined under the command of a centenar, an armed cavalryman whose horse was also protected by armour. The Marshal and Constable of the army had a particular responsibility for organising and co-ordinating the infantry.[33]

There were not only Englishmen in Edward's army. There were a large number of Welshmen, especially from the south of the country. A number of prominent Welshmen allied themselves to the English cause, such as Trahearn ap Madog and Hywel ap Meurig in the mid-Welsh Marches. No doubt they all had their own personal, often selfish, reasons for doing so but their desertion of Llywelyn, taken alongside that of others, clearly demonstrates that Llywelyn did not enjoy a unanimous mandate in Wales from among his own people.

By the time 1 July 1277 arrived, a powerful force, amply supplied, had gathered at Worcester. The gains already made by the Marcher lords had provided a solid platform on which Edward could build. The south and mid-Welsh Marches were already to all intents and purposes clear of any dangerous Welsh forces that could distract the invasion. Even the approaches to Gwynedd itself had been largely cleared of resistance. The odds were now overwhelmingly stacked in favour of Edward and his army. Gwynedd lay naked before an aggressive foe. All that Llywelyn could hope was that Edward would follow the example of many of his predecessors and throw away an overwhelming advantage through incompetence or distractions elsewhere. The time for preparation was now at an end; the time for all-out war had come at last.

CHAPTER FIVE

The Campaign of 1277

Have you no belief in God, foolish men?
See you not that the world is ending?[1]

Gruffudd ab yr Ynad Coch

When Edward's army eventually assembled at Worcester, it was a formidable force indeed. The earl of Hereford was there as Constable, and the earl of Norfolk as Marshal. Their role was to note the forces that had arrived, so that the king was aware of the extent of the manpower at his disposal. Worcester was the main mustering point but some men were allowed to report elsewhere. Some went to south Wales, while the men at Montgomery – a strategically sited point from where renewed pressure could be applied if Edward wished – were allowed to send in their names rather than present themselves in person. Those already at Chester could also stay where they were. The city would be Edward's main base for the forthcoming campaign and he could pick up the men there on his way towards Gwynedd. There was no point in involving troops, or horses for that matter, in superfluous manoeuvres.

It has been estimated that Edward had about 1,000 horsemen available to him.[2] This includes the men available to Edward's brother, Edmund of Lancaster, who was on campaign in south Wales, as well as those men with the Marcher lords who were not registered with the feudal host at Worcester, only those due to Edward from the lands that they held in England being noted in the records. Of these 1,000 cavalry, about 160 horsemen were with Edmund of Lancaster and 40 with Roger Mortimer. The rest were theoretically available to Edward's main invasion force. In practice, however, they would not all be available at the same time. A number would be detached for such duties as escorting movements of men and provisions. Even allowing for this, it was still a sizeable force to have at his disposal.

The force with Edmund of Lancaster would operate to all intents and purposes independently of the main army. Edmund would launch an attack of his own, pushing northwards from Carmarthen. Edmund stayed with this force until 20 September, when his army was disbanded as it was no longer required and he returned to England, leaving construction of the castle at Llanbadarn in the hands of Roger de Molis.

The main army at Worcester presented an intimidating array but Edward experienced the kind of problems inherent to every campaigning army of the period. The fact that there were still so many men provided as part of the feudal levy was problematic for Edward. It meant that the men involved were within their rights to withdraw their services after the 40 days required under feudal law had expired. Not all of them would invariably exercise this right; some would remain with the king beyond this period in the hope that they would benefit from the share-out of spoils at the end of the war. But it introduced an element of risk into the equation. If a number of these men withdrew at a critical time in the campaign, it might seriously compromise the outcome. It would perhaps take a brave man to hold the crown to ransom in this way but the right to do so was one that was jealously protected by the lords of the realm, and it was by no means unheard of that they would exercise their prerogative at a particularly inconvenient moment.

Another problem was that of co-ordinating the forces involved. The men provided under the terms of the feudal levy owed their allegiance in a practical sense to their immediate lord. They therefore worked under his orders to all intents and purposes rather than those of the king, the ultimate commander-in-chief of the force. This would make it difficult for Edward to ensure that his forces worked together. With men acting in such an independent fashion, battle tactics would inevitably be rudimentary. Such difficulties could be partly overcome if the men were taken into pay rather than retained as part of the feudal levy but this would imply a degree of subordination that many of the more powerful lords involved disliked, and a number of them were consequently resistant to the idea. The motivating factor for this was not only the desire to maintain a proud independence from the king's overall command, real though this motivation was for a number of the lordly caste. It was also about the much greater gains that they might win from the division of lands at the end of the war as opposed to the wages they might be paid.

The infantrymen, the unsung and usually unnamed participants in medieval warfare, were noted as being 2,576 men strong.[3] This misleadingly precise figure would be subject to frequent and often large variation. Men would come and go as their period of service expired and they left, to be replaced by others. Desertions would be frequent; these were not professional soldiers and they had left homes and domestic duties behind them, which must, for all the hardships of the times, have normally appeared preferable to the squalor and drudgery of camp life. Others would be lost, either temporarily or permanently, to the ravages of disease. Most of them would be poorly trained but there were some exceptions. Imbert de Monte Regali was at the head of a force of nearly 300 crossbowmen, 20 of whom were mounted. One other group deserves special mention. These were a party of 100 archers from Macclesfield. They were clearly of above average quality. They remained in the pay of the crown throughout the campaign, and they were paid at the special rate of 3d per day, the normal rate of pay for infantrymen being 2d.

There is one other aspect of the campaign that must be considered. Edward was clearly well aware of the importance of sea power to the success of his enterprise. Provisioning the advancing army across the difficult terrain of north Wales exposed his line of communications to attacks from guerrilla forces. This difficulty could be avoided if he could take steps to keep the army provisioned by sea, where the English would enjoy virtually unrivalled supremacy. Though treacherous and lacking safe anchorages, the coastline of north Wales lent itself to such a policy, which Edward would later institutionalise by building his castles whenever possible by the sea or on the banks of a navigable river.

Edward therefore enlisted a number of ships into his service. Under the terms of the feudal levy, they were required to serve with the king for fifteen days, that period starting when they arrived on station. They were later taken on to the crown's payroll, the date that this was done implying that they arrived off the coast of north Wales in the middle of July 1277. Most of the ships (of which there were twenty-seven in total) were from the Cinque Ports, though there was one from Southampton and another from as far afield as Bayonne. They were under the operational command of Stephen of Penecaster, Warden of the Cinque Ports, who was also listed as a knight in the service of the earl of Norfolk. They were small craft by modern standards, most of them carrying about 20 seamen, though the great galleys, of which there were two, carried 50. In addition, there were a number of marines on board, archers and crossbowmen, over 100 of them. They were distributed in an ad hoc manner according to the size of each of the ships.[4]

The seamen did not as a rule enjoy their period of service with the crown. Their ships were primarily involved in trading and, while they were absent from their ports, trade would invariably be disrupted. The consequent loss of profit was most unwelcome to their home ports. Despite this, Edward was able to keep the ships in his pay for two months after their feudal service was over, which was undoubtedly of great benefit to the success of the expedition. The willingness of the ships to remain off the Welsh coast in support of Edward is perhaps explained by his generosity towards them, the records noting the awarding of a 'grant to the barons of the Cinque Ports, who have come to the king's aid to the army in Wales, that they may convert to their own use whatever goods they take from the Welsh rebels, except goods of Welshmen who have or may come into the king's peace'.[5] This legalisation of piracy in controlled circumstances was clearly sufficient to appeal to the profiteering instincts of the ships' masters and their crews. In addition to the larger ships in the fleet, eight smaller boats were hired locally to support them, craft so small that they were manned by only half a dozen crewmen. In all, there were about 726 men in the fleet.[6]

Edward's plan of campaign was not new. He would advance along the narrow coastal plain towards the mouth of the Conwy. From here, he would be in a position to advance upriver if he so wished, towards the heart of Gwynedd itself. He could also decide to push forward towards Anglesey. The island was strategically vital. Gwynedd relied heavily on crops grown in Anglesey. If Edward were to take the island, he would deprive Gwynedd of its granary. Edward could simply threaten to starve Llywelyn into submission.

The first stage in the main campaign saw the king's army advance from Chester to Flint. Immediately, it became obvious that this expedition would be very different from previous English adventures in Wales. The coastal plain was, in those days, heavily wooded. Wykes says that 'between Chester and Llywelyn's territory there lies a forest so broad and dense that the king's forces were unable to pass through it without risk'. The trees gave the Welsh ample opportunity to ambush the invading English army. Such hit and run tactics had been the linchpin of previous Welsh successes against invaders. Edward was fully aware of this fact, and set out to cancel out this threat.

Edward had taken into his service a large number of labourers and woodsmen. Their task was a quite simple, though undoubtedly arduous, time-consuming and dangerous one. They were to remove the forests so that Llywelyn's men could no longer use them for cover. This would make the progress of the English army a much easier and safer prospect. To facilitate their passage, the labourers would construct roads along which the army could travel more conveniently; these would also help to keep the lines of communication open back to Chester so that any provisions that could not be carried by sea, or any troops that were on their way to reinforce or replace men currently with Edward's army (for men were coming and going all the time as their periods of service expired) could be despatched in relative security. In this way, 'a considerable area of the forest was cleared or cut down, leaving a broad way into Prince Llywelyn's land for the king and his men. Through this gap they entered in triumph.'[7]

Edward's methodical approach was to create a stranglehold around Gwynedd which became ever tighter as time passed. It did not appear, however, that all the woodsmen with his army were there of their own free will. A number would have been pressed into service and a close watch was placed on them, as much to prevent their desertion as to protect them from raids from the Welsh (though the latter were a real threat and the danger of them was undoubtedly unsettling for the woodsmen involved).[8] They were however paid for their service. The foremen were paid the handsome sum of 6*d* per day (this compared to a trooper who could earn 1*s* per day and a knight at 2*s* per day), while the skilled workmen received 3*d* or 4*d* per day, broadly commensurate with the wage of a crossbowman. Unskilled labourers were paid 2*d* per day, the same rate as a foot soldier.

It did not take Edward long to advance to Flint, where he had arrived by 26 July. Here he halted while large numbers of men made their way up to join him. He intended to construct a forward base from where further advances along the Welsh coast could be made, ultimately threatening to isolate Gwynedd completely. He erected a castle at Flint, built of wood. Edward placed his crossbowmen and the archers from Macclesfield on guard while his engineers got to work erecting the edifice. There must surely have been Welsh counter-attacks while all this was going on, though there is in truth precious little detail concerning this. It is likely that the Welsh continued to launch guerrilla raids in the time-honoured fashion but Edward's meticulous preparation had seriously limited their effectiveness. At any event, matters were well enough under control for Edward to absent himself from the building of the castle at Flint and return to Chester for a time to make sure that all was in order there.

* * *

Edward eventually returned to Flint in August 1277. Here, he agreed to divide Llywelyn's lands with Dafydd.[9] The degree of flexibility Edward retained over the lands he hoped to keep for himself may have annoyed Dafydd. In addition, there were also other prominent Welshmen with the king who might expect to share in the division of spoils at the end of the war, threatening to dilute Dafydd's portion in the process. Dafydd also complained to the earl of Warwick, Edward's captain at Chester, that he was unhappy at the way his men were paid and that they should be free to plunder in the forthcoming campaign. The indications are that, even at this early stage, Dafydd was far from happy with his lot.

Edward now pushed on to Rhuddlan, arriving there on 20 August. His policy was clear and simple; he would advance methodically, in stages, moving inexorably closer to Gwynedd. His arrival at Rhuddlan gave him the opportunity of striking into Gwynedd itself. As an approach the

Edward of Caernarfon being made Prince of Wales. (BL Cotton Ms Nero D11, f19v.)

King Edward I addressing his bishops. (BL Cotton Vitellius Ms A XIII, f.6v)

A noble and his guests feasting. (BL Additional MS 42130)

la ueille de la pntecou
ste qnt tout li compaig
non de la table roñde fu
rent uenu a camaelot ⁊ il orent

A thirteenth-century king and queen entertaining at a feast. (BL Royal Ms 14 E111, f.89)

The ferocity of medieval warfare. (BL Ms Add 47682, f.40)

English archers training.
(BL London Ms. Ass 421.30,
f.147v)

*A crossbowman – these weapons
were especially valued by Edward I.*
(BL, Additional Ms. 42130,
f.56)

A criminal going to his execution. (BL Harl. 4375, f.140)

A medieval king consulting his master masons. (Life of St Offa English Ms Cotton Nero D1, f.23v)

Masons constructing a castle. (BL Royal Ms Ms15 D.111, f.15v)

Armaments being transported: such scenes would have been a regular feature of the campaigns in Wales. (Bodleian Library Ms 264, f.102r)

The Tower of London in the medieval period. (BL London Ms Roy 16 F11, f.73)

campaign perhaps lacked glamour but it was a devastatingly effective strategy. Edward would not fritter his advantages away by committing his army to daring, high-risk strikes against Llywelyn. He would instead ensure that he played the cards in his hand to maximum effect. The progress of the war thus far already had an ominous quality about it as far as Llywelyn was concerned. Developments from here on in would do nothing to put his mind at rest.

Shortly afterwards, Ruthin was taken. The army then moved forward again, advancing further towards Conwy. The continued progress of the English was now assuming serious proportions as far as the viability of any defence on Llywelyn's part was concerned. The movement on Conwy threatened the lines of communication between Gwynedd and Anglesey. If Edward were not rebuffed soon, his position would be decisive.

More English reinforcements arrived. Some of the infantry who had started out with Edward still remained with the force, and these were joined by new levies from Lancashire, Derbyshire, Rutland and Cheshire. In all, there were now 5,860 infantry from England in Edward's force. The size of this army was about to increase exponentially as a huge body of infantrymen, some 9,760 strong, was brought up from the southern Marches of Wales. The composition of this force is revealing, demonstrating as it does the large number of Welshmen who fought for the English army. There were for example 2,700 troops from Radnor and Brecon and another 1,000 or so from Abergavenny.[10] There was also a contingent led by Lewis de la Pole, son of Gruffydd ap Gwenwynwyn (the family would eventually take the name de la Pole permanently, showing how thoroughly anglicised they had become). This was a substantial army, in reality far too large to be truly effective, and it must have contained by the law of averages a number of troops who were really not up to the required standard. Nevertheless, its sheer volume must have emphasised to Llywelyn the huge challenge that he was up against. The build-up of forces was inexorable, in stark contrast to the paucity of resources available to Llywelyn.

Towards the end of August, the period of feudal service required of those who had joined without pay was at an end. A number of the cavalry were dismissed; their upkeep was expensive and the limited opportunity to use the charge of heavy horse against the men of Llywelyn meant that they were something of a luxury. It also meant that Edward could hand-pick the forces that he wished to remain with him. Some of the leading lords of the realm stayed on without pay, no doubt hoping that they would benefit from generous handouts of conquered Welsh territory when the war reached the favourable conclusion that looked increasingly likely. But equally there was incontrovertible evidence that a number of cavalry were taken on to Edward's payroll. One such group was led by Reginald Grey, and consisted of ninety horsemen. They were taken into pay for forty-two days, for which they were paid £256. They were apparently employed to defend Flint against any Welsh counter-attack, though such a contingency by now seemed more and more unlikely. They were also to patrol the forests to ensure that there were limited opportunities for guerrilla attacks on the lines of communication back to England. For this purpose, 50 crossbowmen and 850 archers were allocated to work alongside them.[11]

The English advance continued apace, arriving at Deganwy, just across the river from Conwy, by the end of August. Llywelyn had retreated into Snowdonia, hoping by his actions to lure the invaders into terrain that was ideal for hit-and-run warfare. Here the Welsh could use their local knowledge to the full. The very size of the English army must work against it in Snowdonia. The weather would break in two or three months. The English army could find itself with its lines of communication seriously stretched, as some of their armies had done in the past. In such a situation the English would be faced with two equally unpalatable options: starve or retreat.

For this to happen of course Edward was required to act in a certain way. But Edward was unlikely to recklessly commit his forces to terrain which suited the Welsh tactics. It was he who was effectively in command of events, not Llywelyn, and his next move was the one that checkmated his adversary. The records demonstrate that at about this time the size of the main English infantry force with Edward dropped dramatically. The reason for this is clear enough; the main English army was no longer at Deganwy, it was now in Anglesey.

The records are largely unhelpful concerning the size of the invasion army that moved on Anglesey but there is no doubt that the attack was in overwhelming force. Whether there was much in the way of a Welsh defence is uncertain but if there was it was doomed from the start. Some Welsh chroniclers assert that the English destroyed the harvest that was then ripe for the picking but they are surely wrong. This would have been a singularly foolish thing for an invading army in need of provisions to do. It is far more likely that the English helped themselves to this welcome new source of food. For all Edward's thorough attempts to keep the army amply supplied, the logistics of medieval warfare meant that invading armies invariably had to live off the land through which they passed, to a greater or lesser extent. The records suggest that 360 men were sent over to reap the harvest, a far more sensible approach than destruction of the crops and denial of their use, not only to the Welsh, but also to the English who needed them just as much.[12] The grain stocks secured, allied to the cattle captured as the English advanced on the mainland, were a significant bonus for Edward and his campaign.

There were rumours that the invading army had threatened to run out of control during its advance. Modern views of war crimes are an inappropriate benchmark to apply to an age when armies were difficult to control and composed of men who were not part of a standing force and therefore lacked discipline. This was a brutal age, where the rights of the common people were minimal in times of war. Violence against civilians was commonplace for those unfortunate enough to find themselves caught up in the path of an advancing army. But the offences committed were serious enough in this particular instance for Bishop Anian to threaten to excommunicate those responsible for them. There were allegations of sacrilege and rape. Church property had been destroyed. The Archbishop of Canterbury, Robert Kilwardby, was perturbed enough to formally order the earl of Warwick to ensure that nothing took place which would jeopardise the ecclesiastical blessing he had given the campaign.

Llywelyn's position was now perilous in the extreme. A strong English army lay before him at Deganwy, while in the area to the south, around the mid-Welsh Marches and across to Aberystwyth, the English had been all-conquering. With Anglesey now taken, not only were his supplies of food in doubt but an attack could be launched on Gwynedd from the rear. Edward had spun a web around Llywelyn and he was by now hopelessly entrapped at the centre of it. His position was dire. One chronicler noted that 'so constrained were the Welsh inhabitants that, as their food supplies ran short, they were forced unwillingly to retreat to their last major stronghold, Snowdonia, with no further thoughts of resistance or rebellion'.[13] In the meantime, the English fleet sailed along the coast with impunity, enabling Edward to deliver further supplies to his army without hindrance. It now looked unlikely that the English would attempt to strike into Gwynedd itself in an attempt to secure a quick win. It seemed that Edward would instead be content to stare Llywelyn out. The Welsh prince decided that there was little to be gained from prolonging the war and sued for peace.

Llywelyn had a number of concerns that collectively led to his approach for terms. He faced a loss of support within Gwynedd itself. How widespread this was is not clear but as early as 21 July 1277, a document was drawn up by a Dominican brother, confusingly named Llywelyn ap Gruffudd, saying that he had advised several prominent figures within Gwynedd to do homage to Edward. The friar himself was a man of some interest. He had almost certainly accompanied Eleanor de Montfort on her ill-fated voyage to Wales. He was therefore sympathetic to Llywelyn but he was in a difficult position. His support for the Welsh brought him into conflict with the views of the Archbishop of Canterbury and other church leaders, and he now opted to change his allegiance and also persuaded his brothers, Rhys and Hywel, important men in the hierarchy of Gwynedd, to do so as well.

Rhys was captured before he could make his way to Edward but his brother did manage to inveigle his way out of Gwynedd and is later listed as being in royal service. With him went men such as Hywel ap Goronwy, of the 'finest lineage' of Gwynedd, and Gruffudd ap Iorwerth, a famed warrior. These were important figures and their desertion was notable. They had clearly seen which way the wind was blowing and reckoned that Llywelyn's cause was now lost. If men such as these saw this to be so then so too must the prince of Wales himself.

A quick conclusion to the war suited Edward well enough. He was not by now apparently set on a campaign of conquest. If he was, then he would surely have pushed on until Llywelyn was utterly defeated. It was rather a case of attempting to discipline a recalcitrant baron. For all that Llywelyn bore the rather grandiose title of 'prince of Wales', to Edward he was in most ways another feudal subject. He had refused to honour his obligations towards Edward, and for that the English king had been forced to take steps to bring him into line. But Edward was not intent on obliteration of Llywelyn. He had made his point very well indeed, and the Welsh prince would be punished; but his punishment would in the event not destroy Llywelyn, although it would massively downgrade his position in Wales.

Edward would have seen his imminent victory over Llywelyn as one that would enhance his prestige and increase his standing with his people. He had proved to his lords, most importantly, that he would be no soft touch as a king and he had asserted the power of the crown in unequivocal fashion. The victory had been a quick and relatively painless one and it was perhaps best to bring the campaign to a successful conclusion before a full-scale incursion into Gwynedd was undertaken. The likelihood was that, in such a situation, both the casualty lists and the costs of the campaign would rise exorbitantly. It would be better for Edward to secure the most beneficial terms he possibly could before his army grew restless and came under greater pressure.

Negotiations soon commenced. Edward withdrew his advance force from Deganwy to Rhuddlan, not so much a sign of good faith but a reflection of the fact that the latter was now a well-defended base in which the English troops might feel particularly secure. New troops continued to arrive as others left but overall numbers began to fall. By the end of September, Edward felt in a strong enough position to let the fleet sail homewards. He continued to travel around with great energy, ensuring that matters were still being conducted in as efficient a way as possible. There were still supplies to think about even at this stage and the records note the granting of a 'safe conduct, until Christmas, for Robert de Lassindon, merchant of Gloucester, and Richard de Wygomia, merchant of Worcester, in taking victuals to the army of Wales'.[14] To the end, Edward was taking no chances with his supply lines.

Negotiations on Edward's behalf were led by his secretary, Antony Bek, a man who would later become a stern critic of the English king when he was Bishop of Durham, Otto de Grandson, and Robert Tibotot. Terms were finalised in the abbey of Aberconwy on 9 November 1277. Bishop Anian played a crucial role in the discussions, acting as mediator between Llywelyn and Edward. Anthony Bek, Robert Tibotot and a Brother William of Southampton received Llywelyn's oath of allegiance. On the prince of Wales's side, his seneschal, Tudur ab Ednyfed and Goronwy ap Heilin – a man who will appear again at a later stage of our story – were his chief negotiators. Shortly before terms were formally and finally agreed, Edward issued a document which stated that Llywelyn had agreed the settlement of some of his lands on his brother Dafydd.

A massive fine of £50,000 was levied on the prince of Wales. It was hugely beyond his means and Edward certainly never expected it to be paid. He formally removed the fine shortly afterwards. The very size of the fine in the first instance demonstrated well enough the seriousness of Llywelyn's offences against the crown of England, while Edward's suspension of the fine showed the king in a merciful and gracious light. As Llywelyn never could have paid it anyway, Edward in reality lost little in his actions. A smaller fee of 1,000 marks a year was to be paid by Llywelyn for the privilege of having Anglesey restored to him. Hostages were taken as surety for Llywelyn's future good behaviour; for a time, Edward was obviously pleased with his response on this score, as eleven months later they were released. In terms of the land taken, Edward kept for himself two of the 'Four Cantreds', Rhos and Teigingl, and also Cardigan and Carmarthen. These had anyway been disputed by the English for some time and merely legitimised previous English claims. The other two of the 'Four Cantreds', Dyffryn Clwyd and Rhufoniog, were given to Dafydd. It was a prize that was short of that agreed by Edward with Dafydd and this was a factor that clearly gnawed away at him until he perceived the agreement to be a great personal injustice.

There were details in the small print of the agreement which meant that the long-term future for Llywelyn and his descendants was grim indeed. Llywelyn agreed that Dafydd had rights to areas of Gwynedd as part of the peace settlement. However, as the man in possession, he was allowed to retain these areas, though other lands were granted to Dafydd in their stead. But when Llywelyn died, the lands in Gwynedd would revert to Dafydd. It was, the Treaty of Aberconwy noted, only at the king's grace that Llywelyn was allowed to keep Dafydd's territories in Gwynedd. And in Anglesey, Llywelyn's rights were very limited indeed. If he were to die without producing heirs – and he had not even met his wife since their marriage by proxy – then the island would revert to the crown. Edward was confirming that the land belonged to England, and was therefore in his gift. He had emphasised his rights of ownership over Llywelyn's territories. This was, in the view of one near-contemporary account, 'a formal sentence depriving his [Llywelyn's] successors for ever of the title of prince and reserving all the rest of the territories of Wales of which he [Edward] had made himself master of for himself and his successors, the kings of England'.[15]

* * *

The formal agreement at Aberconwy was a bitter moment for Llywelyn. The day after it was signed, Llywelyn crossed the Conwy river. As well as Bek and Tibotot, Bishop Anian was with him. This only added to Llywelyn's discomfort, given their past differences of opinion. It was the bishop's task to remove the sentence of excommunication that had been placed on Llywelyn at the start of the war. They journeyed to Rhuddlan, where Llywelyn met the English king at last. Defeated, his powers hugely reduced, it was a very different meeting from their previous one, before Edward had left on crusade.

Although not on the scale of the later wars in Scotland, or for that matter the next war in Wales, the costs of this expedition were a significant though far from unmanageable drain on Edward's financial resources. An analysis of the records extant shows that the total cost of the war came to £23,149. Much of this was paid out to hire the troops involved, but there were some interesting smaller entries, including £416 for food, which seems a very small figure and cannot have covered the costs of food for everyone, and £532 for the use of the fleet in the campaign. It was not an exorbitant sum, though Edward would certainly have noticed its effects on his budget. However, receipts from taxation and loans from Italian bankers would have amply covered it. It has been estimated that receipts from taxation levied in 1275 should have amounted to about £81,954 and although it is true to say that it would take much organisation and some time to collect all these sums in, it nevertheless demonstrates that the cost of this limited war could be afforded.[16] It was perhaps as well however that the war did not last too much longer or the costs of it would have escalated dramatically. Military campaigning was an expensive business, as Edward was to find out in painful fashion at a later stage in his reign.

Once Edward had refused to be drawn into replicating the mistakes of the past by leading his army in a wild goose chase against the Welsh as they took advantage of their home territory to harass the invaders with hit-and-run tactics, the outcome of the war was virtually a foregone conclusion given Edward's methodical approach. His military leadership had been exemplary, fully justifying the compliment that 'it is probable that [the English] army was the best controlled, as it was the best led, that had been gathered in England since the Norman Conquest'.[17]

But at the conclusion of the war, he was not personally vindictive. Edward has achieved a certain notoriety over the years for being a harsh, spiteful king. On many occasions that was undoubtedly true, as later events in Wales would prove. But even though the terms of the treaty were severe, Llywelyn was not punished to the maximum extent for his defiance. There is other evidence that a number of less prominent rebels were also forgiven for their part in the war, such as the entry on the Patent Rolls from Rhuddlan on 8 October 1277, which noted the granting of a 'pardon to Griffin Seys for his trespasses before the day of his admission to the king's peace, and of any consequent outlawry'.[18]

There are other references that give some insight into the lighter side of Edward's nature. From the mundane records of accounts and legal documents that survive, some tantalising glimpses of the king's concerns for his troops can be found. Accordingly, we find a reference to a group of Shropshire archers being given $1d$ each with which to buy a drink to toast the king's health. Other references record the king giving a sum of $40s$ to a party of wounded archers on their return home.[19] Edward, for all his stern nature and unshakeable belief in the unchallengeable rights of his crown, clearly had a human side, albeit one that his enemies would sometimes find hard to recognise.

Yet Llywelyn would still pay a heavy enough price for his defeat. Edward had taken steps to ensure that he exerted a far greater degree of control over Welsh affairs than had previously been the case. The settlement had, on the whole, been conducted like the military campaign, in a measured, methodical fashion. Edward's remission of Llywelyn's fine, unpayable though it was, was not the action of a vindictive zealot but a small act of statesmanship. But the treaty still resulted in a severe diminution of Llywelyn's powers, a diminution that a man such as him, a proud prince with an heroic heritage to inspire him, would find very difficult to countenance for any length of time. Its effect must not be under-estimated.[20]

Edward returned to London for Christmas, accompanied by Llywelyn. Here, 'in the presence of Edward I and many of the nobles of the realm, Llywelyn rendered homage to the king of England. He swore an oath in respect of himself and the nobility of his land that he would hold all his territory in fief from the king of England his lord for as long as he lived.'[21] There was a humiliating condition attached to this. The formerly abstinent Llywelyn would have to renew his homage annually. This would be reinforced by calling twenty men from each cantref together to swear to the king's representatives that they would ensure that Llywelyn remained loyal and subservient to the king and, if he failed to do so, they would abandon him. Goronwy ap Heilin was permitted to visit Eleanor de Montfort in private and Llywelyn would by now have hoped that his wife would soon be released, though in the event it would be some time before she was.

It has been noted that, throughout the negotiations with Llywelyn, his title of Prince of Wales was used by the English representatives.[22] Even after the war was ended, five leading Welsh lords outside Gwynedd would continue to take an oath of fealty to Llywelyn rather than direct to Edward. Within Welsh territory Welsh law, which was very different from English law, was to apply, though in the Marches Marcher law would hold sway. In some ways, the agreement partly upheld Llywelyn's status, which Edward punctiliously maintained. This was a very Edwardian thing to do; one thing that the king valued above all others was the maintenance of the proper order of things. But even this concession was mainly a sham. One of the five lords, Rhys Fychan ap Rhys ap Maelgwyn, had been completely disinherited and was therefore a spent force. The other four, lords from Edeirnion, were not much better. Two of them had been imprisoned by Llywelyn during the recent war. They were in other words hostile towards him. Their so-called allegiance to him was little more than a way of keeping Llywelyn under close watch by men who were inclined towards Edward's cause.

There were, according to Wykes, hints of some problems at the start of 1278. However, these did not end in a serious confrontation. In September of that year the two men met again at Rhuddlan. The meeting apparently went well. Edward laid on a great feast for the Welsh, which cost him a good deal. Dafydd and Llywelyn also met once more here. It must have been a frosty meeting between the two; Llywelyn, the once great prince, now emasculated due in no small part to the rebellious brother who stood before him. They were joined by Rhodri, another brother, perhaps the last time they would be together. Rhodri appears to have had little personal ambition. His contribution to the proceedings was to persuade Llywelyn to make good on a commitment he had made some years previously to buy out Rhodri's claims to land from him in return for 1,000 marks. Edward even went so far as not only to allow the marriage of Llywelyn to Eleanor de Montfort in October 1278 but actually to pay for the wedding celebrations. It took place at Worcester on 13 October, the feast day of Saint Edward the Confessor, the man after whom the English king had been named.

It was a truly regal occasion. Not only was Edward there, so too was his queen, Eleanor. King Alexander of Scotland and his queen were also present. Wedding gifts were given by Edward and Eleanor, a marker for Llywelyn's prayer book and a kerchief for Eleanor de Montfort. Llywelyn had not long before presented Edward with four hounds. Edward even promised 'to be benevolent and a friend to Llywelyn in all things'. Such pleasant gestures, touching as they might have appeared, were superficial. Beneath the surface, tensions continued to bubble away, waiting to boil over spectacularly again in the future.

It may have seemed that the war was over once and for all. A veneer of normality returned to Wales. The excommunication that had been placed on Llywelyn at the start of the war was lifted. Beneath this outward appearance, however, there had inevitably been a fundamental change in the nature of Llywelyn's relationship with England. No longer would he have free rein to do as he wished in Wales. His wings had been clipped in such a way that the balance of power had irrevocably shifted. Although he retained Gwynedd, the 'Four Cantreds' were lost to him, as well as other parts of Wales. In Powys, Gruffudd ap Gwenwynwyn, as loyal an adherent of the English crown as there could be, was firmly back in possession of his lands. In the northern portion of Powys, Edward had kept the lands of the young sons of Madog ap Gruffudd Mawr effectively under his control. Large chunks of Ceredigion had, in practice, been annexed to the English crown. For all that Edward had not achieved total victory in the war, the terms by which it had ended were severe enough to seriously reduce Llywelyn's power.

Llywelyn had in the past been something of a free spirit, always looking for the opportunity to strengthen his position within Wales. Now his situation had been massively constrained. Even at Llywelyn's wedding celebrations, apparently so magnanimously underwritten by Edward, there was a price to pay. He was forced to sign a paper which stated that he would ensure that English outlaws who fled to Gwynedd were handed back to Edward for justice. It was a sign of the controls that in future he would have to operate under. Such a loss of freedom, such interference in the free government of Gwynedd, was always likely to prove irksome to a man such as him. In reality, it was only ever a matter of time before he sought once again to achieve his independence.

CHAPTER SIX

The Great Conflagration

The memory which they will never lose of their former greatness may well kindle a
spark of hatred in the Welsh and encourage them to rebel from time to time; for they
cannot forget their Trojan blood and the majesty of their kings who once ruled over
Britain, a realm which was so great and a dynasty that lasted for so long.[1]

The war now ended, much more to the satisfaction of Edward than to the
outmanoeuvred Llywelyn, it was time for England to consolidate its
position against her recently defeated opponents in Gwynedd. One of
Edward's first steps was to ensure that the process of cutting back the
forests, so successfully employed during his recent campaigns, was
continued. The existence of thickly wooded areas gave the Welsh ample
opportunity to cause problems: even in peacetime, they offered outlaws
the chance to disrupt law and order. The reduction of the forests was also
a good policy to ensure that, if war were ever to break out again,
Edward's advantage from the outset should be more assured than in the
previous conflict. It was a continuation of the systematic and methodical
approach so much in evidence during Edward's campaign of 1277.

Administratively and legally, changes were also made. The historic
division of Wales into a number of separate regions was to be addressed
and steps were to be taken to introduce the English shire system into the
country.[2] This was an important symbolic, as well as administrative,
measure. It sent a signal that Edward saw the country as being just as
much a part of England as, say, Surrey or Devon were. It was an early
indication that Welsh traditions, which were naturally enough held dearly
by those newly defeated in the war, would count for little to Edward. For
him nothing was more important than the unambiguous assertion of the
rights of his crown.

The diminished status of the principality of Wales, and by definition
Llywelyn, was apparent in many different spheres of everyday life. The
prince was warned not to deprive the Church of its privileges in the
country and was also told peremptorily that if he did not pay Rhodri the
money due to him then the king's officials would enter Llywelyn's lands
and take his chattels to pay the debt. Safe conducts were issued by the

king to travellers to Anglesey, a small enough point in itself perhaps but a niggling reminder to Llywelyn that his territories unequivocally belonged to the king.

Even more significant than this, however, was the review that Edward's officials would conduct of Welsh law and its continued use. This was no bad thing if the exercise was conducted objectively. Just what 'Welsh law' was, though, was a moot point. Its application and content varied in different localities: the regionalisation symptomatic of Wales meant that to talk of the concept as one that was consistently understood and applied was well wide of the mark. Nevertheless, the legal code of a country is perhaps one of the most tangible manifestations of the independence and sovereignty of that nation. Nurtured by centuries of tradition, formulated through a series of time-honoured developments and evolutions, more than anything else it epitomises a country's freedom. Welsh law was very different from its English counterpart. And although Edward had undertaken to ensure that Welsh law continued to be applied in the future, the caveats he introduced around this assurance gave ample scope for interpretation. In the newly won territories, English law would apply, while in the Marches, Marcher law would be used. A major problem with this seemingly straightforward solution was that it made no attempt to define which law would be used when there were border disputes. As these were a frequent occurrence in the Marches, this gave ample scope for confusion and confrontation in the future.

Edward also believed that only just laws should be in use, regardless of whether the territory in question was English, Marcher or Welsh. There was of course one problem with this seemingly equitable approach. It was an Edwardian interpretation of justice that was to be applied. This could not be anything but a subjective assessment and it was understandable that those within Wales who objected to the introduction of English law should do so because they saw in it the opportunity for the English to strengthen their grip on Wales.

This implementation of a revised legal system manifested itself in a number of ways. One of the most obvious occurred when a system of jury trials was introduced in 1280. In that same year, a commission was set up to look at the ways in which Edward's predecessors had governed in Wales so that the precedents could be clearly established. At the head of this commission were Reginald Grey and Walter Hopton. They took evidence mainly in the area that the English had recently acquired, or within the Marcher territories, stopping to do so at Chester, Rhuddlan, Oswestry, Montgomery and Llanbadarn.

If the examination of the legal system was one important manifestation of the changed nature of English influence in Wales, another very tangible sign of it was to be seen in the castles that were erected in the wake of the war. The castle-building activities of Edward in Wales are well known but there were several phases involved in the process. The first of these took place in the aftermath of the war of 1277. The erection of castles such as Flint during the recent campaign showed that Edward deemed the construction of strong fortifications to be an important part of military strategy but these were at the start temporary structures. Something more permanent was needed to guarantee the strength of the English position.

Edward decided, effectively, to move the frontier forward, a sure sign that English policy in Wales would in the future be more aggressive than the approach adopted in the past. Chester had for some time been the prime location from which the English had cast a vigilant eye over the Welsh. But in the future, Flint and Rhuddlan would assume its place, thrusting boldly forward like a dagger always pointed menacingly at the heart of Welsh affairs in Gwynedd.

Work had already started on Flint during August 1277 while the war with Llywelyn was still in progress. A stronger castle was now needed there. Edward also decided that a new castle should be built at Rhuddlan. It would be built to the north-west of the existing motte and bailey-type castle. His choice of architect was to mark the start of a famous collaboration. Master James of St George, the Savoyard, was to be in charge of the construction. From 1278 to 1283 he would oversee the erection of the castles at both Rhuddlan and Flint. The relationship between the king and his master architect was to be vital: most of the Edwardian castles that are now liberally spread across the Welsh landscape owe much to James of St George. Although a large number of castles were constructed, demonstrating a wide variety of architectural features, most demonstrated a number of common attributes. They were notable for the way that they were constructed in strategically sited locations, the remorseless way in which they were built, often with remarkable speed, and the innovations that they utilised. Nor was Edward afraid to abandon castles at Diserth and Degannwy, developed at some cost by his father, when he felt that they were inappropriately situated.

We can reconstruct something of what happened during the building of the castles at both Flint and Rhuddlan. At Flint there were 1,800 ditchers (*fossatores*), employed from areas as far away as Yorkshire, Lancashire, Lincolnshire and Warwickshire. Edward took a personal interest in the building of the castles; in 1278 he and his wife Eleanor arrived at Rhuddlan to examine progress so far. A variety of stone was brought in to construct the castle, records for 1277 and 1278 stating that some of it, purple sandstone, was purchased from Richard, canon of St

Asaph's. Other building materials came from Flintshire, while yet more were shipped in from Cheshire. By 1280, the roofs had been topped with lead and in the following year shingles were added to the roof of the King's Hall. When it was completed, the castle was a fine example of a concentric fortification, that is with its inner walls far higher than the outer walls so that archers could fire on an attacking foe from both walls at once, doubling the concentration of the fire. The castle was subsequently overshadowed by Edward's greater later projects but it was an excellent piece of workmanship in its own right.

Edward's construction projects were not just about the building of castles however. In their shadow towns grew up. For example, in November 1278, a charter of liberties was awarded to Rhuddlan, protecting the rights of the burgesses of the town. Soon after, meadows around the town were enclosed. But at the same time, work on the fortifications that protected Rhuddlan took place. An artificial bank and ditch was thrown up, topped by timber fences (unlike later constructions, stone town walls never surrounded either Rhuddlan or Flint).

The greatest effort went into a remarkable engineering feat at Rhuddlan. The interaction of land and sea power was well understood by Edward, and is a much-remarked part of his strategy. At Rhuddlan, the sea was some distance from the castle. It had not always been so; ships had anchored in the river by Rhuddlan as recently as 1063 but since then it had silted up. It being too great an effort to move the town to the sea, Edward decided to bring the sea to Rhuddlan. The River Clwyd was therefore diverted to provide a deep-water channel between Rhuddlan and the sea, a distance of two miles.

It took three years to complete the exercise, with pay records showing that a sum of just over £755 was spent on the wages of ditchers who undertook the work, suggesting that nearly eighty men were employed virtually full-time on this great task. A bridge was also constructed across the river, probably of a type that could be swung back to allow the passage of ships. Not everything worked as it should, however; by 1303, a mason, Thomas of Caerwys, was instructed to repair the wall abutting the river as it had started to collapse, and was now 'partly destroyed and threatened great ruin'. Clearly, the frequent flooding of the river had undermined the foundations of the walls. New retaining walls had to be constructed to shore up the tottering section of masonry.

The construction of these castles was a very expensive undertaking. Between September 1277 and August 1282, a total of just over £9,613 was spent on the castle, town, bridge and other engineering works at Rhuddlan. In an irony that Llywelyn would surely not have appreciated, these costs were partly financed by the money that he had been forced to pay annually to Edward for the return of Anglesey. Even this cannot have been the end of the expenditure at Rhuddlan, as we know that work was still in progress on the defences of the town in December 1282.

However, Edward was not completely successful in all his plans for Rhuddlan. He wished to relocate the episcopal headquarters of the region from the present location of St Asaph's to Rhuddlan. In 1281, he applied to Rome for permission to proceed with this scheme. The transfer of status from St Asaph's to what was essentially an English town would have been another step in the anglicisation of Wales but, despite the offer of a site for a cathedral and a grant of 1,000 marks, the scheme came to nothing. Edward had also made a gift to the friars of the local Dominican friary, so that they could glaze the windows of their church, but his good works apparently were not enough to convince the wider Church that it could support his plans for the town.[3]

While Edward continued to consolidate his position in the north of the country, he also took steps concerning the governance of other parts of Wales. In the south-west it seemed that Edward originally planned to make his brother, Edmund of Lancaster, custodian of both Cardigan and Carmarthen. However, this plan would soon be amended when Edmund surrendered these lands in return for some in Derbyshire. In his place, Edward appointed Bogo de Knoville as his representative, making him justiciar of South Wales on 10 June 1280. As usual, Edward had an eye to the execution of English law in his territories and provision was made to hold a court for two days in every month at Carmarthen.

The effect of the recent wars was to move frontier territories in the south-west further inland as the areas controlled by the Welsh shrank. The castles at Llandovery, Dinefwr and Carreg Cennen assumed greater importance as a result. The castle at Carreg Cennen had been taken from Rhys Wyndod in the recent wars. It would eventually pass to the ownership of John Giffard, who was also awarded Llandovery. Giffard would play an important part in the future government of Wales.

Work also proceeded apace on a new fortification at Llanbadarn. There were several sums recorded for work on the castle here, including £918 given to the Earl of Lincoln. A later letter from his successor as overseer of the work, William de Valence, asks anxiously for money to be sent to the masons working there, whose pay was apparently overdue.[4] This latter account is an interesting precursor to future events; at a subsequent stage in his career in Wales, Edward would find it increasingly difficult to raise sufficient finance to pay for all his great ambitions in the country, with serious results.

In the south also, not everything went quite as planned. The death in 1278 of Edward's supporter, Pain de Chaworth, who had been one of the king's three captains in the first Welsh war, was a grave blow. He was a much-trusted adviser of Edward's, and had done valued service in the aftermath of the war of 1277. On one occasion, he was given the sum of £285 10s towards the upkeep of Carreg Cennen and Dinefwr, a large sum, providing one example of the king's trust in him. Chaworth had been a wealthy man in his own right, judging by some of the work he had initiated at his castle of Cydweli.

Bogo de Knoville, who assumed his role in the south, does not appear to have been a great success as an administrator. He was an uncompromising individual, widely unpopular. He made a tour of inspection around those regions for which he was responsible in 1280 but, early in 1281, less than a year after taking over in the south, he was replaced by Robert Tibotot, a companion of the king, who had accompanied him on his crusade. Bogo reappeared soon afterwards. He was appointed custodian of Montgomery Castle, a position much reduced in prestige from that which he had previously held, and from which we must assume that he had either made a very poor job of his former role or that he had done something else to incur the wrath of the king.

There had been some significant changes as a result of the war in the Middle Marches. Roger Mortimer had previously held the important castle at Builth but he had lost it to Llywelyn. It had been recaptured in the recent war but Edward had decided that he wished to retain it for himself, presumably because of its strategically important position. In return, Mortimer was awarded the castle at Dolforwyn. He also held other important castles in the area, such as those at Cefnllys and Radnor.

Edward also decided that he would strengthen the defences of Builth. A good deal of detail remains as to how he went about this.[5] The old castle on the site had been effectively obliterated by Llywelyn, which meant that Edward's workmen were in practical terms starting from scratch. The castle, construction on which began in 1277, took about four years to complete. The Exchequer Accounts note expenditure of about £1,600 on it during this period. The most interesting details however were those concerning how it was funded, for it gives us an excellent insight into how Edward's finances worked: £550 came from Edward's wardrobe, in other words from general revenues of the crown; a significant sum was also paid by Henry of Bray; £433 was paid in instalments from income accruing from lands he held in the Marches; £250 came direct from income earned from the lands at Builth itself. In addition, there were several fines that generated income used to pay for the castle. A small sum of 20 marks (about £14) came from a local Welsh lord who had clearly committed some offence in the recent war. A heavier toll was exacted from the men of Builth itself. A £200 fine was levied on them, suggesting that they had played a very active part on Llywelyn's side in the recent hostilities.

The resulting castle was clearly a solid edifice as it managed to resist Llywelyn in later wars. However, it is of interest that the sums recorded as being expended on its building are much smaller than those incurred on Rhuddlan. It is tempting to speculate that the sums spent on the latter demonstrate that Edward was primarily concerned with the domination of Gwynedd itself and that he regarded the area around Builth as one of secondary importance, a reasonable enough approach. But Builth was still important; the men of the town had a recent history of opposition to the English and it was crucial that steps were taken to mitigate this in the future. That Llywelyn may have had realistic hopes of support from the town would be demonstrated later on. During the construction of the castle, Edward sent several of his trusted lords to confirm that the building was proceeding according to plan. Among them were the Earl of Lincoln, Roger Mortimer and Otto de Grandson. Steps were also taken to employ that crucial, unsung, group, the woodsmen, who were engaged in cutting roads through to Mortimer's castle at Cefnllys so that Builth would not be isolated should hostilities break out again.

Edward's policy in the aftermath of the war was clear enough. He actively took steps to consolidate the position of the English crown in relation to Wales by the building or strengthening of defences close to Llywelyn's sphere of influence. Whether he thought these would be sufficient to deter Llywelyn's ambitions is far from certain. That they were not is obvious from the Welsh prince's later actions. Even when rebellion subsequently broke out, however, Edward reasoned that this policy was not essentially wrong; it was just the scale that needed to be addressed. He would correct the problem with stunning results at a later stage.

* * *

The outcome of the war was of course a bitter disappointment to Llywelyn. In its aftermath there were a number of genuine grievances against Edward's officials fuelling his anger. There were consistent complaints that they were heavy-handed and arbitrary in their handling of Welsh affairs. Pain de Chaworth had even been accused of murdering some of the men of Rhys ap Maredudd, ostensibly a supporter of the English, in the aftermath of the war of 1277. It has been speculated that, as Rhys did not join in the revolt against the English that was brewing, these grievances were manufactured, but he did subsequently attempt to throw off English rule, suggesting something of a history of inept handling by the English with regard to his interests.[6]

Particular criticism was levelled at Reginald Grey, who was appointed justiciar at Chester in November 1281. It was understandable that he would wish to bring English laws and administrative procedures to north Wales but the way that he did so was guaranteed to anger the Welsh people whom he attempted to bully into compliance. He resurrected old grievances going back decades, threatening to apply summary justice to those with whom he disagreed. His whole approach was patronising and arrogant. Neither was he the only target of criticism. In the mid-Marches, the constables of Oswestry and Whitchurch were the subject of complaints from the Welsh, while in Flintshire the people were irritated by the way that English customs, such as that of trial by jury, were imposed on them. At Hawarden, Roger Clifford proved himself an unpopular overlord (he was holding the castle in trust until its rightful heir came of age). The local people grumbled that he cared nothing for the rights given them by tradition and law, an accusation that would find an echo over all those parts of Wales which were now under direct English rule. And men like Kenrick Seys, a Welshman who 'rendered [himself] obnoxious to [his] fellow countrymen by [his] masterfullness and treachery', incensed loyalist supporters of the princely dynasty of Gwynedd.

It was with regard to the vexed question of which legal system was to be applied that matters were to come to a head. Morris sees this as a result of the frustration of the Welsh lords, rather than the common folk, holding that 'revolts are commonly due to the offended pride of a local aristocracy, who, as their next step, try to make the rising appear to be national and unanimous', citing in evidence the fact that a number of the Welsh, especially in the Marches, sided with the English in the subsequent uprising.[7]

This is altogether too black-and-white an analysis; that the Welsh were divided among themselves and certainly not united against the English is undoubtedly accurate. But that some of the Welsh, lord and commoner alike, were passionately against English rule, is evidenced by the serious nature of the revolt that was about to erupt. The mistake lies in considering Wales as one political and geographical entity; there was no 'nation' of Wales at this time, rather a number of smaller regions with a common cultural heritage but very much owing their allegiances to a local lord, who might side with either Edward or Llywelyn. And, although Llywelyn the Great and the current prince of Wales had taken significant steps towards giving the Welsh a national, as well as a racial, identity, they had far from completed this process. It was this allegiance to their immediate lord that would be the decisive influence in determining whose side the common folk were on, as well as a healthy and quite understandable fear of being roughly suppressed by the more numerous forces available to the English in any war. But it is also true to say that the evidence suggests that at least some the people affected felt that the implementation of English law was effectively an improvement on the status-based, comparative laws they had known previously.

The commission set up by Edward to examine the application of law in Wales was, it has correctly been stated, something that for Llywelyn 'might prove an asset or a threat'.[8] Not everyone was particularly interested in it. In one instance, a Welsh lord was asked to give evidence on some complex legal matters. In his evidence, he offered the delightful comment that 'of the other articles he knows nothing, because he gives more attention to hunting than to discussion of the law'.[9] Initial impressions nevertheless cannot have been entirely adverse. Hopton's commission (a similar one was set up earlier in the south under Pain de Chaworth but had effectively ground to a halt when he died) was noticeably not empowered to investigate Welsh law in Gwynedd itself; Llywelyn's rights and status as a prince again being meticulously observed. Further comfort was given to Llywelyn when a dispute broke out about which law should apply in the case of the lordship of Yale, on the borders with England. The widow of Madog of Bromfield was unhappy about the disputed ownership of certain estates in the territory. It was unclear whether she should appeal about them to Edward or Llywelyn. Given this uncertainty, she appealed to both. Edward reviewed the case and decided that it was within Llywelyn's jurisdiction to examine, so he passed the case over to him for decision.

These promising beginnings were a misleading portent of what was to come. In the event, virtually no cases were to be referred to Welsh courts for consideration in disputed cases.[10] Inevitably, there were situations when it was hard to decide which was the appropriate legal code to use and in such cases the ultimate decisions were often passed to Edward for decision. The danger inherent in this was that Edward was not seen to be a disinterested, impartial observer and, if a case were to be decided in favour of an English lord and against the Welsh, it was inevitable that his involvement would be seen as biased. Even the impartiality of the judges was suspect when some of them were known as supporters of Edward.

No one, it became clear, was above the law; not even, perhaps especially, Llywelyn himself. In January 1278, he was summarily ordered to present himself to the justices 'to propound the suits of himself and his men and to do and receive justice'.[11] It was not just the act of appearing in such a way that would grate with Llywelyn. It was the tone of the order, which made it completely transparent that Llywelyn was just another feudal vassal of the king. To a man like Llywelyn, used to getting his own way, the diminution in status was obvious, disturbing and, above all else, extremely painful.

A potential catalyst for revolt would be found in the region of Arwystli, in the south of Powys, which was disputed between Llywelyn and Gruffudd ap Gwenwynwyn. In 1278, proceedings began to resolve the dispute. Llywelyn took little time after the treaty agreed at Aberconwy was sealed to start attempts to prove his case regarding the lands he had taken from Gruffudd ap Gwenwynwyn in 1274. However, the case could not even get started until it was decided under which legal code it should be heard. Llywelyn asserted that the correct law to use was Welsh. Gruffudd however would have none of this; he asserted that Arwystli was in an area that formed part of the land he held from Edward as an English baron. The law to be used was not Welsh, nor was it Marcher law which in many cases was now nearly the same thing.[12] It should instead, in Gruffudd's contention, be English law as both men involved were barons owing fealty to the English king. It was not a sustainable argument in the view of at least one group of English judges; when Gruffudd brought a claim against Roger Mortimer based on similar grounds it was dismissed because they adjudged it to be Welsh land involved. But despite the fact that the land in question between Llywelyn and Gruffudd was close to that on which the judgment had been made, no such clear-cut analysis was forthcoming in this dispute. It proved impossible to reach a resolution to these difficulties, so the matter was referred to Edward for arbitration.

The English legal system as adopted in Wales was admittedly somewhat bogged down at the time. There had been a large number of cases to review, given the unique nature of the changes then taking place, and it was understandable that some delays would ensue as a result. But, even allowing for this, the review of the case was a prolonged one. The first skirmishings came when Adam of Montgomery began a case against Gruffudd ap Gwenwynwyn. It has been asserted that this was in fact something of a deception, the sole purpose of which was to demonstrate who had jurisdiction over Arwystli,[13] and this seems a not unreasonable analysis of the approach adopted. A decision would ultimately have to be made by Edward himself; but, when he first heard the case in September 1278, it was adjourned for further investigations. Gruffudd initiated an action of his own in response to Llywelyn's tactics on Arwystli, claiming that not only the land there but also territory in Powys and Meirionydd belonged to him. In addition, he brought claims against Llywelyn for the way that he had been treated by the prince in 1274. It was the start of a long series of delays, prevarications and an increasing build-up of frustration on Llywelyn's part.

The surviving evidence suggests that Edward had been involved in the case since earlier in 1278. He found himself in an acutely difficult position, and certainly wished to avoid anything that might be against the interests of Gruffudd ap Gwenwynwyn. It is probable in fact that he urged Llywelyn and Gruffudd to reach an amicable negotiated agreement but his wishes in this respect were unfulfilled.

Matters then proceeded at a snail's pace. By 1280, little progress had been made and Llywelyn was writing with barely concealed irritation and justification to Edward that 'it seems that three years should suffice for the settling of one article'. By June 1281, Edward was able to tell Llywelyn that the case could now be heard before his justices but the decision was so badly drafted that it was still not clear which legal code would be used. Llywelyn now attempted to force the issue, writing to Edward in terms which indicated that he understood it to be Welsh law that would be used in the case. Further problems followed. Gruffudd argued that, as a baron, it was his right to be issued with a writ before proceedings could begin. Llywelyn claimed that such a writ had already been issued but Edward's officials could no longer find it. From this point on, events overtook the progress of the case. Shortly afterwards, Wales was in flames. The time for talking had passed; the only adjudication from now on was one decided by force of arms.[14]

*　*　*

Edward was in an exceedingly difficult situation. Whatever he did would antagonise a party he was particularly keen not to irritate. He certainly did not wish to upset Llywelyn; far better to have him as a subservient subject than a rebel in arms. By the same token, Gruffudd had been a loyal supporter of the English cause and it would be a strange way to reward him by finding against his point of view in this particular case. But his actions did nothing to defuse the situation. It was of course a thorny issue but one in which his stance seems guaranteed to have made the situation more acute than ever. After all, his tactics essentially worked in favour of the status quo, which was to Gruffudd's advantage and against Llywelyn's. In the event, it is little surprise to find that this particular difficulty did not simply go away but instead was exacerbated by Edward's approach.[15] His dithering in the Arwystli affair did him little credit.

Nor were these the only problems experienced by Llywelyn. Before the conflict of 1277, a ship belonging to Robert of Leicester had been wrecked on Llywelyn's shores. The prince had claimed the right to seize control of the cargo. After the war, some of Llywelyn's men were held in Chester as hostages until the case was resolved. Although Edward promised to release them, Grey either never received orders to do so or, if he did, he ignored them. The evidence concerning this case is suggestive. Grey was to state that he had acted on Edward's orders. Unless he was lying – and it would be a brave, or foolish, man who would set himself at odds with Edward – then the king was fully aware of what Grey was doing as he himself had ordered it. It is tempting to think that it was Edward's officials alone who were responsible for the severity of English rule. However, this appears to be very much an oversimplification of the reality of the situation. The subsequent hanging of two men who, Llywelyn said, were travelling under a safe conduct can have done little to improve the mood of the prince of Wales, nor to increase his confidence in English justice.[16]

These problems were keenly felt by Llywelyn; but there were other, more reactive elements entering the equation, such as the much reduced status that had given the once all-powerful prince of Wales the role of a vassal of the king of England, and the unfavourable circumstances that had changed the status of the man who had once attempted to be the power broker in the wars between Simon de Montfort and the English crown to that of a mere feudal baron with vastly smaller lands at his disposal. The legal issues were important and provided a source of genuine resentment. Arwystli as it happens was not a great prize. The land there was not fertile, and would add little of value to Llywelyn's possessions. But for the prince of Wales there was an issue of principle at stake. In the final analysis, the real problem was one of the division of power in Wales, and of who was to wield it. The Welsh, as Gerald of Wales had pointed out, had a proud and ancient heritage and their reduced status would encourage them, as he had suggested over half a century previously, to revolt.

Llywelyn had not been slow to attempt to improve his position again after his defeat in the war of 1277. The year after this humiliating loss, we find him receiving the homage of a Welsh lord, Trahearn ap Madog of Brecon. The origins of Trahearn are suggestive; it shows that Llywelyn did not think of his sphere of influence as being confined merely to Gwynedd and its immediate environs. In the same year, he also entered into an arrangement with Gruffudd ap Gwen, steward to Gruffudd ap Gwenwynwyn. Even more interestingly, in 1281 we find him coming to terms with Roger Mortimer. The two effectively formed a pact of mutual co-operation by which both men would support each other in the future unless it brought them into conflict with Edward I. The conclusion of this agreement between them demonstrates that it was perfectly possible for individual English Marcher lords still to reach an understanding with the wily Llywelyn. The agreement has been the source of much debate among historians. Some suggest that it provides evidence of a decision on Llywelyn's part that a peaceful settlement of the Arwystli dispute was no longer possible and his purpose in the arrangement was to ensure that Mortimer remained neutral in any conflict that might ensue. But this seems to stretch the available evidence too far. It is more likely that this was just the action of two men in the autumn of their lives, who wished to protect their inheritance and ensure peaceful relations.[17]

Nor was Llywelyn the only important Welshman who was unhappy with the form that English influence in Wales had assumed. One of Edward's chief supporters in the war of 1277 had been the prince's brother, Dafydd. However, he had not received the absolute prize that had been dangled temptingly before him as his potential reward for his assistance, and the disappointment gnawed away at him. In his castle at Denbigh, he fumed at the perceived duplicity of the English king and plotted his revenge. Of his castle, little sign now remains. The stone edifice that now stands at Denbigh is not the result of the efforts of Dafydd but of his eventual conqueror. Dafydd's castle was almost certainly of wood, of the old motte and bailey style. Nothing better illustrates the essential difference between the Welsh princes and their English foes than the modest castles of the former and the massive, modern, menacing citadels that Edward constructed in Wales.

There had also been difficulties between Dafydd and the English. His ambition was not satisfied, even when Edward presented him with the newly reconstructed castle at Hope (also known as Caergwrle). He soon came into conflict with the English, and especially with Reginald Grey, Edward's justiciar at Chester. Dafydd even claimed that there were plots to capture him and take his sons hostage. He was summoned to appear at Chester to answer charges concerning his lands at Hope and Estyn. In 1281, an English knight, William Venables, claimed the lands involved. Dafydd responded that this land was subject to Welsh, not English, law. He was irritated still further when he claimed that the English had interfered with his rights regarding three towns in Dyffryn Clwyd and Rhufoniog.

Tensions were also present elsewhere, especially in the two of the 'Four Cantreds', Rhos and Teigingl, which had been retained by Edward after his triumph in the war. Edward appointed two Welshmen to look after his interests there, Goronwy ap Heilin in Rhos and Hywel ap Gruffudd (later replaced by Cynfrig ap Goronwy) in Teigingl. These men were members of important families in Gwynedd, and it says something for Llywelyn's level of support at the end of 1277 that Edward felt confident enough to appoint them. Both regions were at the heart of the revolt against the English that was about to erupt; both would say that they were deprived of the rights and privileges due to them under the traditional laws of Wales.

There was one factor above all others that was responsible for the increasing tensions in the north. By any objective standard, Edward's appointment of Grey as his justiciar in Chester was a disastrous decision as far as the peaceful governance of Wales was concerned. Within months of his appointment on 14 November 1281, the area was seething with discontent. Goronwy ap Heilin was removed from office and replaced with more tractable officials. The local populace later complained that they were threatened with execution if they dared complain to Edward about Grey's severity.

There was then widespread resentment at the imposition of English law, which to many native Welshmen was little more than colonisation by osmosis. The dispute over Arwystli is the most prominent example of problems within the legal system but there were many other cases when Welshmen protested that the rights given them by history and tradition were being inexorably eroded. Some of these instances may not, in themselves, appear significant. A decision concerning the rights of widows in north Powys here, jurisdiction on disputes between an abbey and a secular landowner there: the cumulative effect was to give the impression that the importance of Welsh law was being undermined and that, eventually, it might disappear altogether. In such a climate, immense pressures were created, eventually manifesting themselves as out-and-out rebellion.

The year 1281 closed, and 1282 began, with a winter of Arctic severity. It seemed as if England was in the grip of an Ice Age. One writer said that 'there was bitter frost and snow, the like of which even the old and the aged of that day had not experienced before in England. The five arches of London Bridge, and many other bridges besides, collapsed under the pressure of the ice. The River Thames was frozen solid all the way from Lambeth to the king's palace at Westminster, and people were able to walk across without getting their feet wet. Fish died in the ponds and birds starved to death in the woods and fields.'[18] It was a suitable portent for the days ahead.

A number of factors combined to ignite the great conflagration that was about to flare up in north Wales. Dafydd was particularly put out by the course of events, a feeling that would surely not have been helped by the fact that an enquiry into his right to hold certain lands had been held at the start of 1282. It was a very tangible sign that what he had, he held only by English sufferance. Even more than his brother, Dafydd was a proud man, conscious of his position; while at the same time harbouring an inbuilt grudge that he had not been awarded the status that he deserved. The time was right for him to express his dissatisfaction with affairs in dramatic fashion.

Easter was a special time to the Christian world of the Middle Ages. Its religious symbolism was so significant that warfare was specifically forbidden during this holy time. As the festival of 1282 approached it was therefore probable that the garrison of the castle at Hawarden was relaxed and had lowered its guard. As night fell on 21 March, Palm Sunday, those resident in the castle retired to rest with little regard to any looming danger, for there had been no obvious sign that any could be expected. The guard this night must have been particularly lax because a party of men approached the castle apparently without its occupants being roused.

All of a sudden, the still night air was disturbed by shouts and screams as Dafydd's men launched themselves at the barely defended castle walls. Before any serious resistance had been offered, the fight was over. The exultant war cries of the Welsh contrasted starkly with the groans of the English wounded and dying. In Matthew of Westminster's account, we read that the Welsh killed 'all they met with, young and old, women and children, in their beds and [devastated] afterwards with plunder and conflagration the greater part of the Marches'.

Allegations of war crimes are commonly spread abroad in times of conflict but this was a violent age in which to live and such accounts are by no means unlikely. The detested Clifford was taken alive; he would make a useful bargaining chip in the conflict which Dafydd surely knew must follow. He was taken away in chains to Snowdonia, an invaluable hostage against the vagaries of the future. Dafydd himself had fought on the other side in 1277; he, better than most, had experienced for himself the efficiency and relentlessness of the English king. Another war was about to begin. This time, however, it would not be another limited conflict fought by England with the intention of reminding the princes of Gwynedd of their place in the feudal hierarchy. Edward's objective was far more extensive and permanent, for this was undoubtedly to be a war of final conquest.

CHAPTER SEVEN

War to the Death

Nothing rejoices the hearts of men so much, nothing inspires them to behave so nobly, as the sheer joy of being free.[1]

The initial success of Dafydd at Hawarden was just the first in a series of spectacular results for the Welsh. So striking were their early victories that two things seem crystal clear. The first is that their forces were co-ordinated and that this was a well-planned uprising that did not just happen by chance, while the second is that the English were caught off-guard by events. In contrast to the rebellion of 1277, the uprising now had a widespread level of support, from all levels of the community, from the poor to the lords of the land. It was violent, intense and deep-rooted. A large amount of booty was seized and there was a ferocity about the attacks of the rebels which left no doubt that there was bitter resentment at English rule.

Given the first factor, that of the coordination of the revolt, it is surely inconceivable that Llywelyn was completely unaware of what was about to happen. If the rising were to be a success, it would need the support of the greatest living Welsh leader; resources were in too short supply to ignore the men that he could put into the fray. Of course, relations between Llywelyn and Dafydd had often been difficult but it would be neither the first nor the last time that two men overcame their differences to fight for a cause that was in their mutual self-interest. Given Llywelyn's influence in the country, it is probable that some discussions involving him took place before the uprising. Although there is no direct evidence that Llywelyn knew of the detailed plans for an uprising – and the chroniclers are certainly divided in their accounts on this point – he was put in an impossible position by it. That Dafydd was the primary orchestrator of the revolt appears highly probable; Edward's treatment of him at the end of the war, and his comments concerning him during it, suggest that he for one certainly believed this to be the case. But once Dafydd was up in arms, Llywelyn was forced to take sides. It would be unthinkable that he would support Edward and he was therefore forced – reluctantly or not we cannot know – to side with his erratic, troublesome brother.

After the first success of Dafydd, the Welsh were quick to follow up with further advances. Oswestry was attacked at more or less the same time as Hawarden, as local Welsh forces took out their frustrations on the town. Reports averred that a great deal of plundering had taken place. Although it seems probable that contemporary reports that Flint and Rhuddlan castles fell are inaccurate – there are no records of any substantial rebuilding works being undertaken subsequently, which would have been necessary to restore them – there appears to have been a general slaughter in the town of Flint itself. Little attempt had been made to integrate Welsh people into the communities that had been created when these towns were constructed and they were therefore substantially populated by English settlers who were seen as part of the attempted anglicisation of Wales every bit as much as castles were, and detested just as much.

Dafydd was going down a very dangerous path with his actions. He had previously been taken into the protective bosom of the English court when relations had been soured between him and his brother. There was little doubt that Edward would regard his rebellion as an act of supreme treachery. When Dafydd bit the hand that had fed him, Edward would have regarded it as a very personal betrayal. Of necessity, this was for Dafydd especially a war to the death from the start. If he were to lose the consequences for him personally were likely to be dire in the extreme. This comes across clearly in one of the contemporary accounts that has survived, where Edward says ominously of Dafydd: 'we had welcomed him when an exile, nourished him when an orphan; endowed him out of our own lands, and favoured him under the cloak of our wings, placing him amongst the great of the palace.'[2]

While the castles at Flint and Rhuddlan held out in the north, protected by their sea-borne links with England, Dafydd turned his attention further south. Whereas the war of 1277 had undoubtedly been of Llywelyn's making, in this war it was Dafydd who was at the heart of the initial outburst. Llywelyn's apparent inertia is unexplained. Whether he was merely showing an understandable loss of energy after decades of hard-fought military activity and political intrigue or whether he realised that the chances of lasting Welsh success were very slim is a matter of conjecture. He may also have been seeking political solutions to his much-reduced position. His alliance with Roger Mortimer and his patience so far with the Arwystli case, despite severe provocation, suggest as much. Certainly, he had now seen Edward in action and, a much more astute man than his brother, he was well placed to judge the merits of his opponent. At any rate, this initial low key approach on his part perhaps suggests that his heart was not really in a war which he knew would stretch his resources to the limit.

The immediate effects of the outbreak further south were just as dramatic as they had been in the north. Llandovery and Carreg Cennen fell to Gruffudd and Llywelyn, brothers of Rhys Wyndod of Dinefwr, in March. In the old region of Deheubarth, Rhys ap Maredudd was the only lord of note to side with Edward. Again, English rule had been imposed here, a regime that grated significantly with many of the local Welsh lords. The treatment of Rhys Wyndod is a particular case in point; he had lost some of his most important lands, and both his status and his wealth had suffered as a result. This was despite the fact that he had submitted to Edward early on in the war of 1277. It was little wonder that men such as him revolted against English rule. Even Rhys ap Maredudd, who of course had no personal sympathy whatsoever for his arch-rival Rhys Wyndod, must have been concerned by this stage at the course events in the region had taken, as they set a worrying precedent for him personally. The English were forced to retreat to their bases at Dinefwr and Cardigan, both of which were dangerously exposed, being adjacent to some of the territories recently raided by the Welsh. Further east, Brecon and Radnor were also in arms against the English, while reports from Montgomery suggested that rebellion was rife.

Rhys Wyndod had been involved in a lengthy dispute with an acquisitive English neighbour, John Giffard. He would later complain when the Archbishop of Canterbury, John Pecham, a 'man of the most perfect learning'[3] who had replaced Kilwardby in 1278, attempted to negotiate an end to the war, that Giffard had deprived him of his birthright. His position was summarised most eloquently by his neighbours, Gruffudd and Cynan ap Maredudd of Ceredigion, who stated that many races were allowed to keep their own law and customs even if they were under English rule – the Jews in England were cited as an example. Why then were not the Welsh permitted to do so? The jurisdiction, and therefore the power, of these men was being eroded by English rule, and therefore that they sought to regain it through rebellion hardly comes as a surprise.

For the English, even worse news was to follow. Much time and effort, not to mention hard-earned money, had been expended on the construction of the castle at Llanbadarn. Symbol of English domination, that too fell to the Welsh on 9 April. When the castles fell, the rebels made no attempt to hold them. Such a tactic would have meant that their resources, in short supply to start with, would be hopelessly overstretched. Instead, the castles were destroyed to deny their use to the English forces.

Edward's response to initial news of this crisis was, as might be expected, a methodical one. Receiving the news of the attack on

Hawarden, he immediately appointed captains to safeguard English interests in the Marches, just as he had done in the first war. His choice of Reginald Grey to look after the northern Marches was perhaps an understandable one given the important position that he already held at Chester but, given the complaints that had already been made against him and his reputation as a harsh administrator, it was also a sign that Edward was in no mood for compromise. It could almost be regarded as inflammatory. The sheriffs of the counties of Lancashire and Derbyshire were specifically ordered to provide him with both men and horses. Roger Mortimer, the logical choice, was to look after the Middle Marches, supported by Bogo de Knoville, while in the south Robert de Tibotot was to be in command, aided by the earls of Hereford and Gloucester.

Edward ordered that a particularly close guard should be placed over the Ely region. It was here that supporters of Simon de Montfort had fled at the end of the civil wars in England. Given Llywelyn's connection to the family, the ghosts of the past continued to haunt Edward. Memories of the civil war stretched back nearly two decades into the past now but the wounds that that particular conflict had opened were still far from healed. In this glimpse of Edward's concern for those associated with the de Montfort cause there is a tantalising insight into just how inflammatory Llywelyn's marriage to Eleanor de Montfort must have been to Edward.

Edward ordered his lords to assemble at Devizes. They met there on 5 April 1282. Edward changed the command of the southern Marches, transferring responsibility for this from Tibotot to Gloucester, a man with whom he had not of course always enjoyed a tranquil relationship. Various other important decisions were also taken. One of them was that Edward would not call out a feudal levy but would rather summon a number of men, again to meet at Worcester, and take them into paid service. Steps were also taken to secure financing from Italian bankers, although the 12,000 marks raised in such a fashion would clearly make only a small contribution towards the campaign. The start to the war had been very different from that experienced in 1277, when Edward's Marcher lords had made significant initial gains, and it must have been apparent to Edward even at this early stage that this campaign would be much more taxing than the previous one.

Nor was the provisioning of the army forgotten. The earl of Warwick was despatched to France, as more horses were once again needed for the army. Edward also sent officials to Scotland and Ireland to gather more provisions for the troops, and men were sent as far afield as Gascony to buy up more supplies. Twelve mounted and forty unmounted crossbowmen were called up from Gascony, not a particularly large number but further evidence that the weapon was highly valued by Edward. Nor had Edward forgotten the importance of the fleet in the first Welsh war. Ships were again called up from the Cinque Ports.

It was also decided at Devizes that members of Edward's household guard would be sent at once to Wales as an advance party to reinforce the hard-pressed English forces currently desperately trying to resist the elated supporters of Dafydd and Llywelyn. Just over 100 horsemen – 15 of them knights – were sent to Chester under the command of Amadeus of Savoy. They were followed in May 1282 by another 45 horsemen in three groups, led by Robert de Tateshale, William Audley and Robert Fitzwalter. With a force of over 150 horsemen at his disposal, Grey must have been confident of rebuffing any further advances by Dafydd in the north.

The situation further south was not ignored. The earl of Lincoln, a seasoned campaigner from the first war, was soon at Montgomery to support Roger Mortimer. The records note the payment of £255 for twenty days' service, which it has been estimated would probably supply 100 cavalry and 600 foot soldiers.[4] At Gloucester, Alan Plukenet had assembled nearly 100 cavalry by the end of April. Here he could support the English troops in the south. They had already received something of a bloody nose in the first month or so of the war, and the situation was about to get worse before it got better.

This was an impressive start to recruitment. With various other forces not yet taken into account, it meant that Edward quickly had 600 cavalry at his disposal. It was a far greater force than the Welsh could ever dream of assembling but, for whatever reason, it did not satisfy Edward. When he reached Worcester in May, he issued orders that he wished the feudal levy to be called out after all, to meet him at Rhuddlan in August. There has been a good deal of debate about why he did this. The notice period was unusually short for feudal service, six months being a much more common length of time. It was also of course unnecessarily short. If Edward had issued the summons at Devizes, the length of time given to assemble the feudal forces would have been over a month longer.

There are several reasons why this apparent change of mind may have happened. The first of these is that he misjudged the scale of the uprising. This seems barely credible. By the time that the assembly at Devizes took place Hawarden, Carreg Cennen and Llandovery had fallen and the town of Flint had been sacked. That this was a very serious revolt, and furthermore one attended by initial Welsh success, was obvious, even given the great haste in which Edward had to respond to the crisis. What would particularly have perturbed him was the geographical range of the revolt. From the 'Four Cantreds' in the north-east of Wales to Deheubarth in the south-west, men were in arms against him. Things were markedly different from the situation in 1277 when he could pick and choose his time to attack. Now he was on the defensive, and that may have thrown him. But given the early news of trouble on a wide front it is unthinkable that someone with Edward's sharp military mind could misjudge the full extent of the uprising.

Edward's initial response – the raising of loans and the calling out of the fleet – shows that the king took this uprising very seriously indeed. Nor can he have been unhappy with the size of the initial response from his paid men; the forces available to him in terms of cavalry gave him an overwhelming advantage in this respect. It has been argued that the change of mind may have come about because Edward's lords themselves put pressure on him to do so.[5] For them, feudal service had its uses. It reminded the king that he was dependent on the practical support of his lords and it gave them real power. Service, rather than pay, was also a way that the lords of the realm could increase their influence by the receipt of lands at the end of the war.

There is perhaps another aspect to consider, which revolves around the personality of Edward. The king was a forceful and immensely powerful individual. He could not rule alone, of course, although on a number of occasions during his reign he would overstep the mark and become too much the autocrat. However, there is no doubt that this war was Edward's war, no matter how much of an interest other men had in it. The response to the Welsh revolt was shaped by his actions and largely his alone. The news from the first two months of the war had continued to be bad. Castles and towns on which he had expended a great deal of money and energy were now in some cases reduced to rubble. Did Edward see the revolt as a personal insult, a direct and insolent challenge to his right to rule? If such a supposition is correct then it is probable that, as he pondered the implications of the revolt, he became increasingly incensed at the temerity of Dafydd and his resentment grew proportionately. As a result, he may have decided, in the time that elapsed between the outbreak of hostilities and his decision to summon a feudal army, that complete subjugation was the only answer.

The introduction of personal emotion into his thinking was entirely consistent with his character. It is undoubtedly the case, given what we know of Edward, that Dafydd's actions 'shocked and infuriated him'.[6] As a result, between the assembly at Devizes in April and the muster at Worcester in May, the scope of the war may have changed in Edward's mind. From a war whose ultimate aim was to restore the natural order of things as Edward saw it – that is, with a Welsh prince subservient to him, though nominally still with some status in his own right – its nature may have changed to that of a war of absolute conquest. Such a war would of course require a large army, hence the need to call out the feudal levy.

In theory, a large number of men could legally be summoned by Edward to join the feudal levy. In practice, there was no way that all the men he was entitled to summon would present themselves; the law did not reflect reality. Therefore, men were called up on a quota basis. During the course of the thirteenth century, quotas were amended to come more into line with practicality: as one example, under old systems of calculation Hugh de Courtenay might have been expected to provide ninety-two knights but in Edward's reign his quota was three. There were still some bizarre anomalies: the feudal duty of one man was to turn up to the levy with a side of bacon. In 1282, he did this, promptly ate the bacon and went home again. But all in all, the improvements made during the course of the century did have the effect of making the levy more realistic.[7]

Whatever the truth of this speculation, the result was clear enough. A substantial force would now be available to Edward. Edward's strategy would be based on the previous war, albeit with a more advanced base to start out from at Rhuddlan. He advanced at the head of his army, first of all to Chester. By the time he arrived, he had 276 cavalry with him, though whether some of these were men who had previously served independently under leaders such as the earl of Lincoln is not certain. It is of interest to note that among those listed as providing ten horsemen to the expedition was one Richard de Bruce, uncle to a young Scottish knight called Robert, with whom Edward was to become very well acquainted many years into the future.[8]

With the cavalry already available to Grey, this meant that there was something like 600 horse in the north, representing three-quarters of the total cavalry available to the English in the whole of Wales and the Marches, providing demonstrable evidence that this sector would see the greatest concentration of the English effort. There were also about 7,000 foot soldiers available to Edward in June 1282. A small number of crossbowmen were included in this figure – some 86 in total – though the ordering of 10,000 crossbow bolts from Bristol at this time, followed by 54,000 from elsewhere in England at a later stage, suggests that there was either a great deal of under-recording in the figures or that a larger number of crossbowmen arrived at a later stage. This sizeable force now stood ready at Chester to advance into Wales and subdue Llywelyn and his brother for good.

Spiritual weapons were also called into play. Archbishop Pecham, using the precedent of the Council of Oxford in 1222, was easily persuaded to excommunicate all those who rose in arms against Edward within two weeks of the rebellion starting. An interesting difference from the war of 1277 was that, on the previous occasion, Llywelyn had been excommunicated by name. Pecham now excommunicated those in arms against their king but named neither Llywelyn nor Dafydd individually. The archbishops of York and Dublin did likewise. The terms of the Council of Oxford had provided that an archbishop might excommunicate any who unjustly disturbed the king's peace and that of his realm. It was easy enough in the current circumstances to demonstrate that these conditions had been amply met. Pecham was, despite his efforts at a later stage to broker a peaceful settlement, a man with a low regard for the Welsh as a people. Pecham repeated his edict a month later. Later on in the year, in September, he would send a Dominican friar to absolve those Welshmen who had been taken back into the king's peace.[9]

The war was thus given something of the nature of a spiritual enterprise. After it was over, Pecham was to say that, if the king had found himself unable to subdue Wales by force himself, he would have appealed to the Pope to give the campaign crusading status. There is no doubt that Edward was convinced of the righteousness of his cause. The Welsh had exacerbated their offences by raising the banners of revolt in Holy Week, the build-up to that most sacred of times in the Christian calendar. If they had grievances then they could have been dealt with through the proper channels he had set up to deal with them. Edward may have convinced himself that this was the reality of the situation. He was not a man given to self-doubt.

* * *

Before the English could advance into Gwynedd it was necessary to drive back Dafydd from the positions that he held which impeded the safe movement of Edward's army. Dafydd held his castle at Denbigh and the fortress captured from the English at Hawarden, and also the castles of Hope and Dinas Bran, the hilltop castle close by Llangollen. The task of taking these was deputed to Grey, who set about his task competently. With him was Owain, brother of Llywelyn and Dafydd, demonstrating yet again what a tangled web family loyalty presented in medieval warfare. Dafydd's tactics were simple. To hold his forward positions was playing into the hands of the English and their superior resources. A set-piece siege could only have one result. Instead, Dafydd resolved to abandon his castle at Hope. He would not merely hand over a serviceable asset to the English, however. Before leaving it to Edward's men, he demolished as much of it as he could so that its usefulness to the English was severely limited, at least until time and effort were expended in restoring it. He also blocked up the wells in the area to deprive his enemies of vital water supplies to hinder their advance.

By 16 June, Grey had arrived and taken possession of the now vacant property. However, it would clearly have to be partially reconstructed if it was going to be of any use to the English. Hugh de Pulford was made constable of Edward's first conquest of the campaign. A substantial force was allocated to protect him, including a huge number of 2,600 archers.[10] This can only have meant that Grey expected trouble. Dafydd was likely to see the English, on the defensive while the castle was rebuilt, as an irresistible target for a counter-attack.

Whether these attacks materialised with any intensity is debatable. Although Grey was reinforced with more cavalry soon afterwards, the number of archers with him dropped to 900. It is probable that the others were urgently needed elsewhere but it may also suggest that the original force was larger than it needed to be to deter the Welsh from attacking. Again, a large number of non-combatants were brought up to assist with the efforts of Grey at Hope. The ubiquitous woodsmen were assembled, nearly 500 of them (this initial batch would later be joined by others), to cut down the forests. Masons and carpenters were also sent to assist in the reconstruction of the castle at Hope. Soon after Hope fell, another fortress, probably that at Ewloe, was taken by Grey's men. According to the records, only seven horsemen were needed to do this, suggesting that this castle had also been abandoned without a fight.

These events helped to pave the way for the advance of Edward's main army. Soon afterwards, the king set out at the head of his army into north Wales, reaching Flint on 7 July and Rhuddlan on the 12th. Here, he received welcome news that the fleet conscripted from the Cinque Ports was now on station, having arrived off the coast on 10 July. It was auspicious timing, coinciding as it did with the main advance, and meant that Edward could be confident that a regular flow of supplies could be maintained. A consistent stream of reinforcements came up, helping the momentum of the English advance. All seemed to be progressing exactly to plan. The only cloud on the horizon was a logistical one. The French king had banned the export of all horses to England, which, given the difficulty that had been experienced in finding suitable mounts for the cavalry and the inevitable rate of attrition in any war, would cause some problems. There is plenty of evidence that top quality horses were in short supply. They were also highly valued as a result; Edward sometimes gave a horse as a present to one of his great lords as a mark of particular esteem. As they were such an expensive commodity, the king was also responsible for compensating his men for any losses that they sustained during a campaign, even for feudal levies who were in other respects unpaid.[11] The situation was currently serious enough for Edward to order that all landowners with land worth more than £30 per year should hold a horse ready in reserve to send to the English army in case of emergency.[12]

It was at this point, when everything appeared to be going to plan, that stunning news came in that there had been a major reverse for the English in the south. By the time that Grey had advanced into north Wales in June 1282 there was also a smaller but still sizeable English force preparing to do the same in the south-west. There were 200 cavalry assembled around Carmarthen and Dinefwr. With them were some notable English Marcher lords, particularly the earl of Gloucester, Edward's 'captain' in the south, as well as William de Valence, the earl of Pembroke (Edward's uncle), and his son of the same name. Riding in support of them was Edward's old Welsh ally, Rhys ap Maredudd. Particularly prominent was Gloucester's predecessor as overall commander in the region, Robert Tibotot, who despite his apparent demotion was still at the heart of much of the organisation of the war.

Gloucester had been given specific orders by Edward. The king consistently took a close interest in the affairs of his individual commanders. In Gloucester's case, he had been ordered to retake Llandovery and hand it over into the safekeeping of John Giffard, as well as restoring Llanbadarn to English rule.[13] Again, this would be a two-pronged assault along the lines of that in 1277, with forces from the west and Brecon converging. On 11 June, a large party of 1,600 foot soldiers recruited from the areas around the English-held castles of Llanstephan and Cydweli, accompanied by 50 cavalry, set out from Dinefwr. Their immediate objective was Carreg Cennen, the remote hilltop stronghold which had been taken by Dafydd in April and left in a ruinous condition.

The expedition quickly took on the atmosphere of a picnic. There was no opposition to the advance of the English, who raided at leisure on their way to the castle. It was undefended and it was accordingly an easy job for the English to walk in and take over, though all they gained was the acquisition of a badly damaged shell. A number of men were instructed to remain in the castle and restore it to a defensible state. The rest of the force started to make their way back towards the coast.

The terrain in the region is hilly; not mountainous on the scale of the north but certainly rugged and more than capable of providing opportunities for an ambush. The English were laden down with plunder from their expedition. The combination of the booty they had acquired and the easy nature of their mission, given the complete absence of Welsh resistance, caused them to drop their guard. The details of what precisely happened next are sketchy but it appears that near Llandeilo Fawr the English force was attacked by a party of Welsh fighters that had been lying in wait for them. The English force had been over-confident, intoxicated by its success, and was ill-prepared to fight off the attack, which was pushed home by the Welsh with vigour. The result was a serious setback for the English. A number of lives were lost, including five knights, among them the younger William de Valence. The outcome was not, from the evidence that survives, catastrophic but it was still very serious for the English, who were forced back on to the defensive in the south as a result.

The Dominican friar Nicholas Trivet, a chronicler of the time, claimed that the result was an English victory. He was presumably misled by the fact that the Welsh guerrillas had retreated as rapidly as they had appeared, hardly a novel feature in guerrilla warfare. That the friar might have been better placed offering his opinion on religious rather than military affairs is suggested by a plethora of factors. The first is that following the so-called 'victory' that Trivet claimed, the English forces in the area were completely inactive for six weeks, hardly consistent with an English triumph. Shortly afterwards, on 6 July, the earl of Gloucester was replaced as commander in the south by the elder William de Valence. It is hardly tenable to suggest that such an abrupt change of command would have been imposed without Edward for some reason harbouring serious reservations about Gloucester as a military leader, which he had not had only a few months before when he had first appointed him. Coming so soon after the engagement at Llandeilo Fawr, which took place on 17 June, this again suggests a serious defeat for the English.

There is other compelling circumstantial evidence too. In the pay records, the number of cavalry drops. Just four days before replacing Gloucester with Valence, Edward instructed the feudal levy from the south-west of England to make their way to south Wales instead of to Rhuddlan, suggesting that they were needed more in the former location. Until fresh troops arrived, there was little that the new commander felt able to do other than remain on the defensive, although a half-hearted attempt was made to reoccupy Llanbadarn. Valence was presumably hampered by what also appears to be the disappearance of Gloucester at around this time, whether through a desire to hurry back to his lands and protect them from possible raids from the Welsh or from umbrage at his dismissal is not clear, though the likelihood is that it was a combination of the two.

But fresh troops did eventually arrive. Edward was fastidious in his assessment of even the smallest of details with regard to these recruits. Morris notes that he was quick to praise one of his men, Geoffrey de Camville, for committing his troops without pay when he was not obliged to, promising him that this would not count as a precedent in the future. At the same time, he rebuke the Sheriff of Somerset for sending him substandard troops.[14] Both comments give us an interesting insight into the workings of the feudal system as it was at this stage in its development. The whole set-up was a complex interaction of rights and obligations. Therefore, it was especially important to men like de Camville to be reassured that if they committed men when they were not legally required to, as a favour so to speak, then they would not be creating a precedent which they would be forced to follow again at some point in the future. However, the increasing use of the quota system, whereby the king's men were only required to deliver a percentage of the men strictly demanded by law rather than the whole levy could, if abused, create problems for the king. Devious lords could hand-pick those that the local community could most afford to do without to fulfil their obligation. Men who did not wish to go could even buy their way out of service. This clearly created the danger that the quality of men available to the king would be reduced as a result. Edward's censure of the Sheriff of Somerset shows that this danger was, on occasion, a very real one.

By the beginning of August, Valence felt confident enough to go on the offensive. Once again, his advance would coincide with a push by Giffard from the east. Giffard was quick to move. His enthusiasm was not fuelled only by thoughts of the greater glory of his king. He moved into lands in which he had a long-term interest. He would, after the war was over, retain some of them for good at the king's gift, much to the discomfiture of Rhys ap Maredudd. It was to the support of Rhys that Valence and his men came. He alone had stayed loyal to Edward, an action which inspired the king to grant him on 28 July the lands of his near neighbours who had revolted. At the time, this may have seemed a mixed blessing to Rhys, who was largely cut off by hostile forces. However, by the middle of August Valence's forces had reached Dinefwr and beyond, effectively securing his position. On the 17th of that month, we find Valence granting a small gift to Rhys's soldiers for the great efforts they had made on behalf of the relieving force.

Edward had, as was his custom, issued some quite specific instructions to Valence. He was to advance on Cardiganshire, where the two most prominent Welshmen opposed to him were Gruffudd and Cynan ap Maredudd. Their lands were to be taken from them in punishment for their resistance to English rule and handed instead to Rhys ap Maredudd. Valence had about 160 cavalry available. An accompanying army of 2,000 foot was also put together. These came from all over the March areas of Wales. There were men from Cardigan and Carmarthen, as well as others from Cydweli, the Gower and Gwent; the fact that these were all, in the strict sense of the word, Welshmen demonstrates again that the Welsh were still far from united.

The region was, from Llywelyn's point of view, dangerously vulnerable. It was a long way from the epicentre of his territories, away to the north in Gwynedd, and although it had often set itself against English rule, it was not traditionally at the heart of his sphere of influence. Given the main thrust of the English advance along the coastline of north Wales, Llywelyn could not afford to commit large numbers of reinforcements to the aid of Gruffudd and Cynan ap Maredudd ap Owain, his leading supporters in the area. They were, in other words, largely on their own against the English.

The two brothers had been prominent in the campaign of 1282 from the outset. In 1277, they had paid homage to Edward early on, along with Rhys ap Maredudd. However, they were quick to support Dafydd's uprising in the current war. The reasons for this change of allegiance are not hard to find. A petition to parliament in 1278 noted that Gruffudd had protested that he had lost half of his lands, despite his early support for Edward. The English king's insensitive handling of a number of Welsh lords (not, it might be said, wholly untypical of his actions in other spheres outside Wales) had in Gruffudd and Cynan's case come home to roost. On 24 March – just two days after Dafydd's night-time assault on Hawarden – Gruffudd had invited the constable of Llanbadarn to dinner, and had seized him and held him captive. Their men then took the castle and the town that had developed around it. They held it for only a short time before they abandoned it, ransacked and burning, with its walls smashed down. But now they had to look to their own salvation.

The English advance that followed was, it seems, substantially unopposed. We must assume that the Welsh lords, seeing the strength of the army moving towards them, melted away rather than commit themselves to a defence which would in all probability have been a futile one. Valence moved up to Llanbadarn, though it was still not permanently reoccupied, reflecting its exposed position. He then moved his men back to Cardiganshire, which was returned to English rule. The English had effectively ridden out the storm and survived the setback at Llandeilo.

One incident in particular typified the nature of warfare in this conflict. A letter from Robert Tibotot told how the garrison of Cardigan had been involved in a raid. They came back with a good deal of plunder though without eighteen of their men, who had been captured. Soon after, spies told Tibotot where Gruffudd and Cynan were. Tibotot marched his men across country at dead of night, accompanied by Rhys ap Maredudd. They attacked before they were spotted and, given the element of surprise, were almost completely successful. The only disappointment for the English was that Gruffudd and Cynan managed to escape. They did however manage to release the eighteen prisoners from Cardigan, and returned with a number of cattle they had taken in the raid, although Tibotot's figure of 3,000 surely owes more to wishful thinking than to accuracy.[15]

By mid-September, Cardiganshire was mainly quiet. By the time October had passed, so was Carmarthenshire. The retention of a strong garrison at Dinefwr shows that the English were concerned at the strength of the threat to them posed by the local Welsh forces. The satisfactory completion of the campaign in Cardiganshire meant that some of the foot soldiers raised by the feudal levy could now be diverted to Carmarthenshire. They were led by a troop of horse, about 40 strong, under the command of Alan Plukenet. The force, once again composed mainly of Welsh foot soldiers (paid at a wage of $1d$ per day as opposed to the English foot, who were paid $2d$ per day) advanced on Gruffudd ap Maredudd's base, taking and burning it. This seems to have been accomplished with great speed, suggesting that it was abandoned rather than defended by the Welsh.

Apart from an interesting reference to the receipt of pay, there is little noteworthy regarding affairs in the south. In October 1282, funds of 1,000 marks arrived. The movement of the money was a major logistical exercise, involving no little risk to the English. Men were sent out to guard it as it progressed. It had originally come from Lincolnshire to Chepstow, and from there on to Cardiff. On this latter stage, three cavalry and 12 foot soldiers were detached to guard it. The uncertain state of the country thereafter is best gauged by the deployment of no fewer than 400 men to protect it on the next stage of its journey to Swansea. The guard was reduced to sixty to bring it into Cydweli, giving a strong circumstantial hint as to where the bulk of Welsh resistance in the area was presently to be found. Another shipment of 1,250 marks received a different kind of protection. It was moved overland to Bristol from London, and then completed its journey by sea to Carmarthen, a very sensible precaution given the threat of an ambush from the Welsh.

The spectacular Welsh victory at Llandeilo Fawr was to be counter-balanced by news of great personal tragedy for Llywelyn. Although it had taken many years for their marriage finally to take place, Llywelyn and Eleanor de Montfort enjoyed a close relationship. She was assiduous in putting his case to her blood relative, King Edward. Just a month before the outbreak of war, we know that she was still in communication with Edward about everyday matters of state, English records noting the granting of a 'pardon, at the instance of Eleanor, Princess of Wales, the king's kinswoman, to Hugh de Ponte Fracto, Hugh le Keir and Philip le Taillur, for certain trespasses alleged against them.'[16] Llywelyn would also have hoped to improve his position by siring a successor. In 1280, his hopes appeared to be on the verge of fulfilment when Eleanor fell pregnant.

The depths of devastation he therefore felt when she died in giving birth to a daughter, Gwenllian, on 19 June 1281 can barely be imagined. There would be no son to take his place, now or in the future. This was a great personal blow. So too was the loss of Eleanor, for whom Llywelyn seems to have felt genuine affection. She had done much to help him in the few years they had spent together. As she was interred at the monastery of Llanfaes in Anglesey, many of Llywelyn's hopes were buried with her. It may be a coincidence of timing but Llywelyn's prosecution of the war is more widely reported after her death than before it. It was as if he now realised that his strategy for a peaceful restoration of his powers, of which dynastic considerations were an important part, was now dead and gone. He had little left to fight for but his pride. But to a man of Llywelyn's status and traditions that was perhaps the greatest motivator of all.

By the beginning of August, Edward was ready to advance in the north. The situation in the south had stabilised after the setback at Llandeilo Fawr. In the middle Marches, although there was probably a good deal of raiding and counter-raiding going on, there is little detail of the fighting that took place. We may therefore assume that the conflict was effectively conducted at a small-scale, local level. The absence of further detail suggests that the English were holding their own in the conflict, and that no serious reverses had been sustained there.

It has been suggested[17] that Edward's plan of campaign was a three-pronged one, with Grey synchronising his attack in the north with Valence's advance in the south and a thrust into the interior of mid-Wales by Roger Mortimer in the middle Marches. It is an entirely plausible scenario, though there is nothing other than circumstantial evidence to intimate that a major forward movement was made by Mortimer. Roger Lestrange would later write to Edward in November 1282, ruling out an advance over the Berwyn Mountains, a sentiment that is understandable to anybody who knows of the ruggedness of the terrain there. Rather, he suggested, 'the greatest damage that could be done to [the Welsh] from this time onwards is to guard the March carefully so that supplies do not pass to them', as a large volume of supplies were slipping through because the border territories were so difficult to guard.[18]

Such a plan would be consistent with Edward's capacity for strategic thinking. The movement of the three separate forces at more or less the same time – precise coordination would have been an impossibility – would have pulled the limited Welsh resources in three different directions simultaneously. The effectiveness of the Welsh defence would be much reduced as a result. Unable to fight on all these fronts concurrently, Llywelyn would be forced to concentrate his forces on Gwynedd, leaving relatively easy pickings for the English elsewhere. Such a scenario would explain the ease of Valence's subsequent advance in the south.

* * *

The scene was set for a final push by Edward. When he had last been in a similar position, in 1277, Llywelyn's defence had quickly dissolved. There seemed little possibility that the situation now would be any different. But there was one fundamental circumstance that differentiated the two campaigns. Llywelyn and Dafydd may have already surmised that Edward was unlikely to take kindly to being, as he saw it, personally crossed by them. Given his view of kingship, he would be very likely to see their revolt as a faithless act, deserving of no mercy on his part. The campaign now was one of conquest, a fight to the death. In such a situation, the only possible option for Llywelyn and his brother was to battle to the bitter end, fuelled by a desperation based on the fact that, for them personally and for their shrinking domains, defeat would inevitably lead to subjugation.

CHAPTER EIGHT

Invasion

[The Welsh] are passionately devoted to their freedom and to the defence of their country; for these they will fight, for these they will suffer hardships, for these they will take up their weapons and willingly sacrifice their lives.[1]

At the beginning of July, Edward's fleet was ready to assist him in his push into Wales. On the 15th of that month, a large detachment of crossbowmen and archers – over 300 in all – were placed on board the ships to serve as marines. This was a larger fleet than in 1277, reflecting the scale of the effort put into the campaign by Edward. There were in total forty ships and two large galleys (the king was theoretically entitled to summon fifty-seven ships). The overall cost of the fleet in the second Welsh war was £1,404. As in the previous campaign, smaller boats were bought locally, five of them in all.

Into August, the number of troops registered at Rhuddlan saw a consistently rising trend. At the start of the month there were 3,360 foot soldiers, increasing first to 4,420, then to 6,160 and finally to 8,180 by the end of the month. There were also approximately 750 cavalry available.[2] The gradual build-up is consistent with the English king preparing for a massive push against Llywelyn. There was once more a sizeable Welsh element included in Edward's forces.

Throughout September and October, the numbers of men at Rhuddlan varied significantly. A party of Gascon mercenaries joined Edward's armies during this time. The Gascons were highly valued though expensive troops. They caused considerable casualties among their opponents. At their maximum strength during the war, there were 210 Gascon horse and 1,313 infantry. The force cost £7,618, a considerable sum.[3] By the end of October, though, the total number of men actually with the king had greatly diminished. The reason for this is simple enough. Edward had sent out three separate columns to attack Llywelyn's domains. One would be under Grey operating from Dafydd's captured fortress at Hope, and another would operate under the command of the earl of Surrey. The third of them, under Luke de Tany, would cross over the Menai Strait and retake Llywelyn's granary in Anglesey.

De Tany had recently arrived from Gascony. He was well known to Edward, being another of his circle who had accompanied him on crusade. Edward instructed him to cross to Anglesey and take the island. In itself, this should not have proved to be too much of a challenge. The forces available to de Tany were more than enough to subdue the island. After that, he was to construct a bridge of boats across to the mainland so that Edward could launch attacks from Anglesey in the direction of Gwynedd. For the successful execution of this plan, the presence of the fleet was crucial. The Welsh were still resisting the English advance stoutly, and Edward would have to eliminate several strongpoints, such as Dafydd's headquarters at Denbigh, before being able to advance into Gwynedd. The ships that he had with him would at least let Edward move on Anglesey from the sea, enabling him to put this element of his plan into effect without completing the subjugation of the northern mainland of Wales and launch an attack on Gwynedd on several fronts.

A sizeable force was nevertheless allocated to de Tany for the conquest of the island. The occupation of Anglesey appears to have gone smoothly enough. Shortly after the English arrived on the island, there was a frenetic outburst of activity at Rhuddlan as vast amounts of supplies were made ready for onward shipment to Anglesey so that work on the construction of the bridge could commence. Quantities of building materials, timber, iron and nails were purchased, as well as more substantial items such as boats. Carpenters were sent over to put the bridge together. The fleet played a vital part in the operation, shipping supplies and men across the seas where they were immune from attack from the Welsh. In a move that would have caused Llywelyn much personal distress, Llanfaes, the last resting place of his recently departed wife, became the major English military base on the island.

By the end of September the bridge was completed. The ships were sent back to their home ports, a sensible step given the propensity of those who owned them to complain that the prolonged absence of their vessels seriously disrupted trade. Archers were placed in boats to guard the newly constructed bridge from Welsh counter-attacks now that the larger ships had gone. De Tany stood ready to await Edward's further orders, the nature of which would depend on how affairs developed on the mainland.

Edward was ready to renew his push on Gwynedd. He moved out from Rhuddlan accompanied by the earl of Lincoln, while Grey at the same time advanced from Hope. Further south, Surrey moved on Dinas Bran. All this was an extension of Edward's strategy to attack on several fronts at once, so that the Welsh defences would be overstretched. Early in September, Grey took possession of Ruthin and Edward, moving past

Denbigh, which was still in the hands of Dafydd's supporters, joined him there. Denbigh was now isolated and its fall was only a matter of time. There was no prospect of relief given Edward's overwhelming numerical advantage. Denbigh subsequently surrendered to the English in October.

The pace of the offensive needs to be noted. This was no quickfire advance, no 'blitzkreig', in modern parlance. It was slow progress into a land which was substantially opposed to the English. The relative slowness of the advance demonstrates two things, probably in more or less equal measure. It illustrates the prudence of Edward's tactics, demonstrating his determination to wait for the optimum moment before pushing forward. Supplies had to be secured, and siege engines brought up. But it also suggests that resistance was fierce, fuelled by widespread resentment at English rule in the area. As far as casualties are concerned, the evidence is scanty. But Edward was to note in October that the cemetery at Rhuddlan was full, which is circumstantial evidence suggestive of a savagely fought war.

Dinas Bran fell, and even at this stage of the campaign, with the end still some way off, the English began to divide up the spoils they had taken so far among themselves. Therefore, Dinas Bran was awarded to Surrey on 7 October, with much of the 'Four Cantreds' also being given to various of Edward's lords, with Lincoln and Grey each receiving significant territories (Lincoln for example was given Denbigh as well as many other parcels of territory, while Grey took Ruthin).

The English were now poised on the verge of final victory. The Welsh had been forced back into Snowdonia, their traditional bastion of last defence. The outer defences to the region were now almost exclusively in English hands. Spies were sent into Snowdonia to track the movements of the rebels. Llywelyn and Dafydd had virtually abandoned the south as a lost cause. Anglesey, with its precious food supplies, was now lost to Llywelyn and the island had become a base from which the English could launch an attack on Gwynedd from yet another direction. The mid-Welsh Marches had also seen some important English successes. It appeared that a noose had been placed around Gwynedd, and all that was needed was for the English to tighten it at their leisure, slowly strangling the life out of their enemies. It was easy to see why the English were confident enough to start to discuss how Wales would be divided up even before the war was over.

Thinking perhaps that the apparent hopelessness of their situation might encourage the Welsh to reach a negotiated settlement, John Pecham, the Archbishop of Canterbury, decided that he would approach Llywelyn to see if peace terms might be agreed. He was so keen to intercede that he had sent a Franciscan friar, John of Wales, ahead of him to begin discussions with Llywelyn while he made his way up through Herefordshire in October 1282. However, it soon became clear that the differences between Llywelyn and Edward were too great to be easily put aside.

John of Wales came accompanied with a document containing seventeen articles that Pecham wished to have considered. His stance was clear; the Welsh were wrong to reject their lawful lord, and should halt their unlawful rebellion. Otherwise, Pecham would have to report their transgressions to Rome, with potentially serious effects for the rebels. He particularly castigated them for committing violence in Holy Week, and further went on to say that they were in some ways worse than Saracens, for they slaughtered their prisoners even when they had received ransom money for them. It was clear from the outset that Pecham was no impartial observer. From the start, the process took on the aura more of a lecture than a negotiation.

Llywelyn responded to his initial overtures firmly but in a measured fashion. He desired peace as much as the next man. All that was needed to bring it about was a recognition of the rights of the Welsh people and the applicability of Welsh law in Wales. This neatly turned the argument on its head; this was the very reason the war had started in the first place. As for war crimes, Pecham should know that churches had been burned, the country ravaged and children killed in their mothers' arms.

Llywelyn then went on to describe his grievances further, and it is worth considering them, as the statement made at this time is the only surviving evidence of his reasons for being at war with Edward. He outlined his resentment at the progress of the Arwystli case. He claimed that the English had imposed English law in areas like Anglesey and denied the Welsh use of their own laws and customs as a result. He also commented that those in the 'Four Cantreds' had seen unjust English laws imposed on them; they might no longer be his direct responsibility but that did not mean that he no longer had any interest in them. He made particular reference to the abuses of Grey. It was a substantial catalogue of complaints. It was a convincing manifesto at any event because, when Pecham received the reply, he urged Edward to consider the grievances objectively.

Edward responded that, if he had genuine complaints to make, then the prince of Wales should have put them before him to arbitrate on rather than resort to arms. It was a disingenuous answer given Edward's refusal to reach a decision on matters such as the Arwystli case. But it illustrated well enough that the king was not to be persuaded to soften his stance, that this particular war would only be concluded on Edward's terms. Instead, it seems probable that, from the outset, Pecham's initiative was less than welcome to Edward as he by now appeared to be in the winning position. Certainly, Pecham made clear to Llywelyn that he had commenced discussions against the king's better judgement.

Pecham decided to journey into Snowdonia for face-to-face discussions. It was a commendable decision on his part, though not necessarily a reckless one. Pecham was first and foremost a member of the church in Llywelyn's eyes, rather than an Englishman, and was therefore likely to receive a more respectful welcome. Nonetheless, Pecham would have made the journey with no confidence whatsoever of a successful outcome. His worst fears were quickly confirmed; Llywelyn would only seek peace on what he regarded as reasonable terms and Edward would offer no terms save unconditional surrender. The two positions were irreconcilable. Pecham returned disappointed.

Subsequently Pecham approached Llywelyn again in writing. Nothing was offered of substance. In secret, some concessions were made but they were extraordinary in concept and completely unacceptable, as Edward must have known they would be. It was never likely that these negotiations would succeed. The secret terms offered by Edward demonstrated little in the way of compromise. The prince would be given lands worth £1,000 per year in England but in return he must give up Gwynedd and his other Welsh lands. It is hardly likely that Edward expected this offer to be taken up; if he did, then he surely completely misunderstood his opponent.

For Dafydd, there was nothing. He was to go on crusade, into exile. He was not to return unless recalled by Edward, something that was unlikely to happen for some time, if ever.[4] The king obviously felt that Dafydd's crime in instigating the rebellion was the greater offence when compared to Llywelyn's subsequent reactions and that he should count himself lucky to escape with his life. There was another ominous proposal involved. Under the terms proposed by the English, Edward would take into his care the children of Llywelyn and Dafydd. While the taking of hostages was far from unusual in medieval times, the proposal does illustrate how Edward was prepared to employ a whole range of methods to achieve his ends.

Dafydd responded negatively, comparing the harsh terms of the offer made to him with the much greater clemency that Edward had shown towards some of his recalcitrant English subjects in the past. Llywelyn responded to Edward's uncompromising terms imperiously. In a wonderfully eloquent reply, his leading supporters told Edward that 'the Prince should not throw aside his inheritance and that of his ancestors in Wales and accept land in England, a country with whose language, way of life, laws and customs he is unfamiliar . . . and even if the Prince wishes to transfer his people into the hands of the king, they will not do homage to any stranger as they are wholly unacquainted with his language, his way of life and his laws'.[5] It was an inspiring rejection of what they saw as an attempt by a powerful neighbour to bully them into surrendering their independence, their freedom and their culture; a refrain one hears in some quarters to this day. It was very much in keeping with the words of a Welshman of the previous century, who had proudly told Henry II of England that he was 'persuaded that no other race than this and no other tongue than this of Wales, happen what may, will answer in the great day of judgement for this little corner of the earth'.[6]

Other reasons for the rejection were given. The Welsh appealed to history in defence of their right to retain their possessions, saying that their claims to the land emanated from Brutus, a fugitive from ancient Troy who had fled to Britain and established the country.[7] Desperate as such a claim might seem, such mythological antecedents were employed on other occasions during the Middle Ages in support of land claims. More convincingly perhaps, they also pointed out that their rights had been confirmed in the reign of Edward's father by the terms of the Treaty of Montgomery and that these had been ratified by the papal legate, Ottobuono. In other words, even the papacy had confirmed the rights of the Welsh to their lands.

Any possibility of a negotiated settlement ended when news came in of a shocking defeat for the English. Luke de Tany had been given specific instructions not to leave Anglesey for an attack on the mainland until ordered to do so by Edward. He nevertheless decided to take matters into his own hands. On 6 November, with a sizeable force of 300 horsemen, accompanied by many infantry, he crossed over to the Welsh mainland. His motives for doing so are unclear. A variety of plausible suggestions have been put forward. One of them was that de Tany was disturbed at the prospect of peace negotiations depriving him of his hoped-for gains in the war, so in an attempt to stake his claim for a higher prize he attempted to win a quick victory over the Welsh. He may also have been encouraged to attack by Roger Clifford, son of the same name of the English lord who had been captured at Hawarden. This was the motive given by the chronicler of the Lincolnshire abbey of Hagnaby. Clifford was with de Tany on Anglesey and would have been keen to ensure his father's release, which he may have hoped a raid would bring about.

Another possibility is that de Tany had been replaced as commander in Anglesey by the earl of Hereford and he was piqued at his demotion. However, we cannot be sure that this was the case; it is known that Hereford had recently joined Edward in the north and there are strong signs in the records that he was sent to Anglesey, though it is not clear from the same records whether or not de Tany was replaced as commander as a result. Yet another version has it that de Tany deliberately intended to sabotage the peace negotiations by his actions.[8]

There may have been elements of truth in some or all of these proffered motives. It would be wrong to assume that, despite his powerful and direct personality, Edward was in a position to dictate de Tany's every move. Even though Edward took control of the campaigns in Wales in a very direct way, he could not be everywhere at once and a headstrong lieutenant could wreck his plans with one ill-judged act. In medieval times, commanders were notorious for exercising their own initiative, often with disastrous results. But by his conduct de Tany gave ample evidence of two things. The first is that, by his uncoordinated action and his refusal to do as he had been instructed by Edward, that is to be patient, he showed a lack of strategic awareness that was all too typical of many medieval warriors. The second is that, by his actual conduct of the raid, de Tany exhibited shortcomings in his tactical ability that suggested that he was poorly fitted to be the commander of an important part of Edward's army.

The chroniclers' detailed accounts of de Tany's precise movements are conflicting, though they all agree as to their outcome. In one account,[9] he crossed over to the mainland when the bridge of boats was not quite completed. His force advanced towards the mountains. As they did so, the tide moved in behind them, severing their escape route back to Anglesey. They were however being closely watched from the mountains. When they were effectively caught between the waters of the Menai Strait which were now blocking their retreat and the mountains, the Welsh 'came over from the high mountains and attacked them, and in fear and trepidation, for the great number of the enemy, our men preferred to face the sea and the enemy. They went into the sea but, heavily laden with arms, they were instantly drowned'. A number of English knights and men of some standing, including de Tany himself and Clifford, perished. In all, sixteen knights – a significant number – were lost as well as other men. One knight, William Latimer, had an amazing escape, only managing to survive by encouraging his horse to swim the Straits. Otto de Grandson, too, escaped death by a hairsbreadth.

This account is convincing in many of its details. Indeed, in many ways it is uncannily similar to the later English defeat at Stirling Bridge in Scotland, when an English army, carelessly crossing a river, was overwhelmed by a large Scottish force hidden in the lee of a large hill. The failure to deploy adequate scouts was a foolish, though oft-repeated, mistake to make when campaigning in hostile territory. However, there are problems in taking this account at face value. It is hard to imagine why Edward would move the fleet and the carpenters when the bridge to the mainland was not complete (the surviving records show that they had already been released by this time), and difficult to understand why de Tany would want to cross the Menai Strait before it was. It is more likely, as other chroniclers suggest, that the bridge collapsed under the weight of the panic-stricken English as they fled from the Welsh; or that they simply retreated in such a disorderly fashion that there was a crush at the bridge as they all attempted to cross it at once, giving the Welsh an excellent opportunity to cause carnage among their massed ranks.

In the *Brut y Tywysogyon* the chronicler notes that the English 'made a bridge over the Menai; but the bridge broke under an excessive load, and countless numbers of the English were drowned and others slain'. In Matthew of Westminster's account, the writer says that 'the king, wishing to advance onwards and supported by his ships, caused a large bridge to be built over the waters of the Conway, which ebb and flow near the mountain of Snowdon; and some of the king's army passing over this bridge for the sake of exercise were set upon and, being alarmed by the number of shouts of the Welsh who came against them, endeavoured unsuccessfully to effect their return into the island of Anglesey, from which they had come, but were miserably drowned in the water'.[10] Matthew goes on to say that the Welsh ascribed this great triumph to a miracle and called to mind the prophecy of Merlin that a Briton would be crowned once more in London.

The battle fought during the retreat was savage. There is definitive evidence of this from a macabre source. Excavations at Hulton Abbey centuries later resulted in analysis of the skeletal remains of William Audley, hacked to death in the battle. The damage inflicted by blows from Welsh swords was clearly evident. A brief examination of his campaign reveals that Audley played an important role. He had joined Mortimer in March 1282 and had received the submission of Owain ap Gruffudd ap Madog in June. By October, he was in command of 500 troops at Rhuddlan. A month later he was dead, his shattered corpse washed up by the grey waters of the Menai Strait.[11]

De Tany's defeat caused Edward to reassess his plans. He would surely have been incensed with de Tany had he survived, for the defeat did cause some amendment to his plans. It is firstly notable that sensible negotiations between Pecham and the Welsh were called off soon after. Pecham's discussions were in any case a vexation that Edward could do without, as they had already introduced an element of delay that must have been irksome to him. The defeat of de Tany had made a peaceful resolution even more unlikely. From Llywelyn's perspective, he must have been encouraged by the reverse. In Edward's eyes, a decisive English victory became even more of a priority now. His vision of kingship, whereby ultimate authority and power were vested in the crown, could not be compromised by showing weakness when events did not go his way. De Tany's defeat made Edward more determined than ever to crush all Welsh resistance.

The king was nevertheless certainly forced to re-evaluate his position in the aftermath of the news from Anglesey. He had been poised to pounce on Gwynedd from all sides before the setback, perhaps hoping to crush it in a vice-like grip before the imminent winter period. Now, however, he stayed at Rhuddlan until he had rebuilt his strength. Soon after, reinforcements from Gascony arrived and, early in December, Edward sent orders to England, commanding that more infantry be sent to Wales. He was clearly even now set on a decisive winter campaign, and the setback experienced in Anglesey was only a temporary inconvenience as far as he was concerned.

Even Pecham decided that no more could be done to halt the war. He reminded the rebels that, in the Old Testament, although the Chosen People were often defeated they always triumphed in the end. Apparently, even God was on the side of the English. It is likely that Pecham now at last decided to excommunicate Llywelyn in person. Although there is no documentary evidence of this, issues concerning the treatment of Llywelyn's body after his death suggest that he died outside the community of the church. Pecham had been careful to hold back this spiritual thunderbolt to the last, and had previously told John of Wales not to mention it as a possibility to Llywelyn as he feared it would jeopardise negotiations. With those discussions now ended, there was no further barrier to him excommunicating Llywelyn personally, particularly as he so obviously believed him to be in the wrong in this affair.

But, just as the war appeared to change direction after the defeat of the English forces on Anglesey, there was to be another dramatic change of fortune that would effectively destroy any realistic hope of the Welsh successfully resisting Edward's campaign. Early in December 1282, news of the utmost import reached Edward. He received a despatch from the mid-Welsh Marches of the greatest possible significance. It was phrased in the most laconic way imaginable, but the plain English could not disguise the significance of the message, which simply said: 'Know, sire, that Llywelyn ap Gruffudd is dead, his army broken, and all the flower of his men killed.'

CHAPTER NINE

Dies Irae

Glory to God in the highest, peace on earth to men of goodwill,
a triumph to the English, victory to King Edward
. . . and to the Welsh, everlasting extermination.[1]

'And there was done the betrayal of Llywelyn in the belfry of Bangor by his own men.' This sinister comment, from the Welsh chronicle *Brut y Tywysogyon*, is all the significant evidence that remains that Llywelyn, prince of Wales, was betrayed to his enemies by his own followers. But it must be said that, even for an era when the accounts of chroniclers are notoriously unreliable and inconsistent, huge question marks remain over the death of Llywelyn. The great Welsh historian J.E. Lloyd was able for example to satisfy himself on where and when the battle where Llywelyn met his death was fought; but, as to whether or not treachery was involved, he would commit himself only to an open verdict, albeit one in which the Mortimer family was possibly implicated in suspicious activities.[2] It has never been authoritatively established why exactly Llywelyn made the ill-fated foray into the mid-Welsh Marches that ended in his death, though some sensible strategic reasons why he may have wished to have done so can be postulated. But establishing the exact sequence of events once he arrived there is like trying to pick a way through an impenetrable fog in a landscape that has few signposts or maps to assist the historian. Chroniclers cannot even agree whether he died in a major pitched battle or in a small skirmish when he was isolated from the rest of his army. The only certainty is that he was killed, and with him died all hope of a viable, independent Wales.

To make any sense of these momentous events, we must first of all try to recreate the atmosphere existing in Wales in November 1282. In that month, two events of great significance occurred. The first of them was the heavy defeat of the English forces at the Menai Strait. This setback changed the picture radically but its results stimulated the need for Llywelyn to act quickly as much as they did Edward to retaliate decisively. The defeat would force Edward to revise his plans, of that there was little doubt, but it also gave Llywelyn a marvellous opportunity to turn a significant victory into something with longer-lasting results. By striking another blow against Edward while he was hopefully off balance as a result of the defeat, his entire campaign might be sent off-course. Such opportunities would be few and far between in the campaign and Llywelyn's chance to take advantage of this one would be short-lived, as English reinforcements would certainly be called up to replace the men lost. Llywelyn could not afford to pass up the chance offered him by the catastrophe that had befallen de Tany.

It was a coincidence of timing that was responsible for the second significant event. Roger Mortimer had been one of the crown's most trusted lieutenants, both for Edward I and for his father, Henry III. He had done much to assist Edward, both in 1277 and during the current campaign. His death late in 1282 was therefore a major blow for Edward. It introduced an element of instability into a crucial region at a time when the monarch could ill afford it. This only serves to make the king's subsequent reaction all the more bizarre.

Mortimer's heir was his eldest son, Edmund. We have good reason to think that the relationship between the king and Edmund was amicable. Just a few months before Roger Mortimer's death, Edward had granted the custody of Oswestry and Arundel to Edmund Mortimer until its rightful owner had attained the age when he could hold it in his own right. But for whatever reason, instead of handing the late lord's lands – which were admittedly substantial – over to Edmund, the king prevaricated. A record of proceedings at Denbigh soon after Roger Mortimer's death noted the 'appointment, during pleasure, of Roger Springehoes, sheriff of Salop and Stafford, to the custody of the castles, lands and tenements late of Roger de Mortuo Mori (Mortimer) the elder, deceased, tenant in chief, to those counties in Wales, and in the Marches of Wales'.[3] In other words, Springhouse was to hold the lands on behalf of the king until Edward had finally decided what to do with them.

There are perhaps two strong motivations for this course of action, of which the second appears the more likely on the basis of what is, admittedly, limited information. The first is that Edmund Mortimer had done something to offend Edward. It has been noted that while the king sent a letter of condolence on his father's death to the younger son, also named Roger, no such letter was sent to Edmund.[4] It is a small piece of evidence on which to construct a theory that Edmund had somehow incurred the displeasure of the king but it is nevertheless an interesting and suggestive observation.

The other explanation is that Edward was waiting to see if he could use the opportunity to strengthen his own position at the expense of what was after all a very powerful Marcher lordship. Such opportunities came along only rarely. That Edward was an opportunist of the first order is beyond dispute. There is no direct evidence that he planned to intervene permanently in Edmund's inheritance at this particular time but such a course of action was at least consistent with his temperament. At any event, Edward's actions did nothing to increase stability in the Marches. Springhouse was to write urgently to the king during November, saying that the local populace was surly and unsettled, and in his view the situation would only be resolved when their rightful lord was confirmed and in situ. Llywelyn would have been aware of this unrest. Further, he had other evidence that matters in the south were not as secure as the English might wish them to be. Humphrey de Bohun, nearby in Brecon, had experienced problems with the Welsh living there earlier that year. A new front further south might well be in his interests. It would distract Edward from the major assault in the north. It therefore made strategic sense to involve himself here, particularly given the unrest prevalent in the area.

But there may have been other reasons for Llywelyn's presence in the area of Builth. Edmund Mortimer found himself in a difficult position when he was not awarded his father's lands as of right. It was an embarrassing and potentially difficult situation for him. His future seemed under threat. Even if he were subsequently to receive his lands, he would not wish to commence his lordship at odds with the king, a dangerous man to antagonise. It was therefore in his interests to do something that would ingratiate himself to Edward. Some chroniclers are quite specific as to what form such actions might have taken. The Hagnaby chronicler states bluntly that Llywelyn was lured into the region of Builth so that he could receive the homage of the Mortimers and was instead led straight into a trap. Other accounts, such as that from the Abbey of Dunstable, make similar accusations. The chronicler from Osney states that Mortimer trapped Llywelyn so that he could 'win the king's heart'.

It is hard to credit that Llywelyn would be taken in by this ruse, were it not for the uncertain situation in the lands of the late Roger Mortimer existing at that time. But there is another piece of evidence that must be introduced to the argument. After Llywelyn was killed, Archbishop Pecham proceeded to hurry down to the area to see for himself how matters stood. Less than a week after Llywelyn died, Pecham was writing to the king and his chancellor Robert Burnell, saying that two things had been found on the prince's body. The first was his privy seal. The second

item was however something far more surprising. He was apparently
carrying with him a treasonable letter, disguised with false names, as
Pecham put it, though we have no knowledge of which men the letter
might have incriminated as unfortunately the original letter has not
survived the ravages of time. At any event, Pecham's main interest seems
to have been in playing down the significance of the letter.[5] His account
was, though, couched in very suggestive terms. He wrote to Edward that
'those who were at the death of Llywelyn found in the most secret parts
of his body some small things that we have seen. Among the other things
there was a treasonable letter disguised by false names.' It is just a pity
that those names have been lost to posterity. Was Mortimer's one of
them?

Other suggestions that treasonable activities were involved in the death
of Llywelyn have less evidence to substantiate them. One writer has
hinted that Archbishop Pecham's own role in the events leading up to
that fatal day near Builth was far from honourable.[6] The existence of a
mysterious figure called Brother Adam, an envoy at Llywelyn's court, who
was ordered to return to Pecham on the very day that the prince was
killed in battle, certainly raises some interesting questions.

Given the lack of concrete evidence, we can do little more than take an
informed guess at what happened in the build-up to that dramatic day.
The man against whom there is most evidence is Edmund Mortimer and
his brother Roger. A number of chroniclers suggest that they were
inextricably involved in these events. Edmund in particular had strong
motives for attempting to ensure that he was in Edward's favour. It is even
mentioned in contemporary accounts that his servants and retainers were
the first to be found swarming around Llywelyn's body after the prince
was killed. The evidence is suggestive, without being strong enough to
stand up in any court of law.

The evidence against Pecham, however, is flimsy and largely circumstantial. What did he have to gain? He had already excommunicated the
apostate prince, the worst fate imaginable; while his ultimate loyalty lay
with the Pope in Rome. Equally, accusations that Llywelyn was betrayed
by one of his own entourage cannot be proved. It is certainly not
inconceivable that there was treason plotted 'in the belfry of Bangor'.
Such treason was far from unknown in the annals of Welsh history. As
one writer has noted, 'the very existence of the [alleged] conspiracy in
1282 suggests that the collapse of Gwynedd was not regarded as an
unmixed tragedy by some, at least, of Llywelyn's influential
contemporaries in Gwynedd'.[7] It is not unreasonable to suggest that
Edmund Mortimer hatched a plot with the aid of some members of
Llywelyn's inner circle, though who these men might have been we

cannot be at all certain. It is a tantalising, even fascinating, mystery and one that leaves many questions unanswered.[8]

It would be reassuring if we could say that we had a much clearer picture of the events of the battle itself than we do of the events leading up to it. Sad to say, the facts of 11 December 1282 are every bit as murky as those described above. There is one point that is beyond dispute, and it perhaps lends credence to the fact that there may have been some conspiracy involved, leading to Llywelyn's death. Waiting for Llywelyn as he moved towards Builth was a substantial English army. Some accounts place every English leader of note from that region of the Marches there. The army was probably led by Roger Lestrange, though the chroniclers do not even concur on this.[9] With Lestrange were Edmund and the younger Roger Mortimer. Gruffudd ap Gwenwynwyn, Llywelyn's bitter rival, was there. So too was Peter Corbet, the man whom Llywelyn had dispossessed of many of his lands a few years earlier. John Giffard was also present. The concentration of such a powerful force suggests that the English were expecting Llywelyn when he arrived.

The *Brut y Tywysogyon* places the battle close to the town of Builth, where the rivers Wye and Irfon converge. Because of this, the conflict became known as the Battle of Irfon Bridge (in some accounts, Orewin Bridge). It is English accounts that supply details of the battle itself, though they are extremely contradictory in the versions that they offer. One of the most significant of them is that of Walter of Guisborough, a northern writer who penned his chronicle a quarter of a century after the events he described had taken place. In his version, Llywelyn came down from the mountains accompanied by just one servant to see whether or not there was support for him in the region. One is immediately suspicious as to the accuracy of the account; it was a remarkably small escort for Llywelyn to take with him into uncertain territory. He left his army guarding a bridge over the Irfon while he was away.

The English army felt unable to force a crossing while the bridge was thus protected. However, a Welsh traitor by the name of Helias Walwyn showed them a ford that they could cross. The English could then surreptitiously ford the river and attack the Welsh from the flanks, driving the defenders away from the bridge, and letting the rest of their forces cross. This they did, with success. The Welsh were driven from the bridge by the ferocity of the attack, and the main part of the English army then swarmed over. They launched an assault on the Welsh, who had hurriedly regrouped.

Hearing the noise of battle, Llywelyn, who was apart from his troops still, rushed back. On his way to rejoin his men he was struck down by an English soldier, who did not recognise him. Unprotected, as he was not wearing his armour – an illustration of how much he had been taken by surprise by events – he fell, mortally wounded. In the meantime, the Welsh suffered heavy losses as the English pushed home their attack relentlessly. At the close of the day, the soldier who had struck Llywelyn down returned to where he still lay. Now, at last recognising his victim, he drew his sword and struck off Llywelyn's head. It was sent to the king as incontrovertible proof that his major adversary was dead.

There are grounds to be suspicious of this account. There are details that Guisborough alone mentions, for example those of the bridge and the ford. Further, it has been pointed out that there are marked similarities between his account of the battle and that at Stirling Bridge against the Scots some fifteen years later (with the admittedly rather important detail that the latter battle ended in a heavy English defeat).[10] It is particularly striking that, shortly before his account of the Battle of Stirling Bridge in his chronicle, Guisborough mentions that a group of Scots surrendered to Edward at Irewyn – one letter different from the chronicler's Welsh battle site at Orewyn: hardly conclusive evidence perhaps but a strange coincidence at least. And his account is not corroborated by any independent source. This version is very different from that of the monk who wrote the chronicle of the Abbey of Hagnaby.

This, it may be remembered, was the version which suggests that Llywelyn was lured into the region by the Mortimers. According to this account, Llywelyn arrived on the field of battle at a time that had been prearranged with the Mortimers, with whom he believed he would be entering into some form of alliance. It was not until he arrived that the full import of what was taking place suddenly struck him. The vast size of the force before him, and their aggressive demeanour, spoke unmistakably of treason. It would quickly have been apparent to the prince that he had been duped. He was, however, as one poet noted 'a man who did not wish to flee the nearest way' and it may anyway have been too late to run. The battle was joined, but the result was a formality. Eventually Llywelyn was trapped, alone with one of his servants, and struck down by his enemies, even though he called out his name so that he would be recognised.

The version found in the Peterborough Chronicle has received strong support in modern times, as an account which it is claimed 'deserves to be treated with respect' and which 'suggests an account based on substantial authority'.[11] It provides some interesting extra detail about the battle. This version claims that Llywelyn made his way to the region around Builth to receive homage from men previously in the service of the Mortimers. However, a number of prominent Marcher lords drew up their forces to bring him to battle. The list includes Roger Lestrange, John Giffard, the sons of the late Roger Mortimer, the sons of Gruffudd ap Gwenwynwyn, John Lestrange and Peter Corbet, as well as other less well-known but still important men. There is interesting corroborative evidence that some at least of these men were in the area and supporting Roger Lestrange in the form of an order from Edward telling them to support him in the area, the order dated 30 October of that year. At a predetermined spot, they came across the rebel army at around the hour of vespers (early evening), killed Llywelyn and cut off his head.

The battle was brutal but totally one-sided. The chronicler claims that 'not one of the prince's horsemen escaped death' (after earlier stating that 160 of them were present at the battle) and that 'three thousand foot soldiers' (out of 7,000) were also slain. At Llywelyn's side fell three leading Welsh magnates, two of whom may be identified as Llywelyn ap Gruffudd Fychan of Powys, who had already lost lands to the Mortimers, and Rhys ap Gruffudd, bailiff of Builth, a man with strong local contacts. It is the chronicler's accounts of English casualties that are especially interesting, as he states that 'none of the English was killed or wounded there'.

The statement that there were no English casualties is in stark contrast to that of the Hagnaby Chronicle, which tells how 'very many fell on both sides', although going on to say that in the end the Welsh were slaughtered in great numbers (they were 'almost all killed'). It does appear to stretch credibility that there were no English casualties whatsoever in a battle of this size, and such claims should be treated with a large pinch of salt. If, however, it is accepted that the Peterborough chronicler's account implies that the English losses were very small, then there is a logical flow to this account. Such a one-sided victory is consistent with an army attacking another with its guard down. The element of surprise achieved by the English is compounded by the fact that they attacked in the fading winter light. It is not without its merits as a hypothesis concerning what really happened on 11 December 1282.

Other versions provide varying sequences of events. In some, Llywelyn is caught by surprise and overwhelmed, accompanied by only a few retainers, in others there was a great battle between large armies. It is virtually impossible to recreate the facts, and no hypothesis can be proved beyond all reasonable doubt. But with the few scraps that we do have it is possible to present a plausible argument, of a young English lord, Edmund Mortimer, probably in league with his brother Roger, who wished to show his king that he was worthy of his inheritance, who subsequently made overtures to Llywelyn, a man with whom his late father had reached an understanding shortly before his death. In this version, Llywelyn, confidently expecting to find a potential ally at that fateful spot near Builth, instead arrives on the field of battle to find the combined might of the mid-Welsh March drawn up, ready for battle. The English forces overwhelm their victim, caught like a fly in the web of a spider, and cut off his head as a trophy for their king. The future of young Edmund Mortimer is now assured.

There are even some suggestions as to the identity of the man who killed Llywelyn. Guisborough says that he was a man named Stephen de Frankton. He was a known associate of Lestrange, and is therefore a feasible candidate for the role. However, another account, by an early fourteenth-century chronicler, Robert Manning, names a knight called Robert Body. In this latter version, the writer notes that Body 'promptly dismounted and cut off Llywelyn's head'. It is perfectly feasible that both men played a part in the death of Llywelyn. The wording of Manning's account means that it was quite possible that Frankton killed the prince, but that later Body came along and cut off his head as proof of the deed.[12] Manning also suggests that Roger Lestrange was in command of the English army and it is known that Roger Body was in his entourage. There is supporting evidence that Body was in Wales at about this time too: four months later we find him with Lestrange at the siege of Castell y Bere. Manning's account is of particular interest because it has Llywelyn captured and killed later in cold blood: more of an execution than a death on the field of battle.

Edward was so eager to let the Pope in Rome know of this signal victory that his messenger reached the pontiff in five weeks even though western Europe was in the grip of winter, half the time of the normal journey. There were, predictably, very different reactions to Llywelyn's demise from those who were for him and those who were against him. Against the crowing sentiments of Stephen of St George (see this chapter's epigraph), a Welsh supporter composed Llywelyn the Last's epitaph:

> Here lies the scourge of England.
> Snowdonia's guardian sure,
> Llywelyn, Prince of Wales,
> In character most pure.
> Of modern kings the jewel,
> Of kings long past the flower,
> For kings to come a pattern,
> Radiant in lawful power.

The Welsh poet Gruffudd ab yr Ynad Coch expressed his grief more eloquently than most, a grief accompanied by an unmistakable certainty that Llywelyn's dreams died with him:

> Have you no belief in God, foolish men?
> See you not that the world is ending?
> Ah God, that the sea would cover the land!
> What is left us that we should linger?
> No place to flee from terror's prison,
> No place to live: wretched is living!
> No counsel, no clasp, no path left open
> One way to be freed from fear's sad strife . . .
> All the weak, all the strong he kept safe:
> All children now cry in their cradles.[13]

This contrasted greatly with the sentiments of an English poet, who wrote,

> Here lies the prince of errors,
> A traitor and a thief.
> A flaring, flaming firebrand,
> The malefactors' chief.

This latter writer did his best to demonise Llywelyn as thoroughly as possible, going on to describe the prince with a mixture of exaggeration and respect for his skills as 'the wild Welsh evil genius'. Even in death, Llywelyn had the power to divide and confuse people.[14]

Llywelyn's head was sent to London, where it was stuck on a spike and crowned with ivy, a mocking allusion to a story that one of the Britons, from whom the Welsh traced their descent, would one day be crowned king of England. As for his body, we cannot be sure, but some chroniclers assert that it was buried in the Abbey of Cwmhir, a peaceful sanctuary of the Cistercians, with whom Llywelyn had enjoyed an amicable relationship. It is probable that he had been excommunicated by Pecham after the peace negotiations had broken down. A cousin of Llywelyn's, Maud Longespee, the wife of John Giffard, wrote to Pecham shortly after Llywelyn's death asking that his body should be given a decent Christian burial. After making various enquiries as to his spiritual state at the time of his death he may well have sanctioned the request. He certainly believed that Llywelyn was concerned for his spiritual wellbeing right until the end, noting that the 'very day he was killed, a white monk [i.e. a Cistercian] sang mass to him'.

The treatment of Llywelyn's head, contrasted with the (admittedly apocryphal) reverential treatment of the rest of his body, illustrates as well as anything the differing emotions he aroused in men, depending on whether they were friend or foe. But, whatever the observer's perspective, there was no doubting that his death was a hammer blow to the Welsh.

* * *

Llywelyn had been the driving force behind the power of Gwynedd for thirty years and more. He was an astute politician and a capable military leader. In earlier years he had been possessed of great energy though his less prominent role at the outbreak of war in this latest campaign suggests that he was slowing down.

He was not without his faults. The fact that there were few obituaries for Llywelyn among Welsh chroniclers has been noted by historians,[15] and suggests that there were many, even among his own countrymen, who were unconvinced of his merits. He could be harsh even with his own people, reflecting the fact that although he was richer than his predecessors, he did not have sufficient funds to fulfil his ambitions and subjected his people to punitive levels of taxation. He could be high-handed, and he managed to alienate a number of lords whom he should have tried to keep as his supporters. In this respect at least, he was a kindred spirit of the English king. The similarities between Llywelyn and Edward were marked. One epitaph of Llywelyn describes him in the following terms: 'He was able to make use of the opportunities created by others and reap a rich harvest', and 'where persuasion and common interest failed to win support, he was prepared to rely on discipline and coercion'.[16] Those comments would not be out of place in any analysis of Edward I.

Llywelyn was a man of steely determination, wedded to the attainment of his own ambitions at all costs. He has also rightly been described as 'a man of resilience, willing to bide his time and use the bitter experience of defeat to reconstruct the basis of his power'[17] – and indeed his ability to remain determined despite severe setbacks would have earned him the admiration of his near-contemporary, Robert de Bruce of Scotland, who endured similar vicissitudes. But his judgement let him down. He made enemies among his own people, even his own family. One assessment states categorically that 'the great majority of their [i.e. the princes of Gwynedd's] vassals opposed the imperialism of Gwynedd and were too often inclined to side with the Crown against the pretensions of her princes: it cannot be too strongly emphasised that the ultimate failure of Gwynedd's efforts to solve the Welsh political problem was due as much to the opposition of the Welsh lords as it was to the power of Edward I'.[18] Llywelyn alienated the Marcher lords and united their considerable powers against him. Most of all, he completely misjudged the temper of

Edward I of England, a man with many of the qualities of obstinacy and sensitivity about his own position notable in Llywelyn – but with the resources to back them up.

It is surely right to say that, from a Welsh perspective, no one could take Llywelyn's place. One analysis of the situation is that 'the day's events [i.e. the Battle of Irfon Bridge] were remembered in history not only as the end of an independent Wales but also as the final event in the history of the British nation. English and Scottish chroniclers alike saw in Llywelyn's death the extinction of the glory of the Britons, and its permanent acquisition of the nation by the English.'[19] But it is equally difficult to avoid the conclusion that his death now made little difference. The campaign had been conducted in such a manner that the superior English resources had been used to create a decisive advantage. If men were lost, Edward could replace them. In the November of 1282 – the month of de Tany's disastrous foray across the Menai Strait – he had, for example, received into his service a large number of new men from Gascony: 21 knights, 52 mounted crossbowmen and 533 infantry.[20] Edward would have maximised that advantage whether or not Llywelyn was still alive. All that Llywelyn's supporters could have hoped for, had he lived, was a more favourable peace settlement.

At about the same time as Llywelyn's disastrous foray, there was another rising in Cardiganshire. Little was to come of it. Bodies of cavalry and foot soldiers were sent to William de Valence to help him resist the outbreak, which he did with apparently little difficulty. This gave the English a firm foundation from which to advance once more on Llanbadarn. A force duly set out, arriving there on 14 January 1283. Roger Mortimer was made constable of the castle. It was the start of a permanent re-occupation of Llanbadarn, and another tightening of Edward's grip around Gwynedd. The English success was cemented by the surrender of two Welsh lords who had previously been hostile to the English, Rhys ap Maelgwyn and Cynan ap Maredudd. Edward was magnanimous towards them, pardoning their rebellion and returning them to Cardiganshire on condition that they should now help the English to defeat other Welsh rebels.

On the wider stage, Edward was not completely without his problems, despite his recent successes. The English king was to experience one problem time and again throughout his reign; that of inadequate finance. He was a man with grand ideas, but this meant that he required funding on a grand scale. Regularly his ambition overreached his available resources. The campaign in Wales had been a significant one. Edward had already benefited from a number of loans, the records of the time noting the receipt of 11,000 marks from areas as far afield as

London, Newcastle, York, Lincoln and Yarmouth in September 1282.[21] But the money had now run out and the king would need a substantial boost to his coffers before he could finish off the Welsh campaign in the months ahead. He therefore had no option but to go to Parliament and ask for their blessing for his plans to raise further taxes.

In order to obtain this, a Parliament was summoned for January 1283. Its format was unusual in that it was held in two parts, one in York, the other at Northampton. Many of the leading lords were present with Edward on campaign and the assembly was therefore disproportionately composed of members of the clergy. The clergy were not happy; they had already paid over significant amounts towards the campaign. The laity, however, voted tax of a thirtieth, which Edward's officials duly set about collecting.

The subsequent collection of funds for the campaign was not without interest. A few members of the clergy made small gifts to Edward but he was clearly not satisfied. Donations had been made to churches as contributions towards the crusades; such gifts were a regular part of medieval life. There was clearly little prospect of a crusade being launched from England while Edward had so many other distractions to deal with. Edward therefore helped himself to these funds to finance his Welsh expedition. It was a serious abuse on Edward's part. He had no legal right to the funds. Archbishop Pecham refused to sanction Edward's excessive action and the king was eventually forced to back down. All ended well enough when the money was paid back into the church's coffers and the clergy voluntarily agreed to a tax of a twentieth for the next three years.

By this time, Edward was building up his forces again for a final push on Gwynedd. There were a large number of mercenaries with the army, many of them crossbowmen from regions of France which must have sounded quite foreign to many of the humble foot soldiers, such as Armagnac and Bergerac, as well as Bordeaux. They were to suffer a very high rate of attrition in the war.[22] Edward also sent orders to England, commanding that more infantry be sent so that he could advance again in January. The troops in Anglesey were now led by Otto de Grandson. They were reinforced and the bridge of boats was strengthened so that a new push could be made on the mainland.

As January came and went, Edward was ready to advance into the hinterland of the north. A large number of infantry had arrived from Shropshire, Cheshire and the south-east Marches. There were some 5,000 in all. There were about 400 cavalry and 1,500 mercenaries from Picardy and Gascony. In addition, there were again a large number of woodsmen to hack a road through the Welsh forests. All was set for the final push.

This time, Edward went for the very heart of Gwynedd rather than attempting to isolate and slowly suffocate it. The Welsh castle of Dolwyddellan stood between Betws-y-Coed and Blaenau Ffestiniog. It had a special place in Welsh history, being the birthplace and early home of Llywelyn the Great. It does not appear to have held out against the English for very long. There are no records that the castle was ever subjected to a close siege and we may surmise from this that the castle was surrendered without much of a fight and may even have been given over to Edward by its constable by prior agreement. However, conspiracy theories should in this instance not be overplayed. There were certain features which typified medieval siege warfare. Generally, garrisons might expect to be treated relatively well if they surrendered without a fight. If they resisted they could expect much harsher treatment if the castle were to fall. And castles would only resist in normal circumstances if they were capable of holding out for some time and there was some genuine prospect of relief. In the current situation, such an outcome seemed most unlikely. It was pointless resisting if there was no real purpose in such an act, and the castle was therefore handed over quickly. One of the keys to Gwynedd, the capture of Dolwyddellan on 18 January 1283 left Snowdonia, the refuge of last resort, wide open. The castle was garrisoned with men equipped with white winter clothing and a siege engine was brought up from Betws to help keep it secure against any counter-attack.

Hindsight is a gift that is sadly not possessed by those who are living through great events as they happen. However, with the benefit of it, the loss of Dolwyddellan, coming so soon after the death of Llywelyn, marked the effective end of the war. Even at the time, Edward seems to have realised, to a limited extent at least, the significance of the event. Soon after the fall of the castle, many of his infantry were dismissed. It is of course true to say that, with the arrival of winter and the difficulties it created for the provisioning of a large army, it made very sound logistical sense to do this. But the strategic importance of the castle would not have been lost on Edward. Neither would the psychological effect on what by now must have been the very fragile morale of the Welsh who were opposed to Edward. Edward appointed Gruffudd ap Tudor – a Welshman possessed of a name resonant in subsequent English history, who had recently been a supporter of Dafydd – as constable of the castle, and retired to Conwy in March. Here he occupied a spot that would soon become part of his majestic new castle in the town.

The events of spring 1283 gave Edward the opportunity to finish mopping up in Wales. Resistance was increasingly centred in the wilder parts of Gwynedd and the surrounding areas. Further south, most of

Wales was now subdued. In Ceredigion for example the former rebel Cynan ap Maredudd was now trusted enough by the English to be given some responsibilities of his own. There were now a much smaller number of men available to Edward. Some 600 mercenaries were with him, and about 400 cavalry. The number of foot soldiers varied quite dramatically, swinging from 1,200 to 5,000 at any given point in time, though it appears that the higher number was not typical of the size of force normally available to Edward. The conflict was now a bitter one; English troops were paid for the rebels that they killed; they provided evidence by presenting their heads to the king's officials, in return for which they received a shilling.

Dafydd now realised that his situation was hopeless. He assumed all the trappings appropriate to a prince of Wales that he was able to, given his parlous position, but even a cursory glance at the realities that underlay his situation reveals the truth. Early in 1283 for example he made a grant of land to Rhys Fychan. On the surface, it may have appeared that this was the normal action of a prince who wished to reward and encourage a loyal subject. But the fact of the matter was that when the grant was made, Rhys Fychan was in King Edward's pay. It was nothing more than an attempt – which failed – to buy back the loyalty of a man whose allegiances now lay elsewhere. When later in the year English troops and their Welsh allies scanned the countryside, hunting Dafydd down, Rhys Fychan would be among them. Dafydd was in such a serious position by now that stories quoted by the Hagnaby chronicler saying that he sent his wife unsuccessfully to intercede with the king should not be dismissed out of hand, despite the lack of corroborating references from other sources.

As the English king closed in on his prey, Dafydd made a desperate bid for freedom. He fled from the mountains of Snowdonia south-west to the region of Cader Idris, where he set himself up in Castell y Bere. It was a very difficult fortress to approach and Dafydd could have made a nuisance of himself for some time from there. However, it was a purely defensive action and epitomised the hopelessness of the Welsh situation. Edward nevertheless sent out orders that an army was to assemble at Montgomery in May.[23]

The force was not needed. William de Valence made his way up with a body of men from Llanbadarn and joined up with another despatched by Roger Lestrange from Montgomery. Roger Springhouse, the sheriff of Shropshire, raised a party of 100 woodsmen (English tactics by now seemed to be pretty much predictable but none the less effective for that) and a number of engineers. There were over 1,000 infantry despatched by Roger Lestrange as well as an indeterminate number of cavalry. They made their way across the wilds of central Wales to place a close siege round Castell y Bere. On 15 April, this army was massively reinforced by a party of about 1,400 infantry brought up by de Valence. Another force of 560 men was sent to take Harlech, led by Otto de Grandson. The embrace of the English forces was all-encompassing, like the ever-tightening coils of a constrictor, slowly squeezing the last breaths from the dying body of an independent Wales.

While the siege of Bere proceeded in its leisurely manner, its end all too inevitable now, parties of scouts were sent out to look for Dafydd, who had apparently absented himself from the castle. It was not long before Bere itself, under the command of Cynfrig ap Madog, surrendered on 25 April. Lewis de la Pole, son of Gruffudd ap Gwenwynwyn, was made constable of the castle. He was given a garrison of 8 cavalry, 9 crossbowmen and 40 foot.[24] Workmen were brought to the castle to strengthen the defences, and roads were cut through the forests, to become the arteries along which coursed the life-blood of English domination.

Several months passed, time in which control of the mid-Wales region was made secure. So complete did this control become that, by June, de Valence was confident enough to return to Llanbadarn and disband the army that he had raised. Few further incidents of significant note took place. There was an uprising by a Welsh lord, Rhys ap Maelgwyn; one of those who took part in the campaign to crush it was Rhys ap Maredudd. Rhys ap Maelgwyn was later listed as one of the Welshmen incarcerated in Bridgnorth Castle. Also imprisoned in Chester was Llywelyn, son of Goronwy ap Heilin. A loyal supporter of Dafydd right until the end, Goronwy was to die a rebel.

At last, in June, the final blow was struck. Edward had sent a substantial force, some 7,000 strong, swarming all over Snowdonia looking for Dafydd.[25] The Welsh surrendered to the English in their droves. Already, the month before, the castle at Dolbadarn, standing in the very shadow of Snowdon itself, had fallen. It was Dafydd's last remaining castle and it presaged inevitably his final demise. In the end, it appears that Dafydd was not captured by the English patrols but was handed over by Welshmen – 'men of his own tongue' – who were no longer sympathetic to his cause.[26] He was captured in Snowdonia (probably on 22 June 1283)[27] and taken, accompanied by a large armed guard, through Rhuddlan towards England.

So the war was over, concluding decisively in contrast to the first conflict in 1277. The secret of Edward's success was that he was able to marshal his forces in a way that made the most of his markedly superior resources. Edward was not a military genius in the sense that he was an

Edward I. (PRO E 368/72, m.12)

King Edward I. (PRO London Ms e68–9)

Cydweli Castle, home of the Marcher lord, Pain de Chaworth. (Author's collection)

Dolbadarn Castle at the gateway to Snowdon. (Author's collection)

Caernarfon Castle, showing the dramatic walls based on those of Constantinople. (Author's collection)

Talley Abbey – the monastic orders settled widely in Wales. (Author's collection)

Carreg Cennen Castle, home of John Giffard. (Author's collection)

Dryslwyn Castle, the base of Rhys ap Maredudd. (Author's collection)

Cardiff Castle, much developed by the Earl of Gloucester. (Author's collection)

The wilds of Snowdonia, heartland of Gwynedd. (Author's collection)

The walls of Conwy Castle, showing the unusual turrets at the top of the towers. (Author's collection)

Nuns in a convent, the fate of the daughters of Llywelyn and Dafydd. (BL London Ms Add. 39843, f.6v)

The death of Llywelyn ap Gruffudd. (BL Cotton Nero Ms D11, f.182)

innovator. His overall strategy was not dissimilar to that employed by Suetonius Paulinus, the Roman general, when he exterminated the Druids of Mona (Anglesey) over a millennium before. His tactics were not unlike those advocated by Gerald of Wales decades earlier.[28] Edward's approach to war was in many ways similar to his approach to kingship, which is perhaps only to be expected. He was conservative, although not to the point of ignoring all recent innovations. An example of this would be his approach to taking men into his pay rather than relying on feudal service. But even here, although it was once argued that Edward was revolutionary in his attitude to this, recent historians have agreed that he developed an already existing trend in this respect.

* * *

It is an almost uncanny experience reading the accounts of the medieval chronicler Gerald of Wales in the context of Edward's campaign. He had been dead for over half a century when Edward invaded Wales but his description of how the Welsh could be conquered could have served as the king's campaign orders given the similarity between them. Gerald wrote:

> Any prince who is really determined to conquer the Welsh and to govern them in peace must proceed as follows. He should first of all understand that for a whole year at least he must devote his every effort and give his undivided attention to the task which he has undertaken. He can never hope to conquer in one single battle a people which will never draw up its forces to engage an enemy in the field, and will never allow itself to be besieged inside fortified strongpoints. He can beat them only by patient and unremitting pressure applied over a long period.

He went on to say that any would-be conqueror must do all he can to divide the Welsh, by bribes if necessary, and ensure that he has a fleet at his disposal. In the autumn, castles must be built and put under the command of men friendly to the conqueror. Then in the winter, 'when the trees have lost their leaves and there is no more pasturage to be had', a strong infantry force should 'invade their secret strongholds'.

The importance of reinforcements was emphasised by Gerald, as was the disparity in resources available to the English and the Welsh:

> Fresh troops must keep on replacing those who are tired out, and maybe those who have been killed in battle. If he constantly moves

up new men, there need be no break in the assault. Without them this belligerent people will never be conquered, and even so the danger must be great and many casualties must be expected. What does it matter to an army of English mercenaries if their losses are great today? There is enough money to ensure that the ranks of battle will be filled again, and more than filled tomorrow. To the Welsh, on the other hand, who have no mercenaries and no foreign allies, those who fall in battle are irreplaceable, at least for the time being.[29]

Edward's organisational skills showed themselves in a number of ways, but particularly regarding the interaction of various elements of his forces. The victory owed as much to the woodsmen who cut the roads through the forests as it did to the heavy cavalry. Neither should the role of the fleet be ignored, as it was so important in opening up the route to Anglesey, in many ways the key to Gwynedd. Such integration would be by no means typical of medieval warfare, when maintaining co-operation and coordination between the various parts of a force was a strategic challenge of the highest order given the fact that maintaining discipline was such a difficult job.

Most impressive of all perhaps was his attention to the provision of adequate supplies for the large armies at his disposal. This was the Achilles heel of medieval armies but Edward used every tool at his disposal to counteract the inherent threat. Some detailed measures were taken; no markets could be held in the Marches, so that supplies could be directed instead to the armies in Wales. Those on the borders were also given menacing warnings that they must not trade with the enemy; this hardly seems a revolutionary step to take perhaps but it was, by the standards of the time, a necessary one.

Supplies had to be requisitioned far and wide throughout Edward's empire. In April 1282, sheriffs in Essex, Surrey, Sussex, Kent and Hampshire had been commanded to assist in the collection of wheat and oats in their counties. In July, officials were despatched to buy up supplies in Staffordshire, Derbyshire, Nottinghamshire and Lancashire. Large quantities of wheat, oats, barley, beans, peas, salmon and wine were shipped in from Ireland. From Gascony, wheat, oats, beans, peas, bacon pigs and – naturally enough – wine were transported to England. Nor was it just foodstuffs involved. One detail concerns the provision of crosses of St George to issue to the troops as armbands, a primitive form of uniform and a sign of the quasi-religious nature the war had taken on in Edward's eyes.

These supplies were primarily shipped through Chester, the hub in an efficient warehousing and transportation network, where provisions were organised for onward shipment to individual units with Edward's armies. There is an occasional hint of sentiment within the records that survive; the gift of twenty barrels of wine to Otto de Grandson being one such example.[30] Safe conducts were issued to traders, who were sometimes given armed escorts. The use of compulsory purchase (known as 'prise'), by which localities were forced to sell their goods to the crown, was deeply unpopular and later in the reign was to lead to serious problems. Nevertheless, such purchases were an integral part of the king's provisioning policy in the Welsh wars.

There were widespread complaints at the corruption of some of the officials collecting supplies throughout Edward's reign and many allegations of such men keeping back a proportion of what they collected for themselves. There was also anger at the length of time it took to pay for the goods sequestered in this fashion. Extreme measures might be taken to avoid having goods taken, including moving them to 'sanctuary' in a church, though even this was sometimes ignored by over-enthusiastic collectors. Nevertheless, it was an inescapable reality that large volumes of supplies had to be obtained to keep the king's army in the field. The overall organisation in 1282 was much more thorough than in 1277, hinting that Edward was unhappy at the attention paid to the issue in the earlier war, when the problem of provisioning was not considered until a relatively late stage.[31] It was, all in all, an impressive feat of organisation, which was performed so successfully that it has been compared favourably with the victualling of Tudor armies a quarter of a millennium later.[32]

Factors other than logistical skills certainly played their part. Edward was able to keep his focus on the campaign, despite the defeats that were suffered on occasion. Previous English kings had had other distractions which meant that they were unable, or unwilling, to keep their attention on affairs in Wales for any length of time. Some had civil unrest in England to distract them,[33] some had crusades to occupy them (though only one English king actually set out on one, others were involved in the planning of them), most had affairs in France which involved and affected them greatly. This meant that they were not able to devote all of their resources to Wales in the way that Edward did. Even Edward would suffer from these factors later in his reign, and it is notable that the last great Welsh revolt against him, in 1294, would come when he was about to embark on campaign in France as well as being deeply embroiled in the affairs of Scotland.

One other critical factor was the involvement of the Marcher lords. For most of the campaign, they had been fighting with the king. It would be totally inaccurate to say that they shared a common interest; in some fundamental ways their interests were diametrically opposed. But where they were united was in their opposition to the revolt of the Welsh, which threatened both king and Marcher lords. Given the acrimony between Llywelyn and the Marcher lords in the early 1270s, their support for the king was virtually guaranteed, albeit for self-interested, non-altruistic reasons. To this must be added their desire to share in the carve-up of conquered territories, which, they believed, would follow the subjugation of Wales. Llywelyn's failure to foster good relationships with the Marcher lords, however difficult an objective that might have been, was a serious drawback for the Welsh cause.

Against the marshalling of all the forces available to Edward the Welsh had no answer. They fought bravely and for far longer than could have been expected but it was a courage born of desperation rather than conviction. Their time-honoured tactics were simply inadequate to cope with Edward's strategy and force of arms. They relied on Edward acting in a certain way if they were to succeed and he was far too wise a strategist for that. He would not let himself be drawn into the bleak heart of Snowdonia, where his lines of communication could be attacked and his supplies cut off, forcing him into a chaotic retreat. Neither would he let the Welsh use their favoured tactics of ambush, hit-and-run, to destroy the morale and effectiveness of his troops. He avoided these basic mistakes, learning from the errors of the past, and instead conducted the war as if it were a game of chess, moving his pieces only when it suited him and when all the elements necessary for a decisive tactical advantage were in place.

Now that the war was won, it was time to consider the peace. No longer would there be the possibility of any vestige of independence being retained by the Welsh. Instead, the country would be firmly integrated into the expanding English empire, devoid of any meaningful national identity or any real possibility of exercising influence over its own affairs. For one man in particular, a terrible price was about to be paid for his role in the war.

CHAPTER TEN

Annexation

And so, by the providence of God, the glory of the Welsh,
who were thus against their will subjected to the laws of the English,
was transferred to the English.[1]

With the war over the process of annexation could now be completed.
There was a good deal of administrative work to go through before
Edward could be content that he had complete control of Wales, but
there were practical things that he could do in the meantime to
emphasise his lordship over the country and to reduce any future threat
from the Welsh even more than his crushing victory had already done.

One thing he could do was to make an example of Dafydd and he
proceeded to do this with savage effect. There is no doubt that Edward
saw Dafydd's revolt as a personal rebuff, the actions of an ungrateful man
whose cause the English king had previously espoused. As such, his
actions were to Edward treachery of the worst kind. There would be little
sympathy for Dafydd, a man described by one English chronicler as 'a
deviser of evil and most cruel persecutor of England, a deluder of his
own nation, a most ungrateful traitor and the author of the war'.[2]

Edward summoned an assembly to Shrewsbury. It was to meet there in
the autumn of 1283. Top of the agenda was to agree on the fate of
Dafydd. It was a matter of the greatest significance that the clergy were
not to be asked to give judgement. They could not be party to a verdict
that involved the shedding of blood and there was therefore an
unmistakable hint that Dafydd's punishment would be a capital one. The
very language of the summons issued for the Parliament at Shrewsbury
made it abundantly clear that there would be little prospect of mercy for
Dafydd, describing him as 'the last survivor of the family of traitors' and
castigating the Welsh generally, saying that 'the tongue of man can
scarcely recount the evil deeds committed by the Welsh upon the king's
progenitors'. Edward's bitterness at the perceived treason of Dafydd is
apparent from the sentence handed down when he was inevitably found
guilty as charged on 2 October. In recognition of the various crimes he
had committed, he was to be hanged, drawn and quartered.

This meant that he would be hanged but cut down while still alive. Then he would be disembowelled and his entrails burned before him. After this agonising torment had eventually caused him to expire, his body would be cut in pieces and despatched around the country as a warning to others. The exact symbolism of the various punishments was the subject of some debate, though the Dunstable chronicler asserted that he was hanged for homicide, that his bowels were burned because he had committed his crimes on Palm Sunday and that his body was then quartered because he had plotted against the king. All this took place after he had been dragged to the place of execution by horses, this being an additional element introduced as a punishment for treason.

The punishment was not a new one. There are records describing how a man was treated in similarly harsh fashion as early as in 1238 for plotting to kill the king. However, it was none the less savage for that. It presaged the much more famous execution of William Wallace, the Scottish insurgent leader, by some two decades. The sentence was duly carried out by Geoffrey of Shrewsbury (who received a pound for his labours) and the body divided up, with the head going to London, where it would accompany the rotting head of Llywelyn. Dafydd was very much the sacrificial offering. One other Welsh knight was treated in similar fashion but there are no other records of executions taking place, though a number of Welsh knights, such as Rhys Wyndod, were to spend a long period in captivity.[3]

Neither were the children of Llywelyn or Dafydd omitted from the process. Owing to the long delay in consummating his proxy marriage, Llywelyn had just one child, his daughter Gwenllian.[4] She was compelled to join the nunnery at Sempringham in Lincolnshire, where she eventually died over half a century later in 1337. She would later complain that she had been promised £100 a year for her upkeep but was never paid more than £20 a year. Her close neighbour at the nunnery of Sixhills would be Dafydd's daughter, Gwladus, and Gwladus's five sisters.

For Dafydd's sons, Owain and Llywelyn, there was a harsher fate in store. The Patent Rolls record prosaically that, in July 1283, Henry de Lacy, the earl of Lincoln, was ordered to deliver Llywelyn, son of Dafydd, to Richard de Boys, 'to be taken where the king has ordered' with instructions to Reginald Grey to do the same to his brother, Owain.[5] Both were to be kept in close confinement for the remainder of their natural lives. Llywelyn died in Bristol in 1288 but Owain was to spend decades in prison. As late as 1305, Edward commented that the conditions of his captivity were too lax and he should be put into a wooden cage at night. Whatever might be said in favour of Edward, there is no doubt that as a human being he had a harsh edge to his character.

*   *   *

Edward now turned his attentions to the issue of the continuing government of Wales. There were a number of important political agreements made during the thirteenth century: Magna Carta in 1215, the Statute of Merton of 1236 and the Provisions of Oxford in 1259, to name but three. The Statute of Wales, which was drawn up at Rhuddlan in 1284, was a continuation of this trend but was also, in its own way, unique, as it alone referred to the terms of government of a conquered people. It essentially sought to institutionalise aspects of English law in Wales, a step that, in practical terms, moved a long way towards making Wales merely an extension of England.

As a document, it is a good piece of work. Its impressiveness lies, not in its high-level statement of principles, but in the way in which it sets out how the law should be applied. During the course of the thirteenth century writs had developed that became the standard documents in use for the instigation of various legal mechanisms. These writs are outlined in the statute, and their applicability to Wales described, though not in great detail. Rather than being a definitive list of all the writs that could be issued, it sets out a code, a set of guidelines by which the law should operate. In a surprisingly modern and flexible way, it states that the writs should not be applied in rigid fashion but that the spirit of the law is to be deemed as important as the letter of the law.

It was to have important effects on Welsh laws and customs. One of the most marked was in its attitude towards the rights of bastard sons as far as succession to property was concerned. Traditionally, in Wales these were awarded the same right of succession as that enjoyed by their brothers born in wedlock. This caused grave offence to the church and the Statute of Wales specifically put a stop to the practice. Another important issue, vital in the context of the time with regard to the politics of land, concerned the right of widows to hold dower lands. The practice was well established in England but did not form part of Welsh law. The statute also changed this. Both amendments potentially had a significant impact on the nature of landholding within Wales, as did the change introduced by the statute that allowed the female line to succeed to lands when there was no male heir. The changes that were made to the laws of inheritance altered the nature of landholding within Wales. When Owain ap Gwenwynwyn died in 1311, his lands passed to his son-in-law, John Charlton, whereas they would previously have passed to his brother, Gruffudd, under the old Welsh laws. This must have been particularly galling to Gruffudd, considering the help his family had given to the English in the past.[6]

It should however be noted that in no way was the statute a complete transfusion of English law in its totality. There were to be some significant concessions to existing Welsh conventions, some of them including succession rights. The concept of primogeniture was enshrined in English law, in stark contrast to the situation existing in Wales, which provided for inheritances to be divided up between all sons. There was a very real danger, one that had been realised on many occasions, that in the Welsh model the country would be weakened by this practice as the lands divided in such a fashion became increasingly smaller and consequently less viable. Despite this – or perhaps because of it – the statute allowed the practice to continue.

Other Welsh conventions were also protected. Jury trial was recognised as the standard method for dealing with cases, and there was no attempt to introduce English methods, such as trial by battle, into Welsh law, which had not previously adopted such approaches. There were also some practical considerations to take into account. Fines were to be payable based on the value of cattle (three cows or their equivalent would be the standard fine) reflecting the fact that Wales was still substantially a rural, non-monetary-based economy; although, as far back as 1240, significant developments indicating the wider use of money in the Welsh economy can be noted.[7]

With regard to criminal law, however, there was to be little concession to existing Welsh practice, with wholesale adoption of English practices in this respect. The English criminal code was often much more severe than its Welsh equivalent, and at least one writer has noted that later Welshmen, such as Dafydd ab Edmwnd, who lived in the late fifteenth century, would lament the introduction of the English law when his friend was hanged for accidentally killing a man – something that would not have happened under the Welsh code.[8]

Looked at dispassionately, the Statute of Wales is not without its merits. It sought to allow flexibility and recognised the fact that there were some unique circumstances within Wales which precluded total adoption of English law. Such a policy had been adopted before by Edward; he had exercised similar local flexibility in his lands in France.[9] It can therefore be argued that there was much to commend the statute to the Welsh people.[10] This analysis, however, overlooks two important facts. First was the context in which the statute, issued on 19 March 1284, was drawn up. The background to the statute was the English conquest of Wales. It was the imposition of a new way of life on a conquered people, who had no say in its formulation. For all its concessions to Welsh customs, the likelihood is that these were perceived as small issues in the wider scheme of things. No one can expect a conquered people to welcome the document that enshrines their annexation. From now on, the country was known as 'the land of Wales', a phrase that might superficially appear harmless enough but the effect of which was to remove any residual vestige of sovereign power that the Welsh might have felt they still retained. The conquest of the country changed everything forever; by it, 'the whole land, both in demesne and services, was annexed to the crown of England'.[11]

There was also a second, more practical issue. English officials set to govern parts of Wales sometimes exercised their rule harshly. Much resentment had been created as a result. The recent war had after all partly been caused because of the detestation of the methods of men such as Grey. Given this recent history, there was little reason to be optimistic that the future effects of English rule would be any less harsh than the recent past, whatever the terms of the statute.

One other important change to the government of Wales arising as a result of the statute was the way in which the country was to be divided administratively. The old division of the country into areas whose Welshness was epitomised by their very names – regions such as Gwynedd, Powys and Dyfed – was to be replaced by an English-style shire system. Therefore, counties such as Flintshire, Caernarfonshire, Cardiganshire and Carmarthenshire came into existence. It was a deeply symbolic administrative realignment, another unmistakable sign of annexation and integration into England, although at a more local level many of the older Welsh administrative divisions were retained. All in all, the anglicisation of Wales, though not total, was great enough to lend credence to the objective outlined in the preamble to the statute that Wales was to be 'wholly and entirely transferred under our proper dominion'. The changes also reflected the gains made by the crown in the war. The dynasty of north Powys was basically completely dispossessed, as were the lords of Deheubarth. With few exceptions, the major lords of Wales lost their lands irrevocably.

Not even the religious relics of the Welsh were safe. A piece of the True Cross, fragments of which were dispersed liberally throughout Christendom, was much revered in Wales, where it was known as Croysseneyht. The relic had belonged to Llywelyn and it was delivered to the English king at Conwy by one of his clerks, Hugo ap Ythel. This man received a sumptuous robe in return for his actions as well as a sponsored education at Oxford. Edward valued this trophy of war highly, taking it regularly on his travels with him and later on encrusting it with precious jewels. As a conventionally religious man no doubt Edward valued it for reasons of piety. There is equally little doubt, given Edward's character, that he also regarded this precious relic, taken from an enemy who had suffered such a crushing defeat at his hands, as a symbol of conquest.

It was carried by the Archbishop of Canterbury in a great procession that made its way from the Tower of London to Westminster, headed by the king and queen, on his return from Wales in 1285. It was as if this was a Christianised variation of the return of the Caesars in triumph to ancient Rome. Other items of status were taken by the English. The seals used by Llywelyn were melted down and the silver from them used to make a chalice. The coronet used by Llywelyn to signify his regal status was presented by Edward at the shrine of his namesake, St Edward the Confessor, at Westminster.

The division of offices and lands after the statute was issued is revealing in contrasting ways. A justiciar was to be appointed in north Wales, to whom would report a number of other officials, sheriffs, coroners and bailiffs. The justiciar was to be Otto de Grandson, one of the king's most trusted advisers. He would take as his assistant another man from Savoy, John de Bonvillars. Of the sheriffs, there was also a virtual monopoly of non-Welshmen in the various posts available, only one Welshman, Gruffudd ap Dafydd, rising to the position. There was also only one Welshman employed as constable of a castle, Gruffudd ap Tudor.[12] Welshmen could only aspire to the less important positions, the scraps from the English table. All positions of real influence were in the hands of Englishmen, or those allied to the English cause, such as Edward's supporters from Savoy.

But while Edward was quick to advance his supporters into key positions, he was not always willing, with certain marked exceptions, to hand over Welsh lands to them. Some grants of land had already been made to Edward's supporters while the war was still in progress, such as the granting of Rhuddlan and other land in Dyffryn Clwyd and Teigingl to Grey. The earl of Lincoln took over other parts of the 'Four Cantreds' that had not been given to Grey. Other parcels were handed over to a selected group of Edward's supporters like John Giffard in the south, and the Mortimers in the mid-Welsh Marches. The queen also received some lands in Powys, and the Welsh lords of Edeirnion were by and large dispossessed.[13] For Welsh adherents to the English cause there would also be some reward. The disputed land in Arwystli was found to belong to Gruffudd ap Gwenwynwyn after all, which can surely have surprised no one. There were even stories, though no evidence survives to corroborate them, that Gruffudd handed over his lands to Edward and received them back again as a grant from the English crown, marking him out irrevocably as a 'king's man'. Rhys ap Maredudd also received some lands in return for his support for the English cause.

Edward was not universally generous in his awards of land, though. The one indisputable fact is that there was one body above all others that gained territorially from the conquest of Wales, and that was the crown itself. All Llywelyn's territories in Snowdonia as well as Anglesey were retained by the crown or, to personalise matters more, by Edward himself. He also retained Cardiganshire and Carmarthenshire in the south as well as Flintshire in the north. The effects of this were twofold. It meant first of all that a great deal of wealth flowed to the crown. The incomes from the lands involved would subsequently flow straight into the coffers of the king's treasury. But it also gave the king immense power. He could henceforward decide whether to retain those lands for future income or grant them out to followers at some future point in return for services that they had rendered to him.

Edward's actions tell us much about his views of kingship generally and demonstrate some of the foibles of his personality that would cause him so many difficulties later in his reign. A number of those fighting for him were in his pay, and Edward no doubt reasoned that this precluded territorial reward for their assistance. But others were fighting on an unpaid basis, and Edward's treatment of them seems to have been decidedly niggardly. The earl of Gloucester received nothing, perhaps reflecting Gloucester's umbrage when replaced as commander in the south, but neither did the earl of Hereford. Valence received little reward either, which must have irritated him greatly as he had lost a son in the campaign. Edward's actions were parsimonious and they reflected his not particularly well-disguised attempts to increase the power of the crown at the expense of some of its leading subjects. In this respect, it is of more than passing interest that those men who did not receive the rewards that they might have expected were Marcher barons in the south, whom Edward might have seen – not without reason – as a source of potential opposition to any plans he may have had to expand the power of the crown in Wales. But he was swimming against the tide; his actions were typical of those that, later on in his reign, would lead him into opposition with some of his most prominent barons and bring his kingdom to the edge of chaos.

* * *

The birth of a son, who was named Edward, in April 1284 at Caernarfon appeared to put the seal on the king's triumph. The king certainly seemed to be delighted at the safe delivery of a son, rewarding the man who gave him the news, Gruffudd Llwyd, with a knighthood and lands. Bishop Anian of Bangor was also granted lands for christening the child and appointing a Welsh woman, the mother of Hywel y Pedolau, as his nurse. The boy would eventually become the first English prince of

Wales, yet another symbolic assertion of the subjugation of Wales, though the story of the toddler in arms being presented to the Welsh lords as their prince at Caernarfon Castle is, sadly for romanticists, apocryphal. But for completeness it at least deserves to be retold. The legend has it that Edward I promised to give the Welsh a prince of their own 'that was born in Wales and could speak never a word of English'. Prince Edward, being at the time a baby, born at Caernarfon, who could not yet speak any known language, fitted the bill perfectly. While it is tempting to see in the story a superb example of Edward's legalistic mind at work, the story was not committed to writing until 300 years later.[14] There is, in short, no evidence to prove that the young prince was made prince of Wales until 1301 when, as a seventeen-year-old boy and heir to the crown of England, we must assume that he was fluent in his native tongue.

For the king, this was generally a time for celebration. A great tournament was held at Nefyn in July – the festivities that followed the day's events in the evening were so exuberantly celebrated that the floor of the hall in which they were being held collapsed. At around this time, another Welsh treasure, a crown reputed to have belonged to King Arthur, was presented to Edward. The king had a sentimental attachment to the Arthurian legends and this symbolic link between two great monarchs, one of the glorious past and one of the triumphant present, would surely have delighted him. His interest in Arthur was demonstrated in 1278 when he had arranged for the tomb of Arthur and Guinevere in Glastonbury to be opened and examined. Indeed, he was personally compared to Arthur and praised for his achievements, which, it was claimed, outmatched even those of the legendary king of old. In words that would have seemed deeply ironic to the Welsh, with their affection for Merlin, the early fourteenth-century canon of Bridlington, Pierre de Langtoft, pondered over Edward's achievements in Wales and elsewhere:

> Ah, God! How often Merlin said truth
> In his prophecies, if you read them!
> Now are the two waters united in one,
> Which have been separated by great mountains;
> And one realm made of two different kingdoms
> Which used to be governed by two kings.
> Now are all the islanders all joined together,
> And Albany reunited to the royalties
> Of which King Edward is proclaimed lord.*

*an allusion to his campaigns in Scotland.

Cornwall and Wales are in his power,
And Ireland the great at his will.
There is neither king nor prince of all the countries
Except King Edward, who has thus united them;
Arthur never held the fiefs so fully.[15]

Edward decided that he would make a great royal progress through his newly won realm and show himself to his Welsh subjects. This allowed him to see Wales at first hand and to impose his own brand of rule upon it. For someone who showed an active interest in the government of his realm, this was an excellent opportunity to stamp his own particular style of kingship on Wales. It was also a way of showing himself to the people, of reminding them that he was their king and, by putting on a show, to impress upon them the futility of refusing to accept his authority. So that they might be better able to appreciate his power, the king chose a high-powered entourage to accompany him. So, with him he took Otto de Grandson, his appointee as justiciar in the north, William de Valence, who had played an active role in the recent war in the south-west, and Robert Tibotot, who had also assumed a prominent role in the government of the south.

An important part of the king's strategy was the establishment of towns around some of the castles that he intended to build. Here, English settlers could be established. Some, such as Pecham, even believed that the growth of towns would help to counteract the traditional rural basis of Welsh life, which was thought to have led to the wild nature of the Welsh – though such sweeping generalisations ignore the fact that the Welsh themselves had started to establish their own towns, albeit that the process was at an early stage of evolution.[16] The first stage in implementing this strategy was for Edward to formally establish boroughs at Caernarfon, Conwy, Flint and Rhuddlan, which he duly did in September 1284. He decided to make the constables of the castles in these places mayors of the towns, formalising the link between the military garrison and the government of the settlements which would grow up around the castle. It was a sensible enough strategy when his army was effectively an army of occupation and there needed to be firm and co-ordinated rule within the lands that he had conquered.

At Conwy, the constable of the castle, William Sikun, was confirmed in his role at a salary of £190 per annum. He was to have a garrison of thirty men, ten of whom were to be crossbowmen. At Caernarfon, John de Havering was to be constable. John was clearly a trusted adviser of the king, as he was also to be Otto de Grandson's deputy as justiciar. John was to have a garrison of forty. Soon after, over 100,000 crossbow quarrels were brought up from Bristol for the castle, as well as over 100 crossbows.[17]

Edward next proceeded down the Welsh coast, into the lands that had been the foremost bastions of Welsh culture until his recent victory. New towns were created along the lines of those further north at Cricieth – an important Welsh castle for many years before the conquest – as well as Harlech and Castell y Bere, Dafydd's refuge of last resort in the recent war. William Leyburn was made constable at Cricieth and Hugh de Wlonkeslowe was placed in charge of Harlech, with both men to have garrisons of thirty men at their disposal, as well as a salary of £100 per annum. Walter of Huntercumbe, who was to be a staunch supporter of the king in future campaigns in Wales and Scotland, was confirmed in charge at Bere, and given a salary of 200 marks and a garrison of forty.

Edward then moved on to Llanbadarn, arriving there on 10 November, and next to Cardigan, which he reached on 22 November. He was apparently in the debt of Robert Tibotot, as he not only appointed him justiciar in the region, but also let him hold in his own name a number of castles, allowing him to keep the revenues from them for himself. This came as a grave blow to the ambitions of some of Edward's other supporters in the region, such as Rhys ap Maredudd, and such frustrations go some way to explaining his future actions. Tibotot was quick to place his own men in positions of influence across these territories.

Edward then reached territory that for some time had formed part of Marcher lands. He arrived at Cydweli in December, where Matilda, the daughter of the late Patrick de Chaworth, who had not yet attained the age at which she could inherit his lands, was in the wardship of Edmund of Lancaster, the king's brother. While in these Marcher territories, he could witness at first hand some of the smouldering quarrels between various Marcher lords, disputes which gave him wonderful opportunities to attempt to reduce the powers of this independent and troublesome class of baron. One such confrontation was between John Giffard and the earl of Hereford; Giffard having been granted much territory in the area around Llandovery and further east towards Builth.

Edward had been attempting to populate a number of newly won lands with his own 'king's men' as a counter-balance to the powerful Marcher lords, especially those in the south of the country, such as Gloucester, Hereford and Valence. The granting of these lands to men such as Giffard and Grey was a way of achieving such an end. Giffard naturally set about the task of consolidating his territorial gains. At some point (probably after 1289) he re-created the castle at Carreg Cennen on an altogether grander scale than the previous fortification that stood there. Giffard received the commote (the primary Welsh administrative division of the time) of Carreg Cennen after the defeat of Llywelyn and Dafydd in return for the service of one knight's fee. It was also a condition that the 'bailiff and men of his commote should come on summons of us and his heirs as often as necessary and stay in our service for three days at his expense'.[18]

However, the granting of these lands to Giffard was a direct challenge to the earl of Hereford's claims. The latter had received some of the lands from the sons of Rhys Fychan when they surrendered to him. According to Marcher custom, this meant that they passed legally to Hereford. This was a difficult problem indeed; both Giffard and the earl were legally entitled to the land, the one having received it by royal grant, the other through Marcher custom. The only way that the problem could be addressed was to appoint a commission to examine the evidence and adjudicate accordingly. Such a body was duly set up. It found in favour of Giffard and therefore in support of the king. It was an important development in the law, with the precedent now established that the king's law was to hold sway over Marcher custom.

Edward completed his journey by entering the earl of Gloucester's lands in Glamorgan. This was the most significant part of the king's progress into March territory. Relations between the earl and the king had often been strained. The two men had nearly come to open blows after the defeat of Simon de Montfort nearly twenty years before, and Gloucester had been unceremoniously dumped from the command of Edward's forces in the south during the recent campaign. Of all the Marcher magnates, Gloucester was the most powerful, as his magnificent castle at Caerphilly amply demonstrated. He had also spent a great deal on strengthening other castles in the area, substantially extending the defences of Cardiff Castle, for example.

Gloucester received Edward with great pomp and ceremony. The reception accorded to Edward might have seemed to the naïve observer the actions of a subject keen to demonstrate his loyalty to his sovereign. Anyone who seriously believed this knew neither man very well. The grandeur of the reception was exaggerated to such an extent that Gloucester's tactics were clearly designed to make a particular point. The point in question was that, in Marcher lands, Gloucester and his fellow barons were autonomous and free from the rule of the crown to a far greater extent than a feudal baron in England itself would be. It was a situation of which Edward was acutely aware. Outwardly, all was sunshine and light between the two men. Inwardly, neither was fooled. When Edward crossed the border into England proper, reaching Bristol soon afterwards (where he celebrated Christmas and held a parliament), it must have been with a greater determination than ever to contain the power of the Marcher lords.

Edward's view of the Marcher lords was, on the surface at least, ambivalent. He was prepared to accept the status quo but, at the same time, he wished – as in all things – to see his supremacy acknowledged. He had, from early on, demonstrated his willingness to intervene in Marcher affairs, a reference in 1275 noting that 'in the Marches of Wales, or in any other place where the king's writ does not run, the king who is sovereign lord will do right . . . to all such as will complain'.[19] He was thereafter quick to intervene in situations where he felt that his rights or royal dignity were at stake. He sent commissioners to examine the functioning of the legal process in Marcher lands. Marcher barons were summoned to his presence to explain their actions to him. His most extreme actions concerned Gloucester and Humphrey de Bohun, earl of Hereford, who, for a short time in 1292, had their lands confiscated and were imprisoned by him. Generally his actions, justified or not, created great tensions with the Marcher lords, a manifestation of the pressures in those difficult years which were to culminate in a time of great crisis in England itself during the late 1290s.[20]

Generally, with Wales finally subdued, there was a hardening in Edward's attitude. Now that he had less reason to court the Marcher lords, the king set himself increasingly at odds with many of them. In this attempt to curb their powers a variety of tactics were used. In 1283, for example, he arranged for one of his daughters, Joan, to marry the earl of Gloucester. This was no peace-offering. It was an attempt to gain Marcher lands should the earl's bloodline die out in the future. All heirs from Gloucester's previous marriage were disenfranchised and, if no children arrived as a result of this match, then a good deal of land would pass to Joan in person on Gloucester's death.

This does not mean that Edward had lost interest in Wales; far from it. He would continue to expend great amounts of energy – and money – on tightening his grip on the country. But his future involvement would, with one significant exception when a serious uprising forced him to return in person, be conducted from a distance. The war was finished, his lieutenants were in place, plans were well advanced to secure the country firmly. It was now time for this ambitious and driven king to turn his attention to his next project, the next step in the consolidation and development of his empire.

To ensure the security of English rule, Edward devised a plan by which he aimed to ensure that the Welsh would never be able to throw off his overlordship. It involved what was, collectively, probably the most ambitious military engineering project in medieval Europe. A chain of castles, state-of-the-art constructions embodying the latest thinking in construction techniques, would be erected in a ring around Gwynedd, a stone collar around the neck of Wales. Individually, they were not unique. Nor were they so strong that they were invincible. But they were symbolic of one country's domination of another in a way that few other castles ever have been. They effectively deprived the Welsh of any realistic hopes of independence. For them, the only consolation – and this was surely scant indeed – was that the construction of these castles would, along with Edward's many other projects, stretch the finances of England to breaking point.

In the meantime, Archbishop Pecham set about protecting the rights of the Welsh church over which, as Archbishop of Canterbury, he would have much more control now that all of Wales was in English hands. He was assisted in his task by the trustworthy bishop of Bangor, Anian (not to be confused with the Bishop of St Asaph's, who bore the same name but was a much more problematic character for Pecham to deal with). He did succeed in negotiating over £1,730 in compensation for the damage done to properties owned by the Welsh church in the recent war, a not insignificant charge to Edward's hard-pressed treasury. Pecham's anti-Welsh prejudices, though, seemed to be confirmed when he reviewed the state of the Welsh clergy. He was shocked at the poor levels of literacy demonstrated, as well as the general secularisation of the Church in Wales. He also exhibited his racial bias by his ejection of the Welsh monks at Talley Abbey and their replacement by English brothers. Church taxes were collected far more rigorously than before. But not all developments were negative. In most cases, bishops of Welsh origin were appointed to the Welsh bishoprics, and St Asaph's Cathedral was substantially rebuilt.

In May 1284, Pope Martin IV granted absolution to all those Welshmen who had been involved in the recent war against Edward. The king soon after set up a commission to investigate the losses incurred by the Welsh clergy in the recent war. When it reported back, a significant amount of compensation was paid over. The attempts to protect the Welsh church from loss of privileges were not apparently wholly successful and, in the next year, the English church was to complain that the rights of their brethren in Wales had not been adequately maintained. However, Edward's reply that it now enjoyed more freedom than it ever had before, while not a wholly appropriate or satisfactory response, was nevertheless not without foundation. It seemed that, if there were justified grievances about the protection of church rights, they came about more because of the tardiness of the king's officials rather than any conscious scheming of the king himself.

There was one very practical problem that had to be dealt with, though. One of the most sacred of all Welsh holy sites was the abbey of Aberconwy. It was a Cistercian site, and the 'white monks' had a special affinity for Wales. Given their love of wild, remote and beautiful places they perhaps felt a natural attachment to the country. In any event, the abbey at Aberconwy was a special place for the Welsh, for some of their great men, including Llywelyn the Great himself, were buried there. But someone else coveted the site. It stood right by the River Conwy, in a position of great strategic importance and as such an ideal spot to build a fortification. In short, Edward planned to build a castle on the very spot where the abbey currently stood.

At a distance, it might appear that the absolutism of a medieval king, especially one in the mould of Edward, might allow him to simply help himself to the land. Nothing could be further from the truth. The medieval period is one continuous story of a struggle between the secular element of society and the clergy to achieve pre-eminence. Both were extremely influential and both weighed heavily in the balance of power. At one point or the other, one side might have an advantage but it would never be overwhelming or conclusive. This was the environment that Edward, as much as any other king, lived in and if he wanted the site of the abbey for his own use, then he would have to negotiate for it.

Crucial to the debate was Bishop Anian of St Asaph's. He had sided with Edward when, a few years previously, the king had tried to persuade the Pope to approve the transfer of the cathedral from St Asaph's to Rhuddlan. However, Anian's role in the recent war had been somewhat ambivalent. In Edward's eyes, he had been far too slow to issue the orders of excommunication in Wales, when he was commanded to by Pecham. On the other hand, when a group of English soldiers had set fire to the cathedral at Bangor he seemed very keen to excommunicate those responsible. Given the bishop's very uncomfortable position, right on the frontier between Wales proper (as it formerly was) and the March, he was in a very difficult situation.

Pecham put pressure on Anian to try to get him to support the king's plans to transfer the abbey from Aberconwy to Maenan. Pecham himself was none too sure that he wished it to move to Maenan specifically. It would mean that there would be five Cistercian foundations in the diocese of St Asaph's and, in a letter to Edward, he wrote that 'Cistercians are the most difficult neighbours that parsons and prelates can have'[21] – an interesting insight into the strength of internal church politics at the time. But the plan was given approval to proceed. Anian was persuaded to support the scheme and in return Pecham attempted to convince the king of the bishop's loyalty, apparently with success.

This was not the only instance where Edward expropriated lands. As well as taking over one of Llywelyn's courts at Caernarfon, he commandeered another at Abergwyngregyn, and the timber-framed hall at Ystumgwern in Anglesey was removed to the new castle at Harlech. But all this involved expense. Money was a constant constraint for Edward. The Welsh wars of 1282–3 had been expensive. With the vast additional expenditure required to complete the king's ambitious castle-building projects in north Wales, the problem would only get worse. These financial difficulties would come home to roost in particularly serious fashion at Edward's last castle in Wales, Beaumaris in Anglesey.

Edward adopted a number of measures to help finance his Welsh adventure. He sent John Kirkby on a tour of England to negotiate loans as an advance against the taxes that had not yet even been agreed. Kirkby was to ask a number of people, especially religious houses, how much they were prepared to give – although one chronicler noted sarcastically that it did not do them much good, as he then assessed them at whatever level he felt to be appropriate anyway.[22] Kirkby raised about £16,500 from his initiative, a useful sum but not enough given the enormous levels of expenditure that Edward required.

Money to pay for all this was a constant anxiety for Edward. The branch of his household known as the Wardrobe was responsible for the organisation of affairs during the Welsh wars. Normally, money was handled by the Exchequer but, in times of war, the Wardrobe operated largely independently of this, which gave Edward much greater flexibility, an immensely useful quality at such times. Among other tasks, the Wardrobe, through an official known as the cofferer, would pay the infantry weekly, though if times were hard and funds scarce, there would be delay. But there was a massive increase in costs during the second Welsh war as opposed to the first: some £150,000 against £23,000 in 1277. In addition to the former amount, about £80,000 would be spent in the next decade on castle-building in Wales.

Against these amounts, we can compare the crown's income. As one gauge of the huge expense of the war, it has been estimated that never more than £1 million of coinage was in circulation at any one time during Edward's reign, with £800,000 a more typical figure. Further, the king's regular income was totally insufficient to pay for the wars. Income from crown lands was maybe £14,000 per annum. Money from the administration of justice and customs added perhaps £10,000 or so, with total revenue for 1284 as one example being estimated as about £27,000. This of course left a massive shortfall in funds for the second Welsh war, which was covered in two ways. The first was by raising taxation, which had to be approved by Parliament. Collection was erratic and collectors could be bribed but taxation was a crucial source of revenue, raising over £81,000 in 1275 and nearly £43,000 in 1283. In addition to secular taxes, taxes could also be raised from the clergy, normally based on the rental value of estates.

The second way of raising finance was through loans. Some small amounts would be raised from private individuals; for example, in the second Welsh war Robert Burnell lent 1,000 marks, John Kirkby £548, John de Bohun £980 and Robert Tibotot 290 marks. But the bulk came from private companies, especially the Italian banking firm known as the Riccardi of Lucca. The company had lent £200,000 to Edward in the first seven years of his reign. In his early years as king, Edward managed to repay a large proportion of his debts to them reasonably promptly; as time went on, it became increasingly difficult to do so. So crucial were the Riccardi to Edward that they were also allocated other tasks such as organising the collection of taxation. Without them and their credit, the war could not have been fought and the Welsh could not have been conquered.[23]

The castles were a fundamental part of Edward's strategy for bringing Wales to heel and funding had to be found to construct them. Not that castles were new to Wales; the roll call of Welsh-built castles is a long one; Ewloe, Denbigh, Dolbadarn, Dolwyddellan, Cricieth, Castell y Bere are just illustrative examples. Llywelyn the Great and Llywelyn ap Gruffudd had both engaged in castle-building as a way of tightening their control over the territories that they held and as a confident expression of their status. But they were, it has rightly been pointed out, different in character from the English castles that came after them.[24]

On the whole, the Welsh castles were defensive in nature, often remote (Castell y Bere and Dolwyddellan spring to mind in this respect), places to protect oneself in times of crisis. The English castles on the other hand had a quite different objective. Not just to dominate (though usually they did that and, as overt statements of royal prestige, this was a not un-important feature of them) but to act as a base from which the king's armies could operate, and also, crucially, to function as an administrative centre, an integral part of the towns that would grow up around them.

Edward's castle-building programme in Wales was immense. Although the greatest of them were built after the war of 1282–3, we should not forget that many were built earlier. All told, fourteen castles were built by Edward. In 1277, work began on Flint, Rhuddlan, Ruthin, Hope (which Edward must have regretted handing over to Dafydd when it was first completed), Builth and Llanbadarn (Aberystwyth). Work began on Conwy, Harlech and Caernarfon in 1283. The year after, Denbigh, Hawarden, Holt and Chirk were begun. Finally, in 1295 work started at

Beaumaris on Anglesey. In addition, other captured castles such as those at Dolwyddellan, Cricieth and Castell y Bere were substantially renovated.

It should also be noted that this list takes no account of the intense castle-building activity undertaken independently by Marcher lords during Edward's reign, to which belong significant work at places such as Cydweli, Carreg Cennen and Cardiff, as well as the greatest of the 'non-royal' castles, Caerphilly. Collectively, the resources expended on this enormous castle-building initiative underline just how hopeless the Welsh position was. This construction programme, allied to the enormity of the defeat in 1283, meant there was no way back for an independent Wales.

It is unnecessary to detail the construction of each and every castle but an examination of the three fortresses where construction began in 1283 is instructive. Conwy would be the biggest of the boroughs in the north, though the administrative centre of the county in which it found itself after the revisions instituted by the Statute of Wales was Caernarfon. Edward arrived at Conwy on 14 March 1283, and within four days he was arranging the hire of labour to build the castle he intended to erect. By the end of that month, Richard of Chester, a master engineer, was making his way to Chester to arrange for the shipment of tools and the recruitment of masons and stone cutters. The king was at Conwy until May, by which time the future format of the castle would presumably have been more or less finalised. The plan was that the building of the castle would be linked to the construction of a walled town, a model that would be repeated elsewhere. The negotiations to relocate the abbey currently on the site were satisfactorily completed and the abbey church, construction of which had not yet been finished, was to become the parish church of the new town.

Construction was under the supervision of Master James of St George. With him were several other important figures in addition to Richard of Chester, such as Henry of Oxford and Laurence of Canterbury, master carpenters, and John Francis, a mason who probably also came from Savoy. The latter had worked with James of St George some time previously in 1262 on a walled town at Saillon in Switzerland, which bears some similarities to Conwy. Edward had arranged with Count Philip of Savoy, who was then James's employer, that Master James would join Edward's service at some time in 1278. He was certainly at the heart of Edward's castle-building venture, and is known to have had controlling input at most of the king's new castles from 1278 onwards. Something of his worth to Edward can be gauged by the fact that he was paid 3s a day, more than knights in the king's service.

The cost of completing the work came to somewhere in the region of £15,000. Work went on until 1292, though the bulk of it, judging by the way the money was spent, was completed by 1287. Much of the stone came from local sources. The most common stone in use was Silurian grit, which was quarried locally. In some parts of the walls rhyolite was used, also of local origin. Another local source provided the freestone used for such architectural features as arrow-loops. Slates and sand for making mortar were also close at hand. Other materials came from further afield. Timber had to be shipped in, and lead and coal came from Flint by sea. Iron, steel and nails came from Newcastle-under-Lyme, again completing their journey by water. More unusual items also had to be brought in from England, such as a statue for the castle chapel.[25]

The town walls, some 1,300 metres long, were an integral part of the construction; so much so that in contemporary accounts of the building of the castle and the town walls, the two are often lumped together as one single entity. The healthy collection of records that have survived give us an invaluable insight as to where the workmen came from. There are more signs of continental influence, with the mention of Jules of Chalons, William of Seyssel (from the Rhone region) and Peter of Boulogne. There are also however a large number of English names, such as Roger of Cockersand (from Lancashire), John of Sherwood and Robert of Frankby.

The end result was an immensely strong series of fortifications. The castle was divided into an outer and an inner ward. There were eight huge round towers around the perimeter of the castle walls, the four of the inner ward being topped with turrets of most unusual construction. A water gate guarded access from the river, which was to be a crucial source of resupply if the castle were ever to be under siege. Twenty-one towers ringed the town walls, which were split by three gateways with double towers. It appeared to be, and it was, a formidable construction, but its ambitious scale was its weakness. Such immense fortifications require a great deal of maintenance, which in its turn costs money. The scale of the castle-building projects would stretch even England's resources too far. A petition from the townspeople in the early years of the fourteenth century begged for more funds 'to save the walls and towers of the town, which are in great peril from the tides of the river'. By 1321, the trusses of some of the roofs were rotting away as they had not been covered properly in lead and by 1332 it was noted that Edward II 'understands they [many of the castles of north Wales] are ruinous and not fit for him to dwell in should he go there'.

Work at Harlech began soon after that at Conwy. Otto de Grandson had entered the surrounding district towards the end of the Welsh campaign. By 20 May, a sum of £100 had already been brought from the Cistercian abbey at Cymer to Harlech so that construction could start.

Soon afterwards, twenty stonemasons and quarriers made their way to the site of the castle from Conwy, a two-day journey across the mountains that would, only months before, have been an extremely perilous undertaking. They were joined soon afterwards in July by another party of stonemasons, as well as carpenters.

There were several distinct phases to the construction of Harlech. The first of them saw the construction of a wall around the inner ward. There was a break in construction during the winter months and, when work on this phase stopped in 1284, the walls were not yet fully complete. The first priority of the builders was to construct the walls to a height and thickness that would give the workforce a degree of protection should they be attacked at any time. It would be foolish indeed for the English to think that, even with Dafydd dead, Wales was completely subdued. Work on the walls stopped in 1284 and started again at a later date. The walls did not attain their final height and thickness until 1289.

The next stage of the castle to be built was the great gatehouse. The style of Harlech was quite different than that of either Conwy or Caernarfon, and it was the massive gatehouse that distinguished it more than anything else. It dominated the castle every bit as much as did the keeps that were a feature of earlier castles. By 1285, at least some of the rooms in the gatehouse were completed. This was so that the constable of the castle, John de Bonvillars, could take up residence with his wife, Agnes. The gatehouse was to be the main residential area of the castle, with the domestic apartments of the constable, the great hall and accommodation for visiting dignitaries all contained within it. At the same time that work on the gatehouse was progressing, work began on the outer wall at the castle. Harlech would be one of the most perfect examples ever built of a concentric castle. Huge round towers at the corners of the walls in the inner ward further enhanced the scope of the 'killing ground' available to the archers inside the castle.

A number of architectural features betray the connections of the architect with Savoy. These include the use of inclined scaffolding on the south tower of the gatehouse, the use of round-headed arches, an unusual form of latrine shaft which is very similar to that at La Batiaz in Valais, window designs in the gatehouse closely mirroring those at Chillon in Switzerland and evidence that the tops of the battlements were decorated with stone pinnacles (also the case at Conwy).[26]

Expenditure on the building peaked at about £240 per month between September 1286 and November 1287. By 1289, construction was virtually complete. The walls of the inner ward were finally thickened and raised, and a path constructed from the water gate up to the main body of the castle (the sea is now half a mile away from the castle, but during the medieval period it was close to the base). All the domestic buildings, the hall, the chapel, the kitchens, had by now been finished and the structure was ready for full occupation. Again, the international nature to the workforce is of interest, one William of Drogheda being paid in 1289 for the construction of several towers at the rate of 45s per foot, and for the turrets at the rate of 12s per foot. The year after the building was finished, Master James of St George was made constable of the castle (John de Bonvillars having died in 1287), taking up residence with his wife Ambrosia. Agnes, the widow of Bonvillars, had acted as constable since his untimely death. In 1295, Master James was given a life pension in the manor of Mostyn in the north-east of Wales. Although details of his subsequent life are not extensive, it is known that he died at some time before 1309, surviving records from that year describing how Mostyn was 'late of Master James of St George, deceased'.

* * *

The greatest of the castles erected by Edward, certainly in terms of its spectacular appeal, is undoubtedly Caernarfon. In its basic format it is not dissimilar to Conwy, being divided into two wards and surrounded by a series of towers, all of them topped by subsidiary turrets. The construction of the castle, the town walls with which it was integrally linked and the quay, which would also play a crucial logistical part in the function of the whole, were again treated as one exercise. There is a continuity about the fortifications, a 'oneness', that would be obvious generations after it was finished. One awed seventeenth-century traveller wrote how he had arrived at 'Caernarfon, where I thought to have seen a town and a castle, or a castle and a town; but I saw both to be one, and one to be both; for indeed a man can hardly divide them in judgement or apprehension; and I have seen many gallant fabrics and fortifications, but for compactness and completeness of Caernarfon, I never yet saw a parallel.'[27]

One only has to see Caernarfon once to realise that, stylistically, it is on an altogether greater scale than Conwy, or any of the other castles that Edward caused to be built. The towers are multi-angular rather than round. The walls are banded, layers of differently coloured stone being set into them, giving a striking effect. It has often been remarked that the whole bears more than a passing resemblance to the walls of Constantinople, and there is little doubt that the totality of the castle and its overall effect is even greater than the sum of its individually impressive parts. Everything is on a grand scale. The Eagle Tower is much larger than any normal tower and incorporates many of the finest residential parts of the castle, to the extent that it is almost a throwback to the old concept of a keep. The gates, of which there are two major ones, the King's Gate and the Queen's Gate, are massive. It is a castle that sends a message to the people that it overshadows, an unmistakable statement of domination, of control and of a new order that must be obeyed. There were even three statuesque eagles, an imperial motif, perching proudly on top of the turret on the Eagle Tower.

The link with Constantinople was quite deliberate. Under the year 1283, Matthew of Westminster notes that: 'The body of that great prince, the father of the noble emperor Constantine, was discovered at Caernarfon near Snowdon, and by command of the king was honourably placed in the church.'[28] The castle complex, including the town walls that were linked-in to it, was a symbolic assertion that the legacy of the Roman Empire had passed, that a new imperial dynasty had now assumed its place, and with it, the right to govern Wales.

It would be wrong to think that Edward developed Caernarfon from scratch. A motte and bailey castle had been erected there early on in the Norman incursions into Wales. When the territory was recovered by the Welsh princes, it became an important part of their principality. Llywelyn the Great and Llywelyn ap Gruffudd both held court there on occasion. Edward would undoubtedly elevate it to new levels, though. A new castle ditch was dug, reference to this first being made in the records on 24 June 1283. A temporary stockade was then erected around the site to protect the builders while they worked. Timber was shipped in from Conwy, Rhuddlan and Liverpool. Wood was even re-used from the now redundant bridge that had been constructed across the Menai Strait to Anglesey.

Again, nothing was allowed to stand in the way of the castle, though this time there was at least no abbey on the site to worry about. If the wooden houses of any of the populace stood in the way, they were simply pulled down. It was three years before householders received any compensation. One of the first jobs that the workmen had to undertake was to construct temporary wooden dwellings for the king and his queen, who arrived in July 1283 and stayed for a month. By April 1284, according to tradition, the Eagle Tower must have been partially complete, for it was here that Queen Eleanor gave birth to her son, Edward, on the 25th. It is quite possible that the tower was partly finished by this time and therefore this element of the legend at least may be correct.

By 1284, the basic structure of the castle was becoming apparent, as were the town walls. There was still, however, heavy expenditure on the castle in 1286, but by 1287 basic construction work was more or less finished, though significant numbers of men were still being employed on polishing off the finer details of the castle. By 1288, expenditure was considerably lower than in previous years, and by 1292, everything was finished – at least superficially.

The castle today looks virtually impregnable. But the construction we see now is not the one finished by 1292. In 1294, the castle was attacked and sacked and it was obvious that it had been hopelessly inadequate as a defensive structure once the town walls had been breached. Substantial work was undertaken on increasing the strength of the walls and some parts of the defences that had originally been constructed of wood, such as the bridge to the main gate of the town, were rebuilt in stone.[29] Even this does not complete the story, however. Expenditure went on being incurred on finishing works at the castle until 1330, in all perhaps £25,000 being spent on it from start to finish. But the castle never was actually finished. The inside of the Queen's Gate, so impressive when seen from the outside, was never built in its entirety. Neither was the King's Gate which, if completed as planned, would have been monumental, with five doors and six portcullises for any would-be attacker to negotiate before breaking into the upper ward. Some of the surviving structure suggests that walls elsewhere that were meant to be added never were.[30] Edward, so capable at marshalling his resources in times of war, could not repeat the feat in peacetime. His ambitions exceeded his budget.

Caernarfon was to play an important part in the administration of the king's newly won lands. It was to provide the residence of his justiciar in the north of Wales. It would be the administrative centre for three shires, those of Caernarfon, Anglesey and Merioneth. It would also have an important role as a port. The charter issued to the town in 1284 was designed to encourage settlers from England to make their homes in the area, a move deliberately planned to help in the integration of Wales into Edward's empire. In 1285 or 1286, Otto de Grandson was made constable of the castle. He by now had a large income, drawing a salary of £100 for his role as constable as well as a much larger one of £1,000 from his position as justiciar.

Conwy, Harlech and Caernarfon were just three of the castles built or reconstructed by Edward, though they were assuredly the grandest erected immediately after the second Welsh war. The towns that grew up as an integral part of these castles would be copied in the 1290s in Flintshire, at Caerwys, Overton and New Mostyn, though interestingly they were not accompanied by castles,[31] suggesting that Edward felt that this area was by now far enough away from any potential front line to be safe. Elsewhere, a great deal more work on castles took place, albeit on a somewhat more modest scale. Cricieth had been captured from the

Welsh in 1283 – it was in English hands by 14 March. In the next nine years, about £500 was spent on the castle, a still substantial sum. The castle has unfortunately not survived the passage of time as well as some of its more famous contemporaries but what can be gleaned from the elements that remain suggests that improvements took place in a number of areas. For example, it appears that some of the towers were heightened (Welsh castles as a rule never exceeded two storeys in height and Cricieth was a storey higher than this). Work was also done on strengthening the inner and outer gatehouses. Again, significant expenditure on repairing the castle between 1307 and 1325, in the reign of Edward's son, demonstrates that finding the money to keep the castle in a suitable state of repair was a serious drain on the resources of the Exchequer.[32]

At Denbigh, the chief town of the *cantrefs* (administrative regions) of Rhufoniog and Rhos, which had been granted to the earl of Lincoln as his reward for his support for the king, it was the earl himself who was responsible for constructing the castle. The town had been captured in October 1282 and by the end of the month the king was already at the town and thinking about the layout of a new castle. With him was Master James of St George. But once work had started, the king left the earl to his own devices (he employed a similar approach at Hawarden, Holt and Chirk). By 1284, construction had gone far enough for the earl to concern himself with the crucial detail of how he could stock his deer park, and in the next year he granted the town a charter. A large number of English settlers were attracted to the town, much resented by the local Welsh population to the extent that there were outbreaks of violence between the two long into the fourteenth century.

The construction was impressive. It followed a familiar pattern, with a thin outer wall being built first to provide some elementary protection for the workmen. The work then proceeded to a more substantial level. There was a magnificent gatehouse, as well as a number of distinctive octagonal towers. The castle was once more integrated with town walls, which were 1,100 metres in length. Despite the sizeable town that this implies, the walls were not long enough. By 1305, there were 52 houses inside the walls and 183 outside them. But for the earl the castle became a haunted place, with sombre memories. A son died when he fell down a well within the castle in 1308.[33]

This massive programme of castle building was designed to ensure that there would be no more Welsh revolts to concern Edward. Yet there were still inevitably underlying tensions. Despite all the apparent concessions to reasonableness in the Statute of Wales, the true test of whether or not the Welsh would be well treated depended on the sensitivity of Edward's officials. There was little reason for optimism in this respect, given their past record, and their stern attitude continued much as it had in the build-up to the last war. A number of them earned a well-deserved reputation for exploitation. On Anglesey, the king's sheriff, Roger de Pulesdon, was accused of unfair practices in attempting to balance an undoubtedly tight budget. The queen had been given some of Dafydd's old lands, including Hope, and one of her officials, Roger de Bures, was especially odious to the Welsh. Old rights were consistently ignored and rents were raised without justification. Around Denbigh, large numbers of Welsh people were deprived of their land and given totally inadequate compensation in return.

Lest it be thought that it was just the king's officials involved in this repression and exploitation and not the king himself, reference must be made to a series of pronouncements made by Edward in the mid-1290s. These ordered that no Welshmen could hold gatherings without first being granted the king's permission. They could not hold lands in any of the newly founded towns. Furthermore, they could not bear arms in the towns, nor could they offer shelter to a stranger for more than one night. They would only be allowed to sell their goods in market towns.[34] Resentment between English settlers and the native Welsh bubbled away, barely concealed beneath the surface. The Welsh were dispossessed of many of the better lands to the benefit of the settlers, and were given poor quality land in return. The settlers did nothing to soothe their ruffled feelings, self-consciously emphasising their dominance by referring to themselves as 'the English burgesses of the English boroughs of Wales'. As one writer noted, 'and so by the providence of God, the glory of the Welsh, who were thus against their will subjected to the laws of the English, was transferred to the English'.[35]

And so the list of restrictions went on. While some of them might be understandable in the light of the unrest that still existed in Wales at the time, the cumulative effect of all these strictures was to make the Welsh second-class citizens in their own country. But not for the first, nor for the last, time, Edward, and more especially his officials, had misjudged the situation. Even when the odds against an occupied nation are high – in Wales's case impossibly so – oppression can still stoke up the flames of resistance. The Welsh dragon might be in its last throes, lying mortally wounded, but it could still lash out against its oppressor before it finally expired.

CHAPTER ELEVEN

Death Throes

As you know, Welshmen are Welshmen and you need to
understand them properly; if, which God forbid, there is war with France or
Scotland, we shall need to watch them all the more closely.[1]

Despite the apparent finality of Edward I's conquest, there were to be two more Welsh uprisings during his reign. But the two events, one in 1287, the other in 1294, were dissimilar in character, though both in their own way give us clues to Edward's mindset, and his flaws both as a man and a king.

Rhys ap Maredudd had decided to throw in his lot with Edward at an early stage, having concluded that there was little future in resisting the irresistible, and early in the war of 1277 submitted to Edward. In return, Rhys had been confirmed in possession of his castle at Dryslwyn and the surrounding commote known as Catheiniog. Rhys reckoned that by offering his subservience to Edward he increased his chances of being offered lands in Wales by a grateful king. And, indeed, he had a splendid and obvious example on which to base this hope. A century earlier, his ancestor, the great Lord Rhys of Deheubarth, had become the king's man in the region (the king on that earlier occasion being Henry II). In return, Henry had treated him very favourably indeed. As a result of submitting to Henry, the earlier Rhys's position had been significantly advanced rather than compromised. It was an excellent illustration of how a Welsh lord could strengthen his hand while apparently giving in to the English. Unfortunately, it was a wholly inappropriate example for Rhys ap Maredudd to follow. Edward was no Henry, though the two men undoubtedly shared a short fuse in common. And circumstances were rather different now from what they had been a hundred years earlier.

During the war of 1282, Rhys remained loyal, and indeed played an active role in support of the English, involving himself in expeditions in the south-west of Wales from the outset. Edward was quick to make recognition of this, appointing him to some of the lands initially held by rebels in the region in July 1282. But, only five years later, Rhys had decided that he was mistaken in his actions and that his submission to

Edward had yielded insufficient benefits. What, then, had changed?

Part of the answer lies with Edward himself. His leading modern biographer notes that he had little taste for patronage and rarely showed himself to be a generous master.[2] The same observer unequivocally attributes the rising led by Rhys in 1287 to a 'lack of generosity towards those Welsh who had served him in the wars'.[3] Yet it is important to note that the rising of 1287 was, when it came, one that was largely unsupported by other Welshmen. There was no broad groundswell of support for Rhys from elsewhere in the country. This perhaps suggests several things. The first is that the bedrock of resistance to England was still to be found in the north of the country; the south-west was too far away from the epicentre of anti-English feeling to generate a wider response. But even more crucial may have been the way that other Welshmen felt about Rhys himself, a man who had openly thrown in his lot with Edward and had clearly hoped to profit from the disenfranchisement of other Welsh lords in the region. They saw now that his reasons for rebellion were driven purely by self-interest rather than any wider, more altruistic concerns.

It was clear that Rhys was aggrieved at the lack of reward he had been given in return for his support for Edward. It was not that he was completely without wealth. The latter half of the thirteenth century saw some substantial building works in Rhys's major base at Dryslwyn. During that period, a second ward was added to the castle, effectively doubling it in size. The later addition of a third ward by Rhys made it 'one of the largest masonry castles ever raised by native Welsh lords, a structure impressive enough to rival any number of strongholds raised by Anglo-Norman and English lords of the March'.[4] Excavations in the 1980s have given us a very rare insight into the standard of living enjoyed by Rhys ap Maredudd, which give the lie to any preconceived ideas that the Welsh lords of the day lived a basic and spartan existence. Excavators found evidence that the clothes that the inhabitants of the castle wore in Rhys's time were decorated with fine jewellery. Even more intriguing was evidence found of the diet enjoyed by Rhys and his entourage. Bones of cattle, sheep, pig and deer suggest the range of meats available.

Game birds, including partridge, woodcock, snipe and mallard, added to the variety. A large number of fish were also found, including salmon, trout, pike, cod, plaice, herring, mackerel, haddock and hake. Fruits such as raspberries, cherries and blackberries were also eaten. More unusual was the discovery of grapes and figs from Gascony. All in all, it was a convincing intimation that Rhys ap Maredudd lived a relatively comfortable life.[5]

But he had not been granted Dinefwr Castle as he had hoped, which must have been a particular disappointment. Dinefwr was resonant with symbolism as the headquarters of the great Lord Rhys, and Rhys ap Maredudd could never hope to match his claims to prominence while it was not in his possession. Neither was this his only cause for complaint. At the end of the war of 1283, he had been tried by Parliament for taking possession of some lands granted to him by Edward, before they had formally passed to him. It was a classic example of Edward's heavy-handedness. While the king was within his rights to act in this manner, it humiliated a man who had supported the crown loyally in the recent wars. It would have been much more sensible for Edward to have a quiet word in the ear of Rhys and express his displeasure in other, more subtle ways but this would have been a most un-Edwardian way of handling the situation. Rhys was, presumably, deeply unhappy at this very public admonishment.

But what made Rhys realise that he had misjudged the situation was the way that English lords were given lands adjacent to his which effectively ended his ambitions of achieving prominence in a way that matched his illustrious forefathers. Edward handed out many parcels of land in the region to his English supporters, John Giffard in particular, hemming Rhys in. The problem was exacerbated by Edward's justiciar in the region, Robert Tibotot. Rhys also found himself in opposition to Alan de Plukenet. Even some of Rhys's own tenants, it seems, were at odds with him. In short, Rhys ap Maredudd does not appear to have been a man who found it difficult to make enemies. He was ambitious, a fact that was eloquently illustrated by his marriage to Ada, sister of John Hastings, lord of Abergavenny, in 1285 – as part of his wedding gift from Ada's brother, he received the castle of Newcastle Emlyn in the west of the country. But his ambitions were not fulfilled as he would have wished.

The problem finally spiralled out of control in 1287. In that year, Rhys was summoned to appear before the court of Robert Tibotot to answer some long-standing complaints against him. The situation had been festering for a while and, the previous year, Rhys had even visited Edward, who was campaigning in France, asking for his support in resolving the problem. The king had then written to Edmund of Cornwall, who was in charge in England during Edward's absence, asking that Rhys's grievances should be examined and resolved. But although the king was sympathetic, few other men in England were.

Rhys decided that his grievances were not going to be satisfactorily dealt with through discussion and he therefore rose up in arms. On 8 June 1287, he seized Llandovery Castle, a loss soon followed by the fall of the castles at Carreg Cennen and Dinefwr to him. In the attacks, the constables of the castles were killed along with significant numbers of their garrisons. His initial successes suggest complacency on the part of the English, who appear to have been unprepared to deal with the rising. John Giffard fell back on Builth, finding the forces ranged against him too strong. Rhys then advanced on Carmarthen and onwards to Swansea, which he burned. He also turned northwards towards Llanbadarn, although here the castle survived even if parts of the town did not.

The rebellion certainly came at an inconvenient time for Edward, who was still out of the country in Gascony. It could have been an awkward moment for the English if other parts of Wales rose in support of Rhys. In the event, few did; even some of Rhys's own men sided with the English. Edmund of Cornwall reacted decisively. On 16 July 1287, writs were issued to the Marcher lords instructing them to raise their forces. Edmund Mortimer and John Giffard were given specific instructions to hold Radnor and the surrounding area against Rhys. No fewer than four armies were raised and descended on Rhys's main base at Dryslwyn. Edmund of Cornwall called his own men together at Carmarthen; they numbered 4,000, some of them coming from England, while others were raised locally by Robert Tibotot. Tibotot was particularly quick to react to the threat, a perfectly logical response given the proximity of his lands to those of Rhys. He took early measures to ensure that Cardiganshire was capable of resisting Rhys. Tibotot then turned his attentions to Carmarthen, where he concentrated a force of over 500 Welsh infantry.

His forces were already assuming sizeable proportions when Edmund of Cornwall arrived. Edmund had been compelled to amend his line of advance due to the energy of Rhys. He had originally meant to march through Brecon but the English forces there, led by the earl of Gloucester, had been forced on to the defensive by Rhys's incursions into the area. Edmund therefore needed to take his army through Monmouthshire and Glamorgan to avoid the threat. He reached Carmarthen on 8 August. These English forces were joined a week later by a large army of 6,700, led by Reginald Grey from Chester and Roger Lestrange from Montgomery. Grey seems to have been in a particular hurry. He planned to bring 500 woodsmen with him, but in the event only 20 reached Dryslwyn.[6] Edmund had already moved his men up from Carmarthen to Dryslwyn after spending a few days at Carmarthen. Once again, the large proportions of Welshmen in the final 'English' army should be noted, two-thirds of the troops being Welsh.[7]

Gloucester in the meantime had reacted strongly to Rhys's incursions into Brecon. He had recruited a large number of woodsmen from the thickly wooded area of the Forest of Dean to cut roads through the forested mountain areas in the south of the country. He then assembled a huge number of foot soldiers as a further contribution to the war effort, raising some 5,000 in all. The Marcher lords as a body managed to put together the substantial number of 12,500 in their army, an insight into both the great resources available to them and also how they could operate together if encouraged to do so through the exigencies of a perceived crisis that seemed to threaten their vested interests. The stabilisation of the surrounding area was an important part of English strategy, as it allowed lines of communication to the forward base around Dryslwyn to be maintained. The successful achievement of this objective was illustrated by the safe passage of £800 of funds through the area to pay the army around Rhys's main base.

A close siege was laid to the castle at Dryslwyn. There were a large number of craftsmen who had been brought from Chester and they assembled a huge trebuchet, a device that hurled substantial rocks at the walls of the castle. It cost £14 to build, being made of a range of materials including timber, hides, rope and lead. Nearly 50 men were used to shape the huge stone balls which were constructed to be hurled at the castle.[8] The major problem facing the besiegers was how to keep such a large army of nearly 11,000 infantry and perhaps 600 cavalry properly provisioned. It was not long indeed before numbers were significantly reduced, partly because forces were deployed elsewhere, partly because periods of service had expired and partly because of that persistent problem of all feudal armies, desertion.

The besiegers also used other methods to bring about the fall of the castle. They began to mine under the walls in an attempt to bring them down. The action was not an unmitigated success. Although a large section of wall near the chapel was brought down, part of it fell on a group of English lords who were too close, killing a number of them, including John de Bonvilliars.

The English opted to continue the assault from a safer distance. The siege carried on with the trebuchet continuing to batter the walls. Given the disparity in size between the English army and the garrison, there was only ever one likely outcome, and that was made more certain when the earl of Gloucester arrived on 29 August with a large force of 3,500 infantry. Their arrival was welcome to the English, who had been suffering unexpected attrition in the attack. The castle fell early in September, but the English were not operating as efficiently as they might have been and Rhys and some of his entourage escaped. It is almost certainly the case that he had made his way from the castle very early on. Welsh tactics had in the past frequently acknowledged the stupidity of letting English forces surround hugely outnumbered Welsh forces in castles where their only advantages, knowledge of the countryside and mobility, would be completely negated.

The castle at Dryslwyn suffered a great deal of damage in the siege and £130 was spent by the constable Alan de Plukenet in restoring it after its capture. Other funds were expended on constructing a mill for the castle and in felling woods around it. Further afield, Llanbadarn also had to be repaired, an enterprise which cost £320. Garrisons of 24 men were installed at both Dryslwyn and Dinefwr. The garrisons might not appear large but they did not need to be so in order to adequately defend a strong castle, while reinforcements could quickly be summoned to the aid of a besieged garrison. The biggest enemy to the English was complacency, a lesson that was obvious from the initial successes of Rhys. A town grew up around Dryslwyn. It had developed in Rhys's time, a fact confirmed by the granting of its charter by Edward a few years before the revolt, permitting it to hold a fair for four days starting on St Bartholomew's Day. There is evidence that, after the fall of the castle, settlers – English, Gascon or Flemish – moved in; but, during the thirteenth century, the town settled into terminal decline. It was decimated during the Black Death, but was already experiencing a number of problems by this time. An inspection in 1343 identified that £341 needed to be spent on renovating the castle. By the seventeenth century, there were few signs of the town left.

The fall of Dryslwyn effectively marked the end of a significant phase of Rhys's revolt, though not of Rhys himself. He took the castle at Newcastle Emlyn in a surprise attack in November 1287. The castle had been taken over by Tibotot. In capturing the castle, Rhys also gained for himself an important prisoner in the shape of Roger Mortimer, though most of the English garrison were not as fortunate as their commander and died in the battle. Rhys was still more than capable of making a nuisance of himself and returned to Dinefwr, laying siege to the castle, where his surprise attack was unsuccessful. However, this continued activity on Rhys's part owed more to his energy than to any realistic hopes of success. The crushing victory of the English at Dryslwyn served to remind any Welshman who had forgotten the fact of the immense disparity in resources between the two countries. Resistance at Dryslwyn had been gallant and the English had not had an easy time in taking the castle. But even the losses suffered by the English served to emphasise their advantages, as more men had subsequently arrived to take the place of those lost in the assaults.

After the fall of Dryslwyn, the earl of Cornwall was confident enough of English superiority not to summon large numbers of troops to subdue Rhys. Tibotot was largely left to manage the situation locally. By the end of November, he set out to the relief of Dinefwr with just over 1,000 local infantry and a few cavalry. It was a very small force compared to those employed in the first stage of Rhys's revolt but it was more than enough to encourage the insurgents to move away from Dinefwr. Possibly slightly nervous after the initial successes of Rhys, Plukenet at Dryslwyn substantially increased his garrison at Dryslwyn, increasing it to forty-eight and adding thirty-eight crossbowmen.

Having pushed Rhys back, the English now moved to recover Newcastle Emlyn. They were led by William de Braose and by the beginning of 1288 they were in place around the castle. The great siege engine that had caused so much damage at Dryslwyn was brought into use again, being guarded by 500 men en route. Some repairs to it were necessary but by 10 January it was in position. A good deal of documentary evidence survives to add detail to the story of the subsequent siege, such as the fact that 480 stones were carried from the beach at Cardigan for use as ammunition.[9] The besieging force of about 1,000 men was more than enough to convince those inside the castle that resistance was futile and it was surrendered on 20 January, seemingly without a fight. Shortly afterwards, most of the army was disbanded, suggesting that the English were now confident that the revolt was at an end.

Rhys was now forced to adopt the life of a fugitive, living as a refugee in his own country. As early as December 1287, men had been out searching for him. Now they scoured mountain, forest and moor looking for him but he knew the country well enough to stay out of their way. But although he survived, he was an irrelevance, so much so that before long the English were running down their garrisons to very low levels, confident that there would be no more revolts. Rhys was eventually betrayed by one of his own in April 1292 and subsequently suffered the same horrific fate as that dealt to Prince Dafydd of Gwynedd, dying a terrible death at York. His betrayal is a poignant and perhaps a fitting epitaph. His revolt was fuelled primarily by frustrated ambition, a motivation that was so blatant that few were encouraged to join him. For so long an ally of the English, and a determined enemy of those Welshmen who wished to defeat Edward I, many no doubt felt that his frustrations were no more than his just deserts. A man who made too many enemies, both among his own people and the English, the legendary heritage of the ancient lords of Deheubarth was a prize that was far beyond Rhys's powers or reach.

But there were lessons for the English too. They may have been reassured by the fact that there was so little local support for Rhys in the rebellion but they had been far too complacent during the events leading up to his uprising. They had clearly assumed that Rhys would not rise in rebellion while Edward was still considering his grievances, and in what appeared to be a sympathetic manner. (Similar considerations had not stopped Prince Dafydd from rebelling in 1282.) They were caught completely off-guard when Rhys had attacked, with significant initial success. Panicked into an overwhelming response, their confidence was perhaps restored by their ultimate victory. But they still needed to take care: Rhys had failed, at least in part, because he had too many enemies among those who needed to be his allies if any revolt was to succeed. He also launched his rebellion in an area that was no longer totally opposed to the English. In both respects, the English had been fortunate. It would have served the English well to guard against complacency in the future, or there might be further rebellions yet to come. It was a lesson that they did not absorb as thoroughly as they ought.

The cost of putting down Rhys's revolt was not excessively expensive. It cost some £10,000 to deal with it.[10] Nevertheless, there was a problem in finding these sums as the Wardrobe, the usual administrative body for handling such matters, was away in France with Edward. Edmund was forced to turn to the Italian banking firms once more to finance most of the campaign. The relatively small cost was nevertheless something of a relief to Edward, involved as he was in continental adventures that were already stretching his limited resources. The subjugation of Wales had already cost him a good deal of money, and he could ill afford to spend any more when so many ambitious projects elsewhere were already causing him financial difficulties.

* * *

In the years immediately following the defeat of Rhys, the main interests of Edward I in Wales were as a source of revenue, and as a political, rather than a military, battleground, on which he fought against the interests and what he perceived to be the excessive power of the Marcher lords. There were few signs of rebellious tendencies from within Wales and, when violence did erupt once more, it struck like a thunderbolt from a cloudless sky. That Edward was keen to ensure he gained maximum advantage from his Welsh possessions is clear enough. Taxes were levied on the country which were in practice far more onerous than those raised in England.[11] The target to be raised was £10,000 across the country and the collectors appointed to gather it in went about their task with irritating enthusiasm. As a relatively poor country, taxes such as those charged to Wales in 1292 must have taken a severe toll of relatively scarce economic resources. But it appeared that the Welsh were unable to do much about their heavy burden other than to mutter under their breath at the injustice of it all. Not all kept their thoughts to themselves, though; one man from near Denbigh, Iorwerth ap Cynwrig, boldly stated that the English would soon become aware of 'such rumours that they will no longer wish to come to Wales'.[12]

Edward's attention had moved on to other matters. In Scotland, where the throne had become vacant, he saw an opportunity to extend his interests. Increasingly, he began to assert what he perceived as his rights over the Scottish nation, a personal trait that many in Wales recognised only too well. But he was also distracted further afield. Friction with France had been evident for a while; in 1294, it became all-out war. Conflict overseas was a serious matter for the English crown. It involved a great deal of organisation, money and men. Manpower was a particular problem. Feudal rights which enabled the king to force men to fight for him for a fixed period did not extend to service overseas. It was therefore a very significant challenge for Edward to raise a sufficiently powerful army to make an impact across the English Channel.

There was one area especially where Edward hoped to recruit forces. Soldiers from Wales had proved their worth on a number of occasions. The Welsh enjoyed fighting and a good number of them made a living of sorts from it. The king therefore looked to the country as a source of men to fight overseas. He needed to do so. Recruitment was going so poorly that Edward was forced to issue pardons to criminals if in return they agreed to join his forces.[13] Specific instructions were given to Reginald Grey at Chester to raise forces and also to Robert Staundon, justiciar of north Wales. Further south, Edward's loyal supporter, Robert Tibotot, was similarly instructed. The men raised were to gather during September, and Staundon's men were to present themselves at Shrewsbury on the 30th. Even before they arrived, a number of leading English lords who held lands in Wales sailed for France. Tibotot for example crossed the Channel to join Edward, and the earl of Lincoln was also out of the country. In the meantime, some Welsh forces moved to join the expedition, one body reaching Winchester on its way to the embarkation point at Portsmouth. But the Welsh troops at Winchester were destined never to take ship for France, for they were abruptly turned around. Their loyalty was now in grave doubt, because Wales was once more in flames.

The full scale of the revolt was not immediately apparent. However, although initial news of the uprising was patchy, subsequent information showed that it was indeed a very serious event. One of the foremost symbols of the ultimate triumph of the English was the castle at Caernarfon. But, despite its imperial grandeur, the complacency of the English in failing to properly finish the castle quickly became obvious. Its defences were incomplete and were overrun by the rebels. It appears that the town walls were substantially finished but those of the castle itself were not. In particular, the north curtain walls and the towers of the castle were not at their full height. Once the rebels had broken into the town, the castle was quickly overrun. Before long, acrid flames leapt upwards into the sky, hungrily consuming everything in their path, while in their shadow the mutilated body of the Sheriff, Roger de Pulesdon, lay battered and lifeless. Caernarfon was to remain in Welsh hands for some six months. Knowing full well that the English would fight back, the Welsh took the opportunity of demolishing as much of the town walls as they could, so that they would not be capable of protecting the English again without a great deal of rebuilding work. The full extent of the great damage that they inflicted upon it is absolutely clear from the extent of reconstruction that later had to take place.[14]

The raid on Caernarfon was far from an isolated incident. All over Wales, castles were attacked. Far to the south, Builth, which had been denuded of troops by John Giffard for the campaign in France, was attacked and officials were put to death. The town of Caerphilly was burned, though the castle itself proved unassailable; unlike the fortress at Morlais, which was taken by the rebels. Both Cardigan and Castell y Bere were also besieged by the Welsh. Denbigh, Ruthin, Mold and Hawarden were all taken, though Flint, Rhuddlan, Conwy and Harlech held out.

The widespread nature of the revolt, and the destruction of the house of the princes of Gwynedd, meant that there were several prominent local Welsh leaders at the head of the rebels. The main leader in the north was Madog ap Llywelyn, who was son of a lord in Meirionydd. Far from exceptionally, he had at one time been in the pay of Edward I and had spent some time living in England. It may well be that, like Rhys ap Maredudd and Prince Dafydd, he felt that he had not been adequately recompensed by Edward for his support and took advantage of his distracted attentions elsewhere to lead the revolt which overwhelmed Caernarfon. Cardiganshire rose under the leadership of Maelgwyn ap Rhys, while in the south-east revolt broke out in Glamorgan, led by Morgan ap Maredudd (not a relative of Rhys ap Maredudd).

Not for the first time in his reign, events in Wales had caught Edward off his guard. But if his intelligence gathering was at fault in failing to predict the crisis, he again showed his martial qualities in his response. He was in some sense lucky that the revolt was launched before he had sailed for France. It meant that he had both troops and provisions at hand with which to commence his fightback. Orders were issued for his levies to meet him at Worcester, while the campaign proper would be launched when forces had assembled at Brecon, Cardiff and Chester. The king would again base his advance on Chester, once more recognising that the greatest challenge to him came from the north of Wales.

Before his forces arrived, however, there was a good deal of local fighting to be done. Edward was also fortunate that one of his most trusted lieutenants was on hand in Wales to ensure that the revolt did not become uncontrollable. Reginald Grey may have been hated by many of his Welsh tenants but he had proved his usefulness to Edward before and proceeded to do so again. By the beginning of October he had 5,000 infantry and 50 cavalry in place to halt any Welsh advance. He placed considerable numbers of these troops as reinforcements for the garrisons of some of the castles in the north-east of the country and possibly helped to save them as a result. Flint had 170 men who stood guard on the walls, while a smaller but serviceable garrison of 40 watched for the rebels from the battlements of Rhuddlan.[15] No doubt anxious to avoid the fate of the castle at Caernarfon, engineers were called up to strengthen the defences of the castles. But the outcome was still uncertain as far as the English were concerned. They were having great trouble finding men to hold back the rebels and recruits had to be summoned from as far away as Cumbria. By 20 October there could be no doubt about the seriousness of the uprising and Edward moved the supplies he had collected at Portsmouth for the French campaign to Wales instead.

Orders from Edward later in the month to John de Havering, telling him to ensure that the castles of the north were to be kept provisioned by sea, illustrate several points. The rebellion was obviously on a large scale and had forced the English on to the back foot. But, by the same token, the foresight of Edward was shown to the full. By ensuring that his chain of castles was constructed in such a way that the links in it could be sustained by supplies shipped in by water, Edward utilised one of England's major advantages over the Welsh. The English had control of the sea and, unless the castles were captured by the Welsh in a surprise attack, in most instances the strength of the defences ensured that the garrisons inside them, even if depleted, had a good chance of resisting the rebels.

This was nowhere better illustrated than at Harlech and Cricieth, two castles that were extremely isolated from England, at the western extremities of Wales. Harlech was completely cut off by land but supplies shipped in from Ireland meant that the castle was never taken by the rebels. And, if the castles could not be taken and destroyed in the initial Welsh onslaught, then the omens for the rebels were gloomy indeed. Any extended campaign could once again only play into the hands of the English and their superior material resources.

But, as the English held on, it was by their fingernails. The earl of Lincoln attempted to take matters into his own hands. Before the king arrived, he advanced towards his main base at Denbigh but badly misjudged both the temper of the country and the strength of the rebels, who drove him and his inadequate force back with a badly bloodied nose. Llanbadarn further south was also closely besieged, the defence being led by the widow of the recently murdered justiciar of west Wales, Geoffrey Clement. The defenders held out, if only just. Then, on 12 November, came the first signs of a determined English counter-attack. John Giffard had gathered around him a small force of some seventy men. Four times they advanced on Builth, attempting to raise the siege that had been laid around it. Then, at the fifth attempt, they finally broke through and rescued the garrison of seventy men, who had been holding out resiliently for six weeks. But this success did not mark the collapse of the revolt. A relieving force was sent to effect a similar result at Castell y Bere. According to some, they were successful in their objective. But recent archaeological excavations reveal a serious fire at the castle at around this time which, along with documentary evidence, tells a different story and suggests that the castle was taken and destroyed.[16]

The English present in the north of the country were able to prevent a complete collapse of their defences there until the king arrived. Edward met up with his forces at Worcester towards the end of November. His original plan was modified: three armies would now gather at Chester, Montgomery and Carmarthen. The force at Montgomery was under the command of the earl of Warwick, while that at Carmarthen would be led by William de Valance and the earl of Norfolk, Roger Bigod. Edward moved through Shrewsbury but did not advance towards Castell y Bere, suggesting that by this stage the castle was either saved or destroyed. The size of the army was massive, its power awesome even by the standard of previous campaigns. There were about 21,000 infantry in the north of the country, nearly 11,000 at Montgomery and about 4,000 in the south. Numbers of cavalry are not known but they must have been considerable. Once these forces achieved momentum, they would roll over any force in Wales that was misguided enough to stand in their way.

Edward led the main force, which pushed forward from Chester. However, he chose to vary his route from those which he had used in the past. Rather than leading his army along the traditional coastal route, he moved towards Wrexham, hoping to crush the rebels who had recently discomfited the earl of Lincoln en route to Denbigh. He arrived in Wrexham on 11 December, where he stopped for a few days, allowing reinforcements from further afield, led by Hugh Cressingham, to join him. Bypassing Denbigh, he arrived at the castle of Conwy in time for Christmas, being joined en route by Reginald Grey.

Edward must have been well satisfied with progress to date. He had with him a huge army and, after the initial successes they had enjoyed, the rebels now seemed to be quiet. The appearance was at this stage illusory, although 10,000 rebels surrendered to Edward during December and agreed to serve in France with him. They also undertook to bring in Madog, leader of the rebels in the north of the country. But when they found him, his appeals to their patriotic emotions were so eloquent that they instead sided with him. Safely ensconced in his magnificent new castle, looking contemptuously down on the River Dee, Edward could still settle down to enjoy the seasonal festivities and prepare for the campaign ahead, now surely a formality given the forces available to him. If such comforting thoughts did indeed cross his mind, they were soon to be dispelled.

After being joined by the archbishop of Canterbury, Edward decided to push forward from Conwy. He advanced with part of his force towards Bangor and his now ruined new castle at Caernarfon. He arrived at Bangor on 8 January 1295. Soon after, his baggage train was advancing to join him through rough country. To experienced members of Edward's army, this must have seemed ideal country for an ambush, close to the wilds of Snowdonia, the heart of Gwynedd. Any misapprehensions felt by the English were warranted, as the Welsh rebels were indeed lying in wait. When they judged the moment to be right, they attacked. They caught the guards protecting the train completely off balance and overran it. This left Edward in a very vulnerable position and he was left with no option but to fight his way back as soon as he could to Conwy. Here he was forced to endure the indignities of a siege by the exultant rebels. It was not in truth a serious position for him. The walls of this imposing edifice were more than enough to provide a good deal of protection. But it did pose some difficulties for Edward. At one stage the castle ran out of wine. Down to its last barrel, the king refused to drink any of it when his troops were without. This was no empty gesture when wine was not a luxury but part of the staple provisions of a castle garrison. The king instead took to drinking water sweetened with honey. But these privations apart, Edward was safe enough, knowing full well that he could be reprovisioned by sea given the castle's location right next to the river.

Edward's position had been made worse by floods around Conwy but as they subsided so too did the hopes of the rebels harassing him. The major effect of the floods had been to stop reinforcements from making their way across to Edward and raising the siege of the castle. Once the floods were gone, a deluge of men could take their place. A large number of reinforcements duly arrived and drove the Welsh away. During January 1295, Edward launched a raid westwards to the Llŷn Peninsula, though whether this achieved anything other than keeping the enemy on their toes appears doubtful. At any rate, when Edward returned to Conwy after this expedition he evidently decided not to take on the Welsh until reinforcements had arrived. In the aftermath of this decision, it appeared that the greatest problem for the garrison was boredom. They were seemingly unhappy at his decision to maintain a defensive posture but it was a sensible approach, given the difficulties of campaigning in Wales during the winter months. He nevertheless decided in March to let his cavalry sortie forth and engage the Welsh in battle. The rebels were apparently caught off their guard and about 500 of them were lost in battle. Some of the items taken when the baggage train was captured were recovered by the English. Encouraged by this success, Edward launched an attack on Anglesey during the next month and then led his men southwards towards Llanbadarn and Cardigan.

After being taken by surprise during the initial revolt, the English were now very much on the rebound. The decisive battle of the war took place in March. The earl of Warwick moved towards Edward in an attempt to bring him some support at Conwy Castle. His progress was blocked by the army of Madog, the leader of the rebels in the north. Madog had decided to widen the scope of the campaign and had moved away from the north of Wales towards the mid-Welsh Marches. The English spies were again very effective. They heard that Madog was at Cydewain, close to Montgomery. The English assembled their forces, completing this process on 5 March. The rebels were waiting for them on a patch of broken ground, and battle was joined. It was a hard-fought affair but the English were triumphant. According to one account, 600 rebels were killed in the main battle. In addition, the baggage train was attacked, 100 rebels killed and a good deal of plunder taken, 120 beasts carrying provisions being captured. English losses on the other hand were light.[17] The same chronicler who gives details of this battle mentions that the rebels 'were the best and bravest Welsh that anyone had seen'. It was certainly rare for Welsh rebels to engage in pitched battle. This may have been an attempt to give even greater glory to the earl of Warwick and to talk up his triumph but, regardless of the rebels' gallantry, this was a serious reverse for them. The losses they incurred were damaging and even the escape of Madog himself from the battle could not hide the fact that Cydewain was an important setback.

An alternative version of the battle places it closer to Edward in the north of Wales. It also maintains that the English won the battle through innovative tactics, interspersing their men at arms with crossbowmen and archers who held off the Welsh. Then, when the rebels had been worn down by the volleys of the archers, the English cavalry charged and routed them. It is an interesting precursor of the tactics used during later battles, such as Crécy and Agincourt, but the version of events that outlines this scenario is difficult to substantiate.[18] Some analysts of the battle see in it an important example of the evolution of English tactics that were to play a great part in later triumphs[19] but this overplays the case. The battle was undoubtedly a fierce skirmish with what appears to be significant rebel losses but, all in all, there is no real evidence of any revolutionary development in tactics taking place as a result of it.

But the battle was important enough in the context of the war. It marked a decisive change in fortune. Soon afterwards, Edward felt that it was time to move out from behind the walls of Conwy and take the battle to the enemy. He now started to move southwards with the aim of crushing any resistance that remained. There was little fight left in the rebels. He spent a short time mopping up around Conwy itself, and then moved on to Bangor. Less than a week later he was on Anglesey. He occupied Llanfaes and, while there, gave orders for the commencement of construction of another castle at Beaumaris. The castle building thus far had been confined to the mainland but it was now time to ensure that the island was kept secure for the English crown. He also conscripted a number of local men to serve in his army and then moved back across the Menai Strait to continue his progress through Wales.

More men joined him as he moved southwards. He stopped at Harlech, relieved a few weeks previously. The rebellion was effectively over, fizzling out after a start that promised to pose many more problems for Edward I than were finally delivered. Edward felt confident enough to let the size of his army reduce significantly. As he advanced, he took a number of hostages as surety for the future good behaviour of the country. His task was made easier because the rebellion was also under control in the south, and he was able to take his time in moving towards this part of the country. Edward rested for a week at Llanbadarn. The castle had been under the command of Roger de Molis. It was in an isolated position and as such under threat of being starved out in any siege, though again its situation close to the sea gave hope of relief from that direction. In the event, ample provisions had been sent to the castle on Edward's command from Bristol and this helped to secure Llanbadarn. If the rebels were still laying siege to it when Edward moved south, they disappeared as he drew nearer.

Having taken time at Llanbadarn to restore the strength of his army, Edward then moved to Cardigan and Newcastle Emlyn and from there across country towards Brecon. By this time, the revolt of Morgan ap

Maredudd was at an end. According to some accounts, Morgan protested to Edward that his argument was not with the crown but was directed against the excesses of the earl of Gloucester. The complaint would have struck a chord with Edward and Morgan survived. Edward ignored entreaties from the lord of Glamorgan that Morgan should be duly punished, happy enough to see his arch-rival irritated by his actions.[20] A few years later we find Morgan in service as a member of Edward's household.[21] More surprising is the fate of Madog, who was also captured. Edward's past history would have suggested that his life expectancy would be short indeed but for some reason Edward let him live, though he was committed to the Tower of London.

On 16 June, Edward was back at Brecon. There was little left for him to do now, and he made his way in a leisurely fashion northwards again. He reached Welshpool and from there made his way back to Conwy, arriving at the end of the month. There is no record that there was any serious opposition encountered during Edward's circular tour of Wales, suggesting that the revolt was already over when he sallied forth from Conwy at the end of March. The timing of the revolt was particularly unfortunate for him, though, coming as it did when he was on the verge of leading his army against the French. It was a symptom of a malady that would increasingly characterise Edward's reign. The malady was over-ambition on the king's part, involving himself on several fronts and eventually stretching the resources of England to breaking point. England was by the standards of the day a wealthy land; or, it was at least organised in such a disciplined manner that the resources of the country were used to best advantage. But cumulative involvement in diplomatic and military campaigns in Wales, Scotland, France and the Low Countries would threaten to bleed the English Wardrobe dry.

The financial problems facing the English crown would not have been helped by this latest diversion in Wales. The records that survive for the time are incomplete. However, a sum of £54,453 is known to have been sent to Wales at this time.[22] It is also known that this represents only part of the sum spent. Edward partly recovered his costs by imposing heavy fines on those who were involved in the rebellion, though this would have covered nothing like the full cost of the war. It is true that the uprising did not pose an immediate problem for the crown as money had already been raised and set aside for the French campaign and this could be diverted to Wales. But this would only be a manageable longer-term solution if the French campaign were abandoned for good. In the event no such outcome would occur, creating yet more financial burdens for Edward, causing strains that would soon lead to the greatest crisis of his reign during the troublesome days of 1297, when funds ran out and the intransigence of Edward's own barons threatened to return England to the dark days of civil war once more.

But the fact that the campaigns that had taken place in Wales over a period of two decades and the castle building that followed each of them had helped to create the financial crisis would surely have been of little comfort to those who wished to see an independent Wales. This last rebellion had much to suggest that it might enjoy some success. The king was diverted and the rebellion took place over a wide area. But it was not co-ordinated and the initial promise was chimerical. Any assertion that this was a national revolt is accurate only in so far as the uprising covered many different parts of Wales. Madog's assertion that he was 'prince of Wales' (he could indeed trace his descent back to the royal family of Gwynedd) was a relatively empty boast and he does not appear to have received support for his claim from across the country.

The ultimate triumph of Edward I shattered the hopes of the rebels once and for all. The campaign had assumed the form of previous expeditions in the country, with the king methodically organising his forces to smother the life out of any who dared resist him. It was, for the Welsh, the last throw of the dice. They had fought valiantly against insuperable odds but they had missed their moment. Divided among themselves, opposed by a formidable foe, the challenge facing them had been too great, the mountain too high to be climbed. The dragon at last was slain, and the 'leopard' was finally triumphant.

CHAPTER TWELVE

Last Rites

*At one time, the Welsh were noble and had sovereignty over the
whole of England. . . . And according to the sayings of the prophet
Merlin they will one day repossess England. Thus the Welsh
frequently revolt in the hope of fulfilling the prophecy; but as
they know not the hour, they are often deceived and their labour is in vain.*[1]

The rebellion was finally subdued, and it was time for Edward to turn his mind again to other matters. Affairs of state demanded his attention elsewhere, particularly in France and Scotland. Wales was now a closed book as far as Edward was concerned. No longer would it be at the centre of his efforts; other, to his mind greater, challenges lay ahead into which he would throw his considerable energies.

There was one final chapter for him to write however. He was determined to complete the great fortifications he had built in Wales so that they would become as close to impregnable as he could make them. In most cases, this meant completing the work he had begun a decade or more earlier; in others considerable repairs were needed because of the damage wrought by the rebels in the recent uprising. There was one castle however that he would order to be built from scratch. Edward well understood the importance of Anglesey to the Welsh. He therefore resolved to make it far more secure than it had been in the past. He had visited the island previously, most notably in August 1283, but he had never built a major fortification there. It was now time to change this.

The major port on Anglesey was Llanfaes, which was also a place of special sentiment to the Welsh as many of their great men and women from the past were buried in the abbey there. The settlement was also home to Welshmen rather than Englishmen, but this obstacle posed no difficulties for Edward. He ordered a new town to be built for the Welsh inhabitants at Newborough a dozen miles or so away, for Edward had decided that by Llanfaes he would build what would prove to be his last major castle in Wales. The area was low-lying and marshy and it was these characteristics that would give the new castle its name; 'beautiful marsh' or, in its French spelling, Beaumaris.

There was only one man good enough to build it, of course. Master James of St George was placed in charge of construction, assisted by Walter of Winchester, who was clerk of works. Edward landed at Llanfaes on 10 April 1295 and stayed there until early May. The sum of 60*s* was allocated as an advance against the building of the castle. The design that would be created at Beaumaris was magnificent in its conception. It would be the most perfect example of the concentric castle ever created in Britain. Towers would be liberally spaced along the walls to add to the crossfire that could be unleashed against any potential enemy. Anyone who wished to take this castle by storm would be faced by an immense challenge.

The rest of that year saw a huge amount of activity taking place on the site. The ambitious nature of the design meant that it would be a very expensive castle to construct. Fortunately, a good number of records survive to demonstrate the grand scale of the work. During the remainder of 1295, £6,736 was spent on the castle.[2] This immense sum included £2,100 for the carriage of materials and £1,468 for the wages of workmen required to build trenches, excavate the moat and construct a barricade around the castle. This latter measure was particularly important as a means of protecting the castle while it was incomplete, and Edward was clearly anxious to avoid a repeat of the disaster visited on his garrison at Caernarfon. The wages of the labourers paid suggest that there were about 1,800 of them. In addition, £1,005 was paid to stonemasons (450 men) and £636 for quarriers (375 men). In addition to the stone brought in, 2,428 tons of sea coal were shipped to Beaumaris to burn lime, along with 640 quarters of charcoal, 42 masons' axes, 3,277 boards, 8 loads of lead, 160 pounds of tin, 314 bands of iron and 105,000 assorted nails. These figures have been quoted in detail to emphasise that the building of such fortifications was a massive logistical exercise as well as being a huge drain on the exchequer (Beaumaris was, as we have seen, just the last in a long line of castles). The number of men involved also demonstrates that the building site would have been a very noisy and cramped place to work. Living conditions must have been difficult and the provision of suitable quantities of food and other provisions to the workforce created organisational challenges.

Edward was back at the site in July 1295, and decided that he would stay there to ascertain how well work was progressing. Construction was at a very early stage and thatched buildings were hastily thrown up to accommodate him. Temporary these constructions might have been, but the king was still not without luxuries, the harpist Adam of Clitheroe being employed to soothe his famous ire. Edward's early visit to the site may be interpreted as a sign of how determined the king was to build his finest Welsh fortification yet at Beaumaris but it was in fact a completely false indicator of what was to come. Hints of difficulties are apparent less than a year later. On 27 February 1296, Master James sat down to write what must have been a very difficult letter to compose. The king was not a man who took criticism, implied or otherwise, lightly, even from a long-time confidant such as his Savoyard master builder.

In plain words, James told the king: 'We write to inform you that the work we are doing is costly and we need a great deal of money.' He told Edward:

> we [the letter was co-written with Walter of Winchester] have kept on masons, stone cutters, quarrymen and minor workmen all through the winter, and are still employing them, for making mortar and breaking up stone for lime; we have had carts bringing this stone to the site and bringing timber for erecting the buildings in which we are all now living inside the castle; we also have 1,000 carpenters, smiths, plasterers and navvies, quite apart from a mounted garrison of 10 men accounting for 70 shillings a week, 20 crossbowmen who add another 47s 10d and 100 infantry who take a further £6 2s 6d.

They were already about £500 in arrears as far as the wages of their men were concerned, and James told the king bluntly that 'we are having the greatest difficulty in keeping them because they simply have nothing to live on'. They said that £250 a week would be needed to complete the castle. In case Edward was in any doubt as to the seriousness of the situation, the postcript at the end of the letter hammered home the point, begging desperately 'for God's sake be quick with the money for the works, as much as ever our lord the king wills; otherwise everything done up till now will have been of no avail'.[3]

A sum of £2,132 was spent on the castle in 1296 but this was a figure that fell well short both of what had been spent in the previous year and of what was actually required. After that the funding dried up almost completely. This left Beaumaris in a dangerously incomplete state. It was not indefensible but it was far from the fearsome fortification that had been intended. At the time that Master James wrote his frantic letter the walls were 28 feet high in places and all of them were at least 20 feet in height. Ten outer and four inner towers had been started and four gates put in place. In line with Edward's policy of ensuring that his castles could be re-provisioned by sea, the sea approaches to the castle had been deepened so that a 40-ton vessel was able to approach it from that direction.

Half a century later, in 1343, William de Emeldon was appointed to undertake a survey of the royal castles in Wales. His report on what he found at Beaumaris is a damning indictment of how overambitious the king's efforts in Wales had been. William relates a sorry tale, of many towers and other buildings 'dilapidated and ruinous', of others in dire need of repair and of yet others not even completed – 50 years after construction began. Timbers were rotting, roofing in some places was missing altogether and a need for replacement lead was in widespread evidence. The cost of repairs in William's estimate came to £684.

Edward's problem was partly that, even in Wales, there were many competing demands on the royal purse. The greatest damage had been done at Caernarfon, a perfect example of what devastation might ensue if the royal castles were left incomplete. The first step here was to rebuild the castle walls, and £1,195 was spent on this in 1295, amounting to something like 50 per cent of the original construction cost, a potent reminder of just how great the damage visited on the castle in the recent rebellion had been. Between July 1294 and the end of 1301, nearly £4,500 was spent on Caernarfon. Much work was particularly done on the great edifice known as the King's Gate, and as late as 1316 the timber-framed building known as the Hall of Llywelyn was moved from Conwy and re-erected at Caernarfon. Edward was long dead by this stage but he would surely have approved of the symbolism. But Caernarfon, like Beaumaris, was never properly completed and corners were cut in paying for its upkeep so that it too fell into disrepair.

In the aftermath of the uprisings of 1294–5, there was a good deal of racial antagonism towards the Welsh. Welshmen were made to feel like second-class citizens in their own land. One churchman was arrested just 'because he was a Welshman' and was only released when Edward intervened personally. The situation was worst of all in the English boroughs that had been created to subdue the country. For example, at Denbigh a charter was granted to the citizens which prohibited the inheriting of any properties there by those who were not of English descent.[4] Furthermore, Welshmen were not allowed to carry arms in the 'English' boroughs of Wales, and Welshmen were only allowed to assemble if given express permission to do so by the king.

If these rules were strict, in view of recent events some of them were perhaps understandable, and there is some evidence to suggest that Edward was more generous towards the defeated Welsh than were some of his Marcher lords. He had been merciful towards Morgan ap Maredudd, though that may well have been in an attempt to infuriate the earl of Gloucester. But he had also been generous towards some of the kinsmen of Madog ap Llywelyn, for instance taking his son into the royal household, where he eventually rose to become a squire. This was not all altruism; in the household, the son would be close at hand to ensure that the father behaved himself – a hostage is still a hostage, however well-treated. Edward was also quick to investigate cases of oppression reported to him. Investigations were carried out in the north of the country in 1295 and in the west in 1297.

But the relatively balanced stance of the king after the revolt represented, as much as anything, a new pragmatism on both sides. Most people wanted peace in Wales by now. Edward needed it because of his distractions elsewhere. Not only was he heavily involved in military operations in France and Scotland, but he was also at the heart of diplomatic intrigues in the Low Countries and, not least of his problems, there was trouble brewing at the heart of his kingdom in England. Peace was therefore a very desirable commodity as far as he was concerned.

But the Welsh, too, needed peace. The country had been pulled in all directions during the previous few decades. Not every man of Welsh blood had sided with the native princes of Wales in the recent wars; a substantial number had either remained ambivalent or had sided openly with the English. There were few unifying forces present in Wales now, other than that offered by the English crown and the prospect of union with the larger power. Peace would allow something approaching a normal life to be resumed. The fighting spirit of the Welsh had not been completely exhausted by the battles that had been fought and the campaigns that had been waged – but it was now tired and needed time to refresh itself.

The Welsh also needed something else. In recent years, the princes of Gwynedd had given the native Welsh a rallying point. Following the destruction and dismemberment of Gwynedd as an independent native entity, a new focus was needed for their nationalistic aspirations. Thus it was that Edward decided in 1301 to invest his son, the future Edward II, as Prince of Wales. The appointment may appear to have been a symbolic one but it cannot be denied – there is enough circumstantial evidence to suggest it – that it was a gesture that was to become a matter of some pride for the Welsh. As a monarch, Edward II would prove to be one of the least successful of all medieval English kings. But although he would ultimately die an undignified and painful death, murdered by his own countrymen in Berkeley Castle, the Welsh generally supported him when many others did not. He built up a network of ties in the country and those who were linked in service to him from Wales, on the whole, stood at his side when his reign tottered on the edge of oblivion. In return, Welshmen received some preferment, which they had not in previous years. Some of them started to be appointed to administrative posts in Wales and native Welshmen were made sheriffs of Merioneth (1300), Caernarfon (1302) and Anglesey (1305).

But such achievements should not be exaggerated in their effect. In the generation after the conquest of Wales, sixty-eight out of the eighty-four sheriffs appointed in Wales had English surnames.[5] Taxation in Wales was much harsher than similar areas in England experienced. Levels of taxation on many levels of Welsh society increased markedly as a result of the conquest. Even if numbers of inhabitants in certain areas fell, that region was still required to hand over the same level of taxes to the king's collectors. The difficulties were increased by the crown's desire to be paid taxes in money rather than in kind, a not insignificant challenge for an economy that was still far from being entirely a monetary-based one. Even those who had supported the crown did not necessarily benefit from their loyalty. In 1311, for example, the lordship once held by Gruffudd ap Gwenwynwyn passed into English hands to his son-in-law John Charlton, from where it eventually passed into the Grey family.

Problems still lurked not far below the surface. A long list of grievances was presented by the men of north Wales in 1305 and both the north and the west in 1316. Despite any superficial appearance of calm, the under-currents were still volatile. In 1315 the country was once more on the brink of revolt. There were several inspirations for this state of affair. One was a dreadful famine that hit Wales, a relatively poor country, particularly hard and fomented discontent. But there were political considerations that added to the pressure. Most prominent among them was the success of the Scots against the forces of Edward II. When the flower of English chivalry was decimated at Bannockburn in 1314, not only did a number of leading English warriors perish: so too did any misconceptions that might have existed concerning the invincibility of the English within the British Isles.

Buoyed by their success, the Scots sought to take their anti-English revolution further afield to the other Celtic regions of Britain. They took themselves over to Ireland where Edward Bruce, brother of the Scottish king Robert, was for a time very successful. His success in the island encouraged him to look across the relatively narrow expanse of the Irish Sea that separated him from Wales. For a time, an alliance with rebellious elements in the country seemed a distinct possibility. The nervousness of the English overlords would not have been helped by the boldness of Scottish sea raiders, who launched a number of attacks on English shipping in the area. Several ships were captured in Cardigan Bay and Holyhead was raided in September 1315.

The English were forced to take counter-measures. Learning from the lessons of the past, castles were strengthened so that it would be more difficult for any prospective rebels to capture them by stealth while their garrisons were under strength. Any malcontents within Wales were encouraged to present their grievances and they were, generally speaking, sympathetically listened to. They were also encouraged to send hostages to the English court. Negotiations between the Scots and potential rebels in Wales however continued, particularly between Robert Bruce and Gruffudd Llywelyn, at the time the most powerful of native Welshmen. Gruffudd was for a time imprisoned by the English.

However, it proved impossible to forestall rebellion. The catalyst for revolt was found in Glamorgan. The area was part of the lands traditionally held in the March by the earls of Gloucester and the death of the previous incumbent, hacked to pieces at Bannockburn, not for the first time left a vacuum that was not satisfactorily filled. His death marked the end of the male line of his dynasty. Sensing weakness in the hiatus that followed, a man named Llywelyn Gwen raised the standard of rebellion in the region. In doing so, he was able to tap into a strong sense of oppression felt by the native Welsh. The imposition of royal officers to fill the gap after the earl of Gloucester had died only added fuel to the embers of rebellion that were threatening to ignite at any moment. They were insensitive to the wishes of the native Welsh and rapacious in their policies. Promises that had been made by the late earl were ignored without compunction and officers appointed by him were removed arbitrarily. There was, as a result, a groundswell of resentment.

There were still men in Wales who were willing to fight for their rights, particularly in the more remote areas of Glamorgan. It was here that revolt broke out. An army of rebels, reputedly 10,000 strong, laid siege to Caerphilly. Some English visitors attending a court at the castle and camped outside its walls were taken by surprise and a number of them killed or captured. William de Berkeroles, who was in command at Caerphilly, was among the prisoners. But the rebellion was short-lived. Two relieving forces set out, one from Cardiff, the other from Brecon, threatening to entrap the rebels in a crushing pincer movement. Fighting in the approaches to Caerphilly was fierce but ultimately the rebels' resistance was broken and the siege raised. That the Welsh rebels were unable to create more difficulties when there were rumours of an alliance with the Scots abroad, and their enemy was not the mighty, indomitable warrior of old but his weak and unpopular son, showed just how far matters had changed in Wales. No longer could the Welsh hope to throw off the unpopular yoke of English overlords. Llywelyn Gwen was executed at Cardiff in 1317 – continuing a now gruesomely familiar tradition he was hanged, drawn and quartered by Hugh Despenser the younger, who, as the husband of the last earl of Gloucester's eldest daughter, had seized as many of his lands as he could – and the Welsh of Glamorgan were fined £2,330 for their part in the rebellion.

It was not the last revolt, of course. The most famous subsequent uprising was led by another legendary Welsh patriot, Owain Glyndŵr in the following century. Although he enjoyed some success between 1405 and 1410 – in conjunction for at least part of the time with rebels in England, who were unhappy at the usurpation of the throne by Henry IV – that revolt too ended in failure, however glorious. So bad were matters for the native Welsh that one of their fifteenth-century poets, Guto'r Glyn, could write in desperation, 'woe unto us born into slavery'. If Welshmen wished for advancement they were in certain instances obliged to forswear their nationality as a result.[6] The passing of draconian penal laws confirmed the Welsh in their 'chains', as second-class citizens.

There was an easing of the situation at a later point in the century. It was not, surprisingly enough, the English king most famously of part-Welsh descent, Henry Tudor, who helped most to improve matters but his predecessor, Edward IV, who was descended from the Mortimer line. By the beginning of the sixteenth century, the March had effectively disappeared and Wales was an entire principality of the English crown. Links with Henry VII have in fact been exaggerated; there was no widespread popular support for Henry when he landed in Wales in his successful attempt to seize the crown. He did not latch on to the Welsh; they, rather, latched on to him.[7] Even Shakespeare it seems misread the script slightly, when he quoted King Harry at Agincourt proudly declaring his wearing of the leek on St David's Day to Fluellen, boasting that: 'I wear it for a memorable honour, for I am Welsh you know, good countryman.'[8] For, in keeping with their divided loyalties towards the English, and a man who was effectively the son of a usurper, the Welsh not only played an important part in the English victory at Agincourt but other contingents fought on the side of the king's French enemy.

The mixed involvement of the Welsh at Agincourt hints at the use that was made of them after the Edwardian conquest. Men of such renowned bravery formed an ideal source of recruits for whoever was able to pay them. Edward I had already tapped into this. Shortly after he had put down the revolt of 1294–5, he recruited massively for his Scottish campaigns. At the Battle of Falkirk, when William Wallace was decisively defeated by Edward in 1298, 10,500 out of 12,500 'English' infantry present were in fact Welsh. But they could be difficult soldiers to control. According to the contemporary chronicler, Guisborough, the arrival of 200 barrels on the eve of the battle encouraged the Welsh to get drunk and start fighting the English. Some interpretations suggest that this showed continuing uncertainty in relations between England and the Welsh.[9] But in the event Edward won his battle, while the Welsh who were causing difficulties were forced back into line by a cavalry charge which killed eighty of them. The Welsh stood to one side until they could see how the battle was going without them. There was perhaps a real danger that they might change sides at a vital moment; but, when they saw that the English were winning, they joined in the slaughter of the Scots.

Although their contribution at Falkirk was of such dubious value to the English, Welsh soldiers continued to form significant portions of English armies, and 5,000 Welshmen were present at Bannockburn, a similar number to those who took part at Crécy. They earned themselves a reputation for ferocity. They pillaged the lands that they passed through vigorously and often killed their prisoners rather than holding them for ransom as was the custom of the time. They also became famous for their capacity to desert, though such accusations are somewhat harsh in an era when infantry desertion regardless of nationality was a major problem for any military commander.

Where does Edward I's conquest of Wales fit in a historical context? The answers to this question can be examined on two levels. At the very least, we need to evaluate what the conquest tells us about Edward I as a man and a king, while on a wider scale we can examine its role in the evolution of Anglo-Welsh relations. The most permanent reminders of Edward's military achievement are the castles that he built to protect his conquest. Collectively, they are as fine an assemblage of military architecture from the period as are found anywhere in Europe. Caernarfon, Conwy, Harlech and Beaumaris all individually rank among the finest castles ever assembled. When they are considered together, along with others of little less merit such as Rhuddlan and Flint, then the overall effect is truly astounding. The castles of north Wales are Edward's lasting monument and they are, in what they represent, apposite memorials to his reign. They are domineering statements of intent, testaments in stone to the king's unshakeable determination to impose his will upon Wales. They are wonderful examples of military architecture, at the forefront of design at the time that they were built. Given their impressiveness and grandeur, it is easy to see why Edward has earned a reputation as a master in the art of castle warfare.

Yet one has to ask whether all this great expenditure – estimated at £80,000 in total[10] – was excessive in the context of Wales. The Welsh were great fighters, it is true, but their effectiveness lay in hit-and-run tactics, not set-piece sieges. They had neither the manpower nor the equipment available to indulge in such luxuries. Far simpler designs could have held off their initial attacks, after which it would only be a matter of time before the English, with their greater material resources, could summon up reinforcements to relieve the castle. And castles, as was demonstrated on more than one occasion, could be taken, even by a relatively small and poorly equipped force, by those determined enough to try, especially if the garrison was unprepared.

The castle building of Edward I then seems more like a statement of prestige and imperial pretension than of military necessity. In building these vast citadels, he was making a statement to all men of his place in the world, a monument that would speak of power in a way that all contemporaries would understand. As such, the castles were not so very different from the great new port of Aigues Mortes that Edward's contemporary, Louis IX of France – a man whom Edward greatly admired – had built a few decades earlier. The very range of styles, evolving as each new castle was built, is suggestive, too, of the ambition of Edward's principal architect, Master James of St George, to consistently better his last effort.

In the final analysis the great cost of building, manning and maintaining the castles was far more than Edward could bear. Caernarfon would, if it had been properly completed, have been virtually unconquerable by any rebel force that might face it. But it was not finished when, in 1294, it was attacked and burned. Again and again we find examples of Edward's greatest castles being unfinished and inadequately garrisoned. Outwardly they were magnificent, but the appearance was deceptive; there were many flaws in them, not because of the inherent design but because of a shortage of funds to finish them properly. Edward's failure to provide the castles with adequate sources of income to make them financially viable was one of his greatest failings. Here was a man who was keen to make a statement but who could not afford to maintain the castles he ordered built over the longer term. Edward I, that most ambitious of medieval English kings, overreached himself. It is difficult to avoid the conclusion that the cost of Edward's Welsh castle-building programme was far more than he could afford to pay.

The conquest of Wales tells us much about Edward as a politician. It was no real surprise that there were frequent rebellions in Wales. The country had a history of resistance towards alien invaders. The Welsh had a reputation for their ferocity and fighting spirit. Therefore, it was natural that there would be some attempts to throw over the irksome yoke of English rule. What was surprising was how unprepared the occupying English forces appeared to be to cope with such difficulties. In 1282, the English were caught totally off-guard by the rebellion originally spearheaded by Dafydd, despite the fact that he had shown himself to be a disloyal adherent to more than one leader in the past. In 1287, Rhys ap Maredudd was initially successful, partly because the castles he attacked had virtually no garrisons to guard them. In 1294, Madog ap Llywelyn overran the ultimate symbol of English imperialism because no one had bothered to finish it. It is a sequence of events that implies that the

English, and by definition their leader King Edward, were complacent, and believed that the threat from Wales was at an end.

Partly it came back to money again; money to finish the magnificent fortifications that Edward had ordered to be built in the country and money to pay the garrisons to guard them. Equally, ambition played its part. Once Wales was conquered, Edward moved his focus elsewhere towards new challenges. It was as if he wished to close not only a chapter in the book but to finish the book itself and move on to something completely new. Life is not that simple. Once the conquest of 1277–8 had been completed, Edward might have wished that insurgent elements within Wales might simply acquiesce to his rule – the relative moderation of his dealings with the Welsh at this time suggests a desire for harmony and compromise, rather than total subjugation – but this was never likely to happen.

The repeated difficulties in Wales illustrate that Edward was not at his best at a personal level. As a man who clearly wished to act like an autocrat, even if circumstances sometimes dictated otherwise, perhaps he thought that he was above such matters and that men would happily recognise the supremacy of the king. A ruler who was intensely aware of his own rights and those of the crown, and who took every opportunity to expand them wherever he could, Edward was often oblivious to the emotions and motivations of other, humbler men. Thus, we can see Llywelyn ap Gruffudd, with whom Edward had enjoyed an amicable political relationship before he left on crusade, turning against Edward in 1277. Then, in 1282 Prince Dafydd, for some years an ally of the English, led the revolt against them. In 1287, Rhys ap Maredudd, one of the closest of England's allies, lashed out in frustration at the lack of reward he had gained as a result. It is far from an unblemished record on Edward's part and echoes of such resentment would be found elsewhere in his lands during his reign.

What cannot be denied, though, is that Edward brought the Welsh into the fold of the English crown finally and irrevocably. Previous monarchs had tried and failed and the major English involvement in Wales prior to his campaigns had been through the Marcher lordships. The triumph of the crown in Wales portended great danger for the Marcher barons. Their raison d'être had been to act as a buffer between England and the hostile lords of native Wales. Now that those once hostile territories were under the control of the king, their reason to exist as a series of small buffer territories had gone. Edward had never felt comfortable with the power and independence of the Marcher lords. Once Wales was firmly under his control, he initiated a series of actions to increase his power at their expense.

In 1292, matters appeared to have come to a head when, in a dispute over the actions of some of the Marcher lords, he had both the earl of Gloucester and the earl of Hereford flung into jail. The men had come to blows over the castle of Morlais. A number of raids and counter-raids ensued, despite the king's injunctions against just such actions. A council at Abergavenny in October 1291 reviewed the case. In January 1292, both men appeared in Parliament and were found guilty of offences against the peace of the land. Their lands were declared forfeit and they were incarcerated. But Edward could not keep them in jail. Their power was still too strong to be ignored. To ride roughshod over the rights of the Marchers would have turned England back to the dark days of civil war. Both men were released. Gloucester was fined the massive sum of 10,000 marks and Hereford 1,000 marks. Gloucester's fine in particular was a stinging penalty but the reality of the situation was that he was now a free man with his privileges, and power base, substantially intact. Edward had to be content to nibble away at the edges of Marcher privileges, a process that ensured that the final eclipse of Marcher power far postdated his own death.

The assessment of Edward so far then is of a flawed king, not without some merits and hardly the worst of English monarchs, but with faults in his character and vision that meant he did not achieve all that he was capable of, though he did pave the way for the creation of union within the British Isles. It would be wrong however to end this review of his campaigns in Wales on an excessively negative note. Balance is one thing, exaggerated criticism another. Edward may not have been novel in his methods. The routes used during his invasions of Wales followed in the footsteps of military commanders who preceded him by more than a thousand years. He had massive advantages to hand in terms of the resources available to him. Yet so had other English monarchs and they failed where he succeeded. They failed because, unlike this king, they did not have the ability to make the advantages they held count to the full. In contrast to them, Edward had been focused on his mission, methodical in his approach and had as a result maximised every advantage that he possessed.

When Edward expired in 1307, a number of orations were prepared in his honour. One in particular stands out as an appropriate epitaph for Edward the man and the conqueror of Wales. Quoting from the Book of Maccabees, the text simply read: 'In his acts he was like a lion, and like a lion's whelp roaring for its prey'. The lion – or, if one prefers the contemporary analogy already offered, the 'leopard' – was triumphant. Independent Wales disappeared into the realms of dream and memory, into a netherworld inhabited by Brutus and Merlin and other mystical leaders of the past, where superhuman heroes mingled with mortals of more recent times, two of them princes of Gwynedd named Llywelyn.

Notes

INTRODUCTION

1. *The Welsh Wars of Edward I.*
2. *Edward I* by Professor Michael Prestwich and *Llywelyn ap Gruffudd* by J. Beverley Smith.

CHAPTER ONE

1. Gerald of Wales (Geraldus Cambrensis), 274.
2. R.R. Davies, 115.
3. R.R. Davies, 120.
4. A story discussed by Geoffrey of Monmouth in his *History of the Kings of Britain.*
5. This view of the hereditary status of the Welsh was borne out in startling fashion in 2002, when researchers from the Department of Genetics at London University declared them to be more than 85 per cent racially 'pure', and undoubtedly the aboriginal inhabitants of the greater part of the British Isles; while the English found themselves labelled by their DNA as mere Friesian interlopers, with later additions.
6. R.R. Davies, 122.
7. R.R. Davies, 156.
8. *Ancient Laws and Institutes of Wales*, ed. A. Owen, 1841, II, 381.
9. J. Davies, 127.
10. J.C. Perks, *Guide to Chepstow Castle*, Department of the Environment, 1955, reprinted 1971.
11. See for example Walker, 105.

CHAPTER TWO

1. Description of Edward I in *Froissart: Chronicles*, trans. and ed. by John Joliffe, London, 1967 (reprinted 2001).
2. *The Song of Lewes*, edited C.L. Kingsford, 1890, 14.
3. See Prestwich, *Edward I*, 17.
4. R.R. Davies, 309.
5. Prestwich, *Edward I*, 25.

6. The activities of the Welsh during the civil wars, which were themselves significant, are discussed in more detail in Chapter 3.
7. *Calendar of Ancient Correspondence*, 30, 53.
8. See page 21.
9. From the *Close Rolls*, quoted in Prestwich, *Edward I*, 42.
10. De Montfort found it difficult to maintain a balance between the competing and contradictory interests of the Marchers and Llywelyn ap Gruffudd. In 1262 for example, most of the Marcher lords had turned against him when they believed that he was becoming too supportive of Llywelyn. It was a political game that de Montfort never quite mastered.
11. Prestwich, *War, Politics and Finance*, 43.
12. Ibid., 49.
13. Ibid., 26.
14. J. Beverley Smith, *Llywelyn ap Gruffudd*, 42–3.
15. R.R. Davies, 288.

CHAPTER THREE

1. Welsh poet Bleddyn Fardd on the death of Llywelyn, translated by A. Conran in *The Penguin Book of Welsh Verse*, London, 1967, 132–3.
2. See Smith, *Llywelyn ap Gruffudd*, 37.
3. *Gwaith Dafydd Benfras* 30, 75–80, trans. Ann Parry Owen.
4. For other comments concerning the link between Henry III's campaigns and those of his son, see for example J. Beverley Smith, *Llywelyn ap Gruffudd*, 62. Smith notes that 'a number of factors in the synthesis of authority and power that Edward I came to represent had their origin in the course of action taken by his father'.
5. From *Close Rolls*, quoted in J. Beverley Smith, *Llywelyn ap Gruffudd*, 69.
6. *Gwaith Bleddyn Fardd*, 24, 94–102, trans. Ann Parry Owen.
7. See 19 above.
8. For the impact of the discussions at Oxford on Welsh affairs, see J. Beverley Smith, *Llywelyn ap Gruffudd*, 119–23.
9. Letter from Amiens, dated 22 July 1262.
10. *Litterie Wallie*, 77–80.
11. For a discussion of the financial resources available to Llywelyn, see J. Beverley Smith, *Llywelyn ap Gruffudd*, 248–54. The terms also prescribed that if ever Henry should amend the situation concerning Maredudd ap Rhys Gryg and require him to give homage directly to Llywelyn, then a further 5,000 marks were payable.

CHAPTER FOUR

1. Gerald of Wales, 271.
2. For further detail on Edward's part in the crusade see Prestwich, *Edward I*, Chapter 3.

3. *Flowers of History*, 468. The strange portents continued. In a significant earthquake on 11 September 1275, the church of St Michael at Glastonbury was flattened.

4. Thomas Wykes, quoted in *Chronicles of the Age of Chivalry*, 114.

5. *Close Rolls*, dated 29 November 1272, 1 Edward I, membrane 11, ordering Llywelyn to present himself 'to make an oath of fealty to the king'.

6. Quoted in Lloyd, *History of Wales*.

7. *Calendar of Patent Rolls*, 3 Edward I, membrane 36.

8. *Calendar of Patent Rolls*, 3 Edward I, membrane 10.

9. *Flowers of History*, 469.

10. J. Beverley Smith, *Llywelyn ap Gruffudd*, 364–5.

11. *Calendar of Patent Rolls*, 2 Edward I, membrane 22.

12. J. Beverley Smith, *Llywelyn ap Gruffudd*, 340–1.

13. See Renn, *Cadw guide to Caerphilly Castle*.

14. For further reading on the dispute between Llywelyn and Gloucester see J. Beverley Smith, *Llywelyn ap Gruffudd*, 338–55.

15. Prof. Prestwich dates this letter to either 1273 or 1274, and links it with the suspension of payment of the monies due under the terms of the Treaty of Montgomery. See *Edward I*, 174. Given the acknowledgement of receipts of money in 1274 (see above) I incline towards the latter date.

16. Morris, 113.

17. Prestwich, *Edward I*, 95.

18. References are to be found in *The Calendar of Patent Rolls*, dated 14 and 24 April 1274, both issued at Westminster. See 3 Edward I, membrane 19.

19. *Flowers of History*, 470.

20. As late as October 1281, Pope Martin IV was writing to Edward urging him to release Amaury from Orvieto, at the same time writing to the Archbishop of Canterbury to ask him to exert his influence to achieve the desired result.

21. R.R. Davies, 327.

22. J. Beverley Smith, *Llywelyn ap Gruffudd*, 386.

23. *Calendar of Patent Rolls*, 4 Edward I, 1276.

24. Prestwich, *War, Politics & Finance*, 41.

25. For further discussion of horses used by the medieval knight and other mounted warriors, see Prestwich, *The Medieval Warhorse* and *Medieval Warfare – A History*, Chapter 9.

26. Edward used both crossbowmen and archers in his armies. The weapons used by each group had advantages and disadvantages. The longbow was cheap and could fire more rapidly than the crossbow. However, the stopping power of the crossbow was much greater. It has been estimated that the drawing power of the longbow was somewhere in excess of 100 lb while with the crossbow it would eventually reach something like 1,000 lb. See Prestwich, *Medieval Warfare – A History*, 142, 205.

27. *Calendar of Patent Rolls*, 5 Edward I, membrane 26.
28. *Calendar of Patent Rolls*, 5 Edward I, membrane 7.
29. *Litterie Wallie*, 104.
30. Morris, p. 121, quoting *Parliamentary Writs*, vol. 1, p. 19 which notes that service here was given not because of duty but 'freely and graciously'.
31. R.R. Davies, 333.
32. See page 43 above.
33. Prestwich: *War, Politics & Finance*, 105–7.

CHAPTER FIVE

1. Quoted from Dilys Gater, *Battles of Wales*, Llanwrst, 1991.
2. See Morris, 127. At the height of his powers in the 1260s it has been estimated that Llywelyn had 300 horsemen available to him. The difference in resources is even starker than first appears from mere statistics. There are no records showing his cavalry strength of the 1270s but it is probable that numbers had declined from attrition. And the Welsh horsemen were as a general rule much less well equipped than their English counterparts, so man for man would be much inferior to their enemy. See Prestwich, *Edward I*, 180.
3. From *Exchequer Account*, E101/3/11.
4. Morris, 107.
5. *Calendar of Patent Rolls*, 5 Edward I, membrane 6, 5 August 1277, issued at Birkenhead.
6. Morris, 128.
7. Wykes, from *Chronicles of the Age of Chivalry*, 116.
8. Desertion was a perennial headache for Edward. The effect of it in the Scottish wars has been examined by Prestwich, *War, Politics & Finance*, 96–8. Prof. Prestwich notes that Welsh troops were less likely to desert than English in the Scottish Wars, a testament to their durability and tenacity.
9. See page 74 above.
10. Morris, 131–2.
11. Morris, 133.
12. Prestwich, *Edward I*, 181, notes that the Exchequer Accounts record the despatch of a messenger by Edward on 9 September to hurry through supplies, an indication that the English were beginning to experience logistical difficulties for all Edward's thorough preparations and energetic involvement in attempting to secure sufficient provisions for the army.
13. Wykes, *Chronicles of the Age of Chivalry*, 116.
14. *Calendar of Patent Rolls*, 20 September 1277, Chester.
15. *Flowers of History*, 473.
16. Morris, 141, quotes a figure of £120,000 from the 1275 tax. I have used the more recent research of Prof. Prestwich in my account; see *Edward I*, 569.

The latter's note of caution should be noted; the sum of £81,954 is the amount assessed, not necessarily that collected.

17. Powicke, *The Thirteenth Century*, 411.
18. *Calendar of Patent Rolls*, 5 Edward I, membrane 3.
19. Morris, 139, quoting from Exchequer Accounts.
20. See J. Beverley Smith, *Llywelyn ap Gruffudd*, 338. R.R. Davies, 335, describes it as 'a comprehensive humiliation for Llywelyn'.
21. Wykes in *Chronicles of the Age of Chivalry*, 120.
22. Walker, 126.

CHAPTER SIX

1. Gerald of Wales, 274.
2. These would reach fruition in 1284 when, in a directive issued from Rhuddlan, Edward would initiate reforms which would set up a number of new counties; see Chapter 10.
3. For further information on Rhuddlan, see the official guide prepared for the Department of the Environment by A.J. Taylor, 1956.
4. See Morris, 146.
5. The statistics quoted are taken from the Exchequer Accounts and are as quoted by Morris, 147–8.
6. Morris, 151.
7. Morris, 151.
8. Walker, 145.
9. From *Calendar of Welsh Rolls*, quoted by Prestwich; Edward I, 186. See also J. Beverley Smith, *Llywelyn ap Gruffudd*, 472–3.
10. See Prestwich, *War, Politics & Finance*, 28.
11. *Calendar of Welsh Rolls*, 163.
12. Roger Mortimer for one agreed that the land involved was covered by Welsh law. See J. Beverley Smith, *Llywelyn ap Gruffudd*, 471–2.
13. See Prestwich; *Edward I*, 184.
14. This is a very abbreviated version of what was a long and complex series of legal manoeuvres. For more detail, see J. Beverley Smith, *Llywelyn ap Gruffudd*, pp. 470–89.
15. That the Hopton commission and the review of Welsh law generally was a disappointment to many is evidenced by the actions of Goronwy ap Heilin, bailiff of Rhos. He was a member of the commission and was not notably unsupportive of either English or Welsh interests. But when the revolt of 1282 broke out, he firmly allied himself with the Welsh cause. Interestingly, Goronwy had been heavily involved in trying to sort out the dispute over Arwystli. It is only fair to point out however that his empathy for the English would not have been enhanced by Grey's threat to remove his head over a dispute he was involved in.

16. See Prestwich, *Edward I*, 184.
17. For the former view, see Prestwich, *Edward I*, 187. For the latter, J. Beverley Smith, *Llywelyn ap Gruffudd*, 493–6.
18. *Flowers of History*, 477.

Chapter Seven

1. Gerald of Wales, 270.
2. From the *Welsh Roll*, 28 June 1283, quoted by Morris, 152.
3. *Flowers of History*, 473.
4. Morris, 157.
5. Morris, 158.
6. Powicke, *The Thirteenth Century*, 420.
7. Prestwich, *War, Politics & Finance*, 79–81.
8. For a detailed table analysing how these troops were provided, see Morris, 189.
9. Powicke, *The Thirteenth Century*, 421.
10. Morris, 161.
11. Morris, 83, notes that unusually the *Exchequer Accounts* for 1283 also record that the king would repay his feudal levies for any arms or armour lost in the war.
12. *Welsh Rolls,* 26 May and 22 June 1282.
13. An entry in the *Calendar of Patent Rolls* (10 Edward I, membrane 15, 9 April at Devizes) notes the 'appointment of John Giffard to keep the body of the castle of Landovery, during pleasure, with order to strengthen the same on account of the present circumstances amongst the Welsh, and the king will repay the cost'.
14. Morris, 168.
15. Prestwich, *Edward I*, 190.
16. *Calendar of Patent Rolls*, 10 Edward I, membrane 18, 1282, 12 February at Cirencester.
17. Morris, 172.
18. From *The Calendar of Ancient Correspondence Concerning Wales*, quoted in Powicke, *The Thirteenth Century*, 423.

Chapter Eight

1. Gerald of Wales, 233.
2. Morris, 174.
3. Prestwich, *War, Politics & Finance*, 108.
4. Crusade was a spiritual undertaking and Edward, as a secular ruler, was assuming powers far beyond those that were legally the king of England's by his stance in this instance.
5. Quoted in J. Davies, 159.
6. Gerald of Wales, quoted in Powicke, *The Thirteenth Century*, 386.

7. The story of how Brutus established Britain is discussed in Geoffrey of Monmouth's *The History of the Kings of Britain*, 75, and was used by Gerald of Wales.

8. *Annales Monastici*, Wykes, vol. iv, 290.

9. Guisborough, *Chronicle*, 219.

10. *Flowers of History*, 476.

11. See J. Beverley Smith, *Llywelyn ap Gruffudd*, n108, 538. Tradition has named the battle as Moel-y-don which is on the narrow part of the Menai Strait. Smith notes the similarity with the Battle of Stirling Bridge but does so for its effect on the overall conduct of the war rather than the tactical similarities.

CHAPTER NINE

1. Stephen of St George (English clerk in Rome).

2. J.E. Lloyd, *The Death of Llywelyn ap Gruffudd*, 349–53.

3. Reference to the granting of lands to Edmund Mortimer is noted in the *Calendar of Patent Rolls*, 8 August 1282, at Rhuddlan, 10 Edward I, membrane 8, while the reference to the appointment of Springhouse is to be found later the same year, 10 Edward I, membrane 3.

4. J. Beverley Smith, *Llywelyn ap Gruffudd*, 559. Smith notes that the king's treatment of Edmund at this time 'is not easy to understand'.

5. Letters to the king and Burnell from Pecham, 17 December 1282.

6. See J. Beverley Smith, *Llywelyn ap Gruffudd*, 553–5.

7. Roberts, 382.

8. For further analysis, see J. Beverley Smith, *Llywelyn ap Gruffudd*, 550–9. Welsh tradition would later provide a name for the traitor, one Madog Min, archdeacon of Anglesey.

9. In a quite dreadful pun, Stephen of St George was to claim that it was very appropriate that 'a knight estranged by name yet close in loyalty should have exacted the supreme penalty from the rebel and traitor Llywelyn who, by the error of his infidelity, is estranged indeed'. Lestrange himself wrote to the king after the battle, stating that he was in command of the forces on the day. Morris, 182, believes that the army was led by John Giffard (a view also shared by Prestwich; see *War, Politics & Finance*, 29) and offers as evidence the fact that he was from then on always in Edward's favour. This ignores the reality that Giffard was a long-time acquaintance of Edward and had supported him years before in the Evesham campaign. Further, he had already held lands taken as a result of the 1277 campaign, long before Llywelyn's death. In my view, the balance of the evidence points towards Lestrange as the leader of the English army on the day.

10. For analysis of Guisborough's account, see J. Beverley Smith, *Llywelyn ap Gruffudd*, 563, and Prestwich, *Edward I*, 193. See also L. Beverley Smith in *Welsh History Review*, xi, 1982.

11. L. Beverley Smith, 211.

12. For further reading on the battle, see J. Beverley Smith, *Llywelyn ap Gruffudd*, 561–7, Prestwich, *Edward I*, 193–4, and Morris, 181–4 and Appendix I. See also L. Beverley Smith in *Welsh History Review*, xi, 1982, 200–13. The theory that both Franklin and Body may have been involved in the death and decapitation of Llywelyn is also mentioned in Stevenson, 78.

13. From 'The Lament for Llywelyn ap Gruffudd' quoted in *Battles of Wales*, Dilys Gater, Llanwrst, 1991.

14. From Rishanger, quoted in *Chronicles of the Age of Chivalry*, 125.

15. See Walker, 131–2.

16. Ibid., 132.

17. R.R. Davies, 317.

18. Roberts, 379.

19. L. Beverley Smith, 213.

20. Morris, 188–9.

21. Morris, 186.

22. Morris, 189, estimates that they were to lose from a third to a half of their forces during the war.

23. Prestwich, *Edward I*, 195.

24. Morris, 193.

25. Powicke, *The Thirteenth Century*, 429, points to evidence from a charter issued by him that Dafydd was at Llanberis on 2 May where he was accompanied by Goronwy ap Heilyn.

26. Some accounts attribute the capture to a Welshman named Dafydd Fychan, who was made constable of Emlyn in south-west Wales as his reward. However, other accounts suggest that it was a son of Prince Dafydd who he captured. See Roberts, 'Wales and England: Antipathy and sympathy 1282–1485', in *Welsh History Review*, 1963, vol. 1, no. 4, 383.

27. J. Beverley Smith, *Llywelyn ap Gruffudd*, 578.

28. Prestwich, *The Three Edwards*, 17.

29. Gerald of Wales, 267–8.

30. Prestwich, *Edward I*, 198–9.

31. Prestwich; *War, Politics & Finance*, 116–20.

32. Ibid, 136.

33. Prestwich asserts that political instability in England was a far more important reason for the military failures of Henry III than any shortcomings in his armies.

CHAPTER TEN

1. Matthew of Westminster.

2. *Flowers of History*, 478.

3. One of the more macabre side-effects of the execution was a dispute between the cities of York and Winchester over the ownership of Dafydd's right shoulder.

4. Some historians have seen in his late marriage a serious dereliction of his duty to his country. The fact that he did not marry younger, it has been suggested, was an error of judgement on his part, and deprived Wales of a secure succession. See Walker, 132. Judged by modern standards this might seem to be an extreme view but marriage and succession policy were an integral part of medieval politics and it is surprising that Llywelyn did not pay greater attention to these, given his flair for politics.

5. *Calendar of Patent Rolls*, II Edward I, membrane 13, 15 July 1283, at Caernarfon.

6. J. Davies, 164.

7. J. Davies, 142.

8. J. Davies, 167–8.

9. See Powicke, *The Thirteenth Century*, 381–2.

10. Interestingly, the Welsh themselves would eventually see some merits in aspects of the English law. In 1322, men from north Wales would argue that they preferred English common law to their own native law. See Prestwich, *The Three Edwards*, 14.

11. *Monasticon Anglicanum*, iv, 660.

12. See Prestwich, *Edward I*, 206–7.

13. There was one significant exception to this. A son of Gruffudd ap Madog, also named Gruffudd, was given some territory after the intercession of Earl Warenne, an experienced adviser to the king. Future English monarchs would have cause to regret this act; one of Gruffudd's descendants would be a future Welsh rebel, Owain Glyndŵr. See Powicke, *The Thirteenth Century*, 424.

14. The first written reference is found in David Howel's *The Historie of Cambria* (1584).

15. From *King Arthur in Legend and History*, edited by Richard White, London 1997, 530–1.

16. Powicke, *The Thirteenth Century*, 433, notes that 'the Edwardian boroughs of Snowdonia, except at Conwy, Harlech and Newborough (Newport on Anglesey) had been preceded by a Welsh town'.

17. Morris, 200.

18. J.M. Lewis, *Guide to Carreg Cennen Castle*, 1990.

19. *Welsh Assize Rolls*, 309.

20. R.R. Davies, 376–9 and Prestwich, *Edward I*, 348–352.

21. Powicke, *The Thirteenth Century*, 434.

22. Prestwich, *The Three Edwards*, 16–17.

23. For further detail on the financing of the wars, see Prestwich, *War, Politics & Finance*, Chapter VII.

24. Prestwich, *Edward I*, 207.

25. Arnold Taylor, *Guide to Conwy Castle*, 1953, republished 1998.

26. Arnold Taylor, *Guide to Harlech Castle*, 1980, reprinted 1997.
27. John Taylor, *A Short Relation of a long journey made round or ovall by encompassing the Principalitie of Wales, etc.*, 1652.
28. *Flowers of History*, 478.
29. See Chapter 12.
30. For further details see the guide to Caernarfon Castle by Arnold Taylor, 1953, reprinted 1997.
31. Prestwich, *Edward I*, 216.
32. Details from Avent, *Guide to Cricieth Castle*, 1989.
33. L.A.S. Butler, *Guide to Denbigh Castle and Town Walls*, 1990.
34. Prestwich, *Edward I*, 217–8.
35. *Flowers of History*, 478–9.

CHAPTER ELEVEN

1. Letter from Master James of St George to Edward I, February 1295.
2. See Prestwich, *Edward I*, 110 and 154 for example.
3. See Prestwich, *Edward I*, 218.
4. Sian E. Rees and Chris Caple, *Cadw guide to Dinefwr and Dryslwyn Castle*, 1999, 12–13.
5. Ibid., 40–1.
6. See Morris, 209.
7. See Morris, 207. Morris, 209, calculates that of a force of 10,635 foot soldiers, 6,820 were Welsh. Most of the English troops came from regions bordering Wales, such as Herefordshire, Chester and Shropshire, though there were a few men from Derbyshire and of the 105 crossbowmen most were from London or Bristol.
8. The archaeological evidence uncovered in modern times includes balls of stone 16 inches in diameter, presumably ammunition from the trebuchet, along with smaller stones, links of chain mail, slingshots, spearheads and arrowheads, including some with long sharp points which were made to penetrate armour.
9. See Morris, 216.
10. See Prestwich, *War, Politics & Finance*, 170.
11. Prestwich, *Edward I*, 218.
12. R.R. Davies, 177.
13. Morris, 240.
14. See Taylor, *The Welsh Castles of Edward I*, 85.
15. Morris, 244.
16. For the view that the castle was saved from the rebels see Morris, 252. Morris's main evidence for asserting that the castle was saved appears to be because of the shortage of documentary evidence stating categorically that it was lost. For the alternative interpretation, see Prestwich, *Edward I*, 221.

17. For further information on the battle see R.F. Walker, 'The Hagnaby Chronicle and the Battle of Maes Maydog', *Welsh History Review*, 1976–7.
18. This version was given by Nicholas Trivet. It is queried by Prestwich; *Edward I*, 223. Modern commentators on the battle now generally agree that it was fought in the region of Montgomery.
19. See for example Morris, 256–8.
20. The long-standing difficulties between Edward and Gloucester were soon to find a natural resolution with the death of the latter on 7 December 1295. His heir, also named Gilbert, was only four years old. He would not gain ownership of the late earl's land, including the castle 'good and well provisioned' at Caerphilly, for twelve years. See Renn, *Caerphilly Castle, Cadw guide*.
21. Prestwich, *Edward I*, 224.
22. Prestwich, *Edward I*, 225.

CHAPTER TWELVE

1. Biographer of King Edward II, quoted J. Davies, 183.
2. The figures quoted here and afterwards for construction at Beaumaris have been gleaned from the *Cadw guide to Beaumaris Castle* by Arnold Taylor, first published 1980, 4th edn 1999.
3. From Public Record Office E101/5/18, quoted in the *Cadw guide to Beaumaris Castle*, 8–9.
4. R.R. Davies, 385.
5. J. Davies, 178.
6. J. Davies, 204.
7. J. Davies, 219.
8. *Henry V*, Act IV, Scene 7.
9. See for example *Under the Hammer* by Fiona Watson, 1998, 67.
10. Prestwich, *Edward I*, 231.

Bibliography

PRIMARY SOURCES

Bartolemaei de Cotton Historia Anglicana, ed. H.R. Luard, Rolls Series, 1859

Brut y Twysgonyon or the Chronicle of the Princes, ed. T. Jones, Cardiff, 1952

Calendar of Ancient Correspondence concerning Wales, ed. J.G. Edwards, Cardiff, 1935

Calendar of Close Rolls, London, 1900

Calendar of Patent Rolls, London, 1901

'Calendar of Welsh Rolls' in *Calendar of Chancery Rolls*, London, 1912

Chronicles of the Age of Chivalry, ed. E. Hallam, London, 2000

The Chronicle of Pierre de Langtoft, ed. T. Wright, 2 vols, RS, 1866–8

The Chronicle of Walter of Guisborough, ed. H Rothwell, Camden Society, ixxxix, 1957

Chronicles of the Reigns of Edward I and II, ed. W. Stubbs, 2 vols, RS, 1882–3

'Chronicon Thomae Wykes', *Annales Monastici*, iv, ed. H.R .Luard, RS, 1869

Chronicon Petroburgense, ed. T. Stapleton, Camden Society, 1849

Flowers of History, especially such as relate to the affairs of Britain from the beginning of the world to the year 1307, collected by Matthew of Westminster, trans. C.D. Yonge.

Froissart: Chronicles, trans. and ed. J. Joliffe, London, 1967 (reprinted 2001)

Geoffrey of Monmouth, *The History of the Kings of Britain*, trans. Lewis Thorpe, London, 1979

Gerald of Wales, *The Journey through Wales/The Description of Wales*, trans. Lewis Thorpe, London, 1978

Gwaith Bleddyn Fardd a Beirdd Eraill o Feirdd Ail Hanner y Drydedd Gunrif Ar Ddeg, ed. R.M. Andrews *et al.*, Cardiff, 1995

Litterie Wallie preserved in Liber A in the Public Record Office, ed. J.G. Edwards, Cardiff, 1940

Matthaei Parisiensis, Monachi Sancti Albani, Chronica Majora, ed. H.R. Luard, 7 volumes, Rolls Series, 1872–83

Monasticon Anglicanum, ed. W. Dugdale, 6 vols, London, 1830–49

Penguin Book of Welsh verse, London, 1967

The Oxford Book of Welsh verse, ed. T. Parry, Oxford, 1962

The Song of Lewes, ed. C.L. Kingsford, 1890

The Welsh Assize Roll 1277–84, ed. J.C. Davies, Cardiff, 1940

Trevet, Nicholas, *Annales Sex Regum Anglie, 1135–1307*, ed T. Hogg, London, English Historical Society, 1845

Wilhelmi Rishanger, Chronica et Annales, ed. H.T. Riley, Rolls Series, 1865

SECONDARY SOURCES

R. Avent, *Cricieth Castle*, Cadw Guide, 1989

J. Bradbury, *The Medieval Archer*, Woodbridge, 1985

——, *The Medieval Siege*, Woodbridge, 1998

R.A. Brown, *English Castles*, London, 1976 edition

L.A.S. Butler, *Denbigh Castle and Town Walls*, Cadw Guide, 1990

J. Davies, *A History of Wales*, London, 1993

R.R. Davies, *The Age of Conquest, Wales 1063–1415*, Oxford, 2000

A. Edwards, *Appointment in Aberedwy*, Tregarth, Gwynedd, 1992

J.G. Edwards, 'The Battle of Maes Moydog and the Welsh campaigns of 1294–5', *English Historical Review*, xxxix, 1924, 1–2

——, 'Madog ap Llywelyn the Welsh leader in 1294–5', *Bulletin of the Board of Celtic Studies*, 13, 1950, 207–10

R.A. Griffiths, *The Principality of Wales in the Late Middle Ages*, Cardiff, 1972

——, 'The Revolt of Rhys ap Maredudd', *Welsh History Review*, 3, 1966–7, 121–43

G. Holmes, *The Later Middle Ages 1272–1485*, London, 1974

D. Howels, *The History of Cambria*, 1584

A. Hyland, *The Medieval Warhorse*, Stroud, 1994

M. Keen (ed.), *Medieval Warfare – A History*, Oxford, 1999

J.M. Lewis, *Carreg Cennen Castle*, Cadw Guide, 1990

J.E. Lloyd, *A History of Wales from the Earliest Times to the Edwardian Conquest*, London, 1911

——, *A History of Wales*, London, 1930

——, 'The Death of Llywelyn ap Gruffudd', *Bulletin of the Board of Celtic Studies*, 5, 1931

M. McKisack, *The Fourteenth Century 1307–1399*, Oxford, 1997 edn

J.E. Morris, *The Welsh Wars of Edward I*, Stroud, 1996 (reprint of 1901 publication)

C. Oman, *The Art of War in the Middle Ages 1278–1485*, London, 1991 edn

A. Owen, *Ancient Laws and Institutes of Wales*, 1841

J.C. Perks, *Chepstow Castle*, HMSO Guide, 1967

F.M. Powicke, *Henry III and the Lord Edward*, 2 vols, Oxford, 1947

F.M. Powicke, *The Thirteenth Century 1216–1307*, Oxford, 1988 edn

M.C. Prestwich, 'A New Account of the Welsh Campaign of 1294–5', *Welsh History Review*, 6, 1972

——, *Armies and Warfare in the Middle Ages – The English Experience*, Yale, 1999

——, *Edward I*, London, 1988

——, *The Three Edwards – War and State in England 1272–1377*, London, 1980

——, *War, Politics and Finance under Edward I*, Aldershot, 1991

C.A.R. Radford, *Cydweli Castle*, HMSO Guide, 1952

S.E. Rees and C. Caple, *Dinefwr Castle/Dryslwyn Castle*, Cadw Guide, 1999

D. Renn, *Caerphilly Castle*, Cadw Guide, 1987, reprinted 1997

G. Roberts, 'Wales and England: Antipathy and Sympathy 1282–1485', in *Welsh History Review*, volume 1, 4, 1963

W. Seymour, *Battles in Britain 1066–1547*, London, 1975

J.B. Smith, 'Edward II and the allegiance of Wales', *Welsh History Review*, 8, 1976–7

——, 'Llywelyn ap Gruffudd and the March of Wales', in *Brycheiniog*, 20, 1982–3, 9–22

——, *Llywelyn ap Gruffudd, Prince of Wales*, Cardiff, 1998

——, "The Middle March in the Thirteenth Century', in *Bulletin of the Board of Celtic Studies*, 24 (1970–2), 77–93

——, 'The Origins of the Revolt of Rhys ap Maredudd', in *Bulletin of the Board of Celtic Studies*, 21 (1964–6), 151–63

L.B. Smith, 'The Death of Llywelyn ap Gruffudd: the narrative reconsidered', in *Welsh History Review*, xi, 1982, 200–14

D. Stephenson, *The Last Prince of Wales*, Birmingham, 1983

A.J. Taylor, *Beaumaris Castle*, Cadw Guide, 1999 edn

——, *Caernarfon Castle and Town Walls*, Cadw Guide, 1997 edn

——, *Conwy Castle*, Cadw Guide, 1998 edn

——, *Harlech Castle*, Cadw Guide, 1997 edn

——, *Studies in Medieval History Presented to R. Allen Brown*, Woodbridge, 1989

——, *Rhuddlan Castle*, HMSO Guide, 1956

——, 'The Death of Llywelyn ap Gruffudd', *Bulletin of the Board of Celtic Studies*, 15 (1953)

——, *The Welsh Castles of Edward I*, London, 1986

J. Taylor, *A short relation of a long journey made round or ovall by encompassing the Principalitie of Wales*, 1652

D. Walker, *Medieval Wales*, Cambridge, 1999

R.F. Walker, 'The Hagnaby Chronicle and the Battle of Maes Moydog', *Welsh History Review*, viii, 1976–7, 125–30

P. Warner, *The Medieval Castle*, London, 1973

W.H. Waters, *The Edwardian Settlement of North Wales*, London, 1935

F. Watson, *Under the Hammer – Edward I and Scotland*, East Lothian, 1998

Index